TORCH BIBLE COMMENTARIES

General Editors

FOREWORD TO SERIES

The aim of this series of commentaries on books of the Bible is to provide the general reader with the soundest possible assistance in understanding the message of each book considered as a whole and as a part of the Bible.

The findings and views of modern critical scholarship on the text of the Bible have been taken fully into account; but we have asked the writers to remember that the Bible is more than a quarry for the practice of erudition; that it contains the message of the living God.

We hope that intelligent people of varying interests will find that these commentaries, while not ignoring the surface difficulties, are able to concentrate the mind on the essential Gospel contained in the various books of the Bible.

Already published

GENESIS I-XI, by Alan Richardson
GENESIS 12-50, by A. S. Herbert
DEUTERONOMY, by H. Cunliffe-Jones
RUTH AND JONAH, by G. A. F. Knight
I AND II SAMUEL, by William McKane
ESTHER, SONG OF SONGS, LAMENTATIONS, by G. A. F. Knight
THE BOOK OF JOB, by Anthony and Miriam Hanson
PROVERBS AND ECCLESIASTES, by Edgar Jones
ISAIAH 1-39, by John Mauchline
ISAIAH 40-55, by C. R. North
JEREMIAH, by H. Cunliffe-Jones
THE BOOK OF DANIEL, by E. W. Heaton
HOSEA, by G. A. F. Knight
AMOS AND MICAH, by John Marsh
OBADIAH, NAHUM, HABAKKUK AND ZEPHANIAH, by J. H. Eaton
HAGGAI, ZECHARIAH AND MALACHI, by D. R. Jones

Apocrypha

THE WISDOM OF SOLOMON, by John Geyer

ST MATTHEW, by G. E. P. Cox
ST MARK, by A. M. Hunter
ST LUKE, by W. R. F. Browning
ST JOHN, by Alan Richardson
ACTS, by R. R. Williams
ROMANS, by A. M. Hunter
I CORINTHIANS, by W. G. H. Simon
II CORINTHIANS, by R. P. C. Hanson
GALATIANS, by John A. Allan
EPHESIANS, by John A. Allan
PHILIPPIANS AND COLOSSIANS, by F. C. Synge
I AND II THESSALONIANS, by William Neil
THE EPISTLES TO TIMOTHY, TITUS AND PHILEMON, by A. R. C. Leaney
HEBREWS, by William Neil
JAMES, by E. C. Blackman
I AND II PETER AND JUDE, by C. E. B. Cranfield
THE EPISTLES OF JOHN, by Neil Alexander
REVELATION, by R. H. Preston and Anthony Hanson

In preparation

EXODUS, by G. Henton Davies
JOSHUA, by J. R. Porter
JUDGES, by J. R. Porter
I AND II KINGS, by R. B. Y. Scott
EZRA, NEHEMIAH, CHRONICLES, by Peter Ackroyd
PSALMS, by J. H. Eaton
ISAIAH 56-66 AND JOEL, by D. R. Jones

I & II SAMUEL

Introduction and Commentary

by

WILLIAM McKANE

SCM PRESS LTD
BLOOMSBURY STREET LONDON

FIRST PUBLISHED 1963

PRINTED IN GREAT BRITAIN BY
NORTHUMBERLAND PRESS LIMITED
GATESHEAD ON TYNE

CONTENTS

INTRODUCTION

COMMENTARY

SAMUEL AND ELI

I 1-3

CONCERNING THE ARK

I 4.1–7.1

SAMUEL AND SAUL

I 7-15

SAUL AND DAVID

I 16–II 1

II

DAVID AS KING

II 2-8

THE NARRATIVE OF SUCCESSION

II 9-20

APPENDIX

II 21-24

PREFACE

So far as was compatible with the aims and emphasis of the series I have tried to furnish this commentary with an adequate linguistic and textual basis. I have used notes sparingly and always with the same purpose—to point the student to the primary evidence or to indicate where he may find a more detailed treatment of important problems than I have been able to offer within the scope of this work. The translation on which the commentary is based is that of the Revised Standard Version.

ABBREVIATIONS

AASOR	*Annual of the American Schools of Oriental Research*
ATD	Das Alte Testament Deutsch (Göttingen)
AV	Authorized Version of the Bible
BASOR	*Bulletin of the American Schools of Oriental Research*
BH	*Biblia Hebraica*[4], ed. R. Kittel and P. Kahle, 1951
ET	English translation
G	Greek version of the Old Testament (the Septuagint)
G^A	Codex Alexandrinus
G^B	Codex Vaticanus
G^L	Lucianic recension of the Septuagint
ICC	International Critical Commentary (Edinburgh)
JBL	*Journal of Biblical Literature* (Philadelphia)
JPOS	*Journal of the Palestine Oriental Society* (Jerusalem)
JTS	*Journal of Theological Studies* (Oxford)
MT	Masoretic Text (Hebrew Bible)
PEQ	*Palestine Exploration Quarterly* (London)
RB	*Revue Biblique* (Paris)
RSV	Revised Standard Version of the Bible
RV	Revised Version of the Bible
S	Syriac version of the Old Testament (Peshitta)
T	Targum (Aramaic paraphrase of the Old Testament)
V	Vulgate
ZAW	*Zeitschrift für die alttestamentliche Wissenschaft* (Giessen)
	See also Select Bibliography

SELECT BIBLIOGRAPHY

Albright, W. F., *Archaeology and the Religion of Israel*[3], 1953 (cited as *ARI*)

Bentzen, A., *Introduction to the Old Testament*, ET[2], 2 vols., 1952

Bright, J., *A History of Israel*, 1959

Driver, G. R., *Canaanite Myths and Legends*, 1956 (cited as *CML*)

Driver, S. R., *Notes on the Hebrew Text of the Books of Samuel*[2], 1913

Eissfeldt, O., *Einleitung in das Alte Testament*, 1934

Gordon, C. H., *Ugaritic Manual* (Analecta Orientalia 35), 1955 (cited as *UM*)

Grollenberg, L. H., *Atlas of the Bible*, 1957 (cited as Groll.)

Hertzberg, H. W., *Die Samuelbücher* (ATD), 1955 (cited as *ATD*)

Johnson, A. R., *Sacral Kingship in Ancient Israel*, 1955

Köhler, L., and Baumgartner, W., *Lexicon in Veteris Testamenti Libros*, 1958 (cited as Köh.)

Noth, Martin, *The History of Israel*, ET, revised ed., 1960

Das System der zwölf Stämme Israels, 1930

Smith, H. P., *The Books of Samuel* (ICC), 1899 (cited as *ICC*)

Smith, W. R., *Religion of the Semites*[3], 1927 (cited as *ROS*)

S. R. Driver, *Notes on the Hebrew Text of the Books of Samuel,* is indispensable for the fundamental study of the Books of Samuel. In addition to the works which are listed above or cited in the introduction and in the body of the Commentary, the following are deserving of mention: L. Elliott Binns, *The Clarendon Bible* II, 1929, pp. 159-192; G. B. Caird, J. C. Schroeder, and G. Little, *The Interpreter's Bible* II, 1953, pp. 853-1176; G. W. Anderson, *A Critical Introduction to the Old Testament*, 1961, pp. 71-81.

INTRODUCTION

THE NARRATIVE OF SUCCESSION

That part of the Books of Samuel which most gives the impression of compactness and inner consistency is the so-called History of Succession (II 9-20) and it is convenient to begin our study from this nucleus. There is general agreement that the Narrative of Succession is a connected and unified piece of writing and it has been customary to suppose that it is the work of a single author and that it is contemporary or nearly contemporary with the events which it describes. It has been asserted that the work of this author marks the appearance in Israel of a new kind of connected historiography and that the emergence of this is to be traced to the upsurge of national feeling and the sense of achievement deriving from the military and political successes of David. David made history and so paved the way for the appearance of history-writing of a new kind.

Eissfeldt[1] has questioned the assertion that the Narrative of Succession has the character of contemporary reporting of events and has pointed to evidences of literary art and poetic freedom in the work (II 13.11-16, the conversation between Amnon and Tamar; 14.4-20, the conversation between David and the woman of Tekoa; 17.1-14, Absalom's conference with Ahithophel and Hushai; 18.10-14, Joab and the messenger). Nevertheless he agrees that the writer everywhere gives the impression of being singularly well-informed and that what he offers us is a soberly realistic and well-balanced account of events.

More important is the question-mark which Eissfeldt[2] places

[1] O. Eissfeldt, *Einleitung in das Alte Testament*, 1934, pp. 151 f. (ET in preparation).

[2] *Einleitung*, pp. 148-50.

against the belief that this narrative had no previous literary history, in the sense that no part of it existed independently until its author sat down and wrote what is now called the Narrative of Succession. This is no doubt what S. R. Driver[3] meant when he said that II 9-20 was plainly the work of a single author. That is to say, the raw material of the work was either the author's observations or the observations of some other eye-witness or eye-witnesses, and we are not to think of the ingredients of the Narrative as having had any previous *literary* existence prior to their incorporation in it.

Eissfeldt[4] notes the difficulty which is experienced in defining the limits of the Narrative of Succession and he argues that, if I 4-6, II 6, 7, 9-12 are said to be connected with the central core of the Narrative of Succession, (II 13-20) this connection must also be held to apply to I 1-3. The position which Eissfeldt is criticizing here is that of Rost[5] who maintains that II 9 must be regarded as part of the Narrative of Succession, because some of the references in II 13-20 and I Kings 1-2 are only intelligible if II 9 is presupposed (e.g. the references to Mephibosheth and Ziba). Eissfeldt holds that this argument also applies to I 1-3, since what is said of Eli and his sons in I 4-6 presupposes the previous treatment of them in I 1-3. Hence the argument which justifies the inclusion of II 9 in the Narrative of Succession would also demand the inclusion of I 1-3 and so it is seen that the limits of the Narrative are not easily defined.

Eissfeldt holds that this vagueness of definition stems from the circumstance that the author stands on the shoulders of the narrators of individual and self-contained narratives which are the ingredients of the Narrative of Succession. Thus the Narrative easily falls apart into a series of independent narratives, each of which is complete in itself and can be understood in isolation from the others. There are thus, according

[3] S. R. Driver, *Introduction to the Literature of the Old Testament*[8], 1909, p. 184.

[4] *Einleitung*, pp. 149 f.

[5] L. Rost, 'Die Überlieferung von der Thronnachfolge Davids', in *Beiträge zur Wissenschaft vom Alten und Neuen Testament* 42, 1926, p. 102.

to Eissfeldt, two ways of looking at the Narrative of Succession. It may be viewed as a unified and compact composition or as a loose association of self-contained stories. It is this relative independence of the individual narratives which makes the literary criticism of the whole so delicate a matter, since it is impossible to determine with certainty whether two narratives which now follow one another were conceived as a unity from the very beginning of their literary existence or whether this adjacency was in the first place accidental and the connection only subsequently made by a secondary link. All this, however, touches only the way in which the final product came into being. We are asked by Eissfeldt to reckon with the possibility that the individual episodes of the Narrative of Succession had an independent literary existence before they became connected parts of the Narrative and that the author may not have created the history all at once from the store of his observations. Either way the final product is a literary unity and is meant to be such a unity, however complicated its literary evolution may have been.

With regard to the date of the Narrative of Succession Eissfeldt[6] suggests that II 20.14 may point to a date subsequent to 900 BC. Here he follows the text of G (MT is probably corrupt) and takes the meaning of the 'proverb' to be that the citizens of Abel remained faithful to the traditions of Israel despite the fact that the city lay in an area of Aramaean occupation. (Abel Beth Maacah means Abel belonging to the Aramaean Beth Maacah.) Since the occupation of the area did not take place until *c.* 900 BC (I Kings 15.20), the 'proverb' must be subsequent to this date, and, moreover, the circulation of such a 'proverb' presupposes that a certain interval of time had elapsed since the Aramaean occupation.

THE INSTITUTION OF THE MONARCHY

We now pass to the other pole of the Books of Samuel

[6] *Einleitung*, p. 152.

where the reader is most conscious of disconnectedness and even contradiction, namely, the account of the institution of the monarchy (I 8-12). In order to explain this phenomenon a two-source theory has long been in existence and a source favourable to the institution of the monarchy (I 9.1–10.16, 27b; 11.1-15) has been differentiated from another whose attitude is unfavourable (I 8; 10.17-27a; 12). The favourable narrative has generally been regarded as the earlier and as historically credible; the other late and, if not historically worthless, certainly a representation of history which has been shaped by later dogma. These two accounts are not simply divergent, but are also in ideological conflict with each other. The one views the monarchy as ordained by Yahweh to save Israel from her enemies and the other sees it as a departure from the primitive faith and a rejection of the kingship of Yahweh. Elsewhere in the book, where there is evidence of two or more narrative strands, this aspect of ideological conflict does not seem to be so markedly present. It is simply a case of variant accounts of the same events. This is seen in the two explanations of the proverb 'Is Saul also among the prophets?' (I 10.11; 19.24); in the two accounts of the introduction of David to Saul (I 16.14-23; 17.1–18.2); in the two descriptions of David's escape from Saul (I 19 and 20); in the double account of David's desertion to the Ziphites (I 23.19-28; 26.1 f.); in the differing stories of the death of Goliath (I 17; II 21.19); in the contradictory information about the children of Absalom (II 14.27; 18.18); in the double account of the sparing of Saul's life (I 24 and 26); in the double account of Saul's rejection by Yahweh (I 13.7b-15; 15); in the double prediction of the fall of Eli's house (I 2.27-36; 3); in the two variant accounts of Saul's death (I 31 and II 1).

These features are generally accounted for by a two-source or a three-source documentary hypothesis. Budde[7] held that the J and E documents, which he traced through the Heptateuch, extended into the Books of Samuel. Thus the older

[7] K. Budde, *Die Bücher Samuel* (Kurzer Hand-Kommentar zum Alten Testament), 1902, pp. xii-xxi.

narrative of the inauguration of the monarchy is assigned to J, as also is the Narrative of Succession, while the younger and unfavourable account of the inauguration of the monarchy is assigned to E. The other doublets which have been detailed are apportioned between J and E. Eissfeldt's[8] approach is similar, but he postulates a third L (Lay) source which he has also detected in the Heptateuch, and Snaith[9] agrees that a third source is needed in order to achieve a complete critical analysis of the account of the institution of the monarchy. In this section Eissfeldt attributes to L I 10.21b-27; 11.1-5, 6b-15 and with this should be compared Bentzen's[10] suggestion that I 11 may be a special tradition in which Samuel is described on the model of the 'judges' in the old legends. Other passages assigned to L by Eissfeldt are the stories of the ark in I 4-6 and II 6; certain biographical details in I 14.49-51; II 3.2-5; 5.13-15; 8.16-18 and David's lament over Abner (II 3.33-34). The Narrative of Succession is given to J.

S. R. Driver[11] thinks it very questionable that the earlier narrative of the institution of the monarchy belongs to J, but he regards it as an example of the best style of Hebrew historiography. He observes that the later narrative has notable affinities with E and that it is probably pre-Deuteronomic. Driver's analysis thus has a general similarity to that of Budde. Bentzen[12] is more reserved in his position and refers simply to two narrative strands. He does not believe that there is enough evidence for a documentary hypothesis and he is uncertain whether or not the two strands are a continuation from the Heptateuch of J and E. In any case the two strands extend only as far as II 8 and the core of the Books of Samuel is the Narrative of Succession (II 9-20).

[8] *Einleitung*, pp. 309 f.

[9] N. H. Snaith, 'The Historical Books', in *The Old Testament and Modern Study*, ed. H. H. Rowley, 1951, p. 98.

[10] A. Bentzen, *Introduction to the Old Testament* II, p. 93.

[11] S. R. Driver, *Introduction*, pp. 177 f. Cp. A. R. S. Kennedy, *I and II Samuel* (The Century Bible), 1905. Kennedy holds an elaborate documentary theory, but he does not identify any of his sources with J and E.

[12] Bentzen, *Introduction* II, p. 94.

Weiser[13] has similar doubts about a documentary hypothesis and sees the Books of Samuel rather as a collection of heterogeneous literary traditions which have originated in different literary circles and have been placed side by side without any attempt to adjust the discrepancies between them or to bring them under the control of a comprehensive ideological scheme. The three main independent literary units are: (*a*) The Narrative concerning the Ark (I 4-6; II 6); (*b*) The Story of Saul's rise (I 9–10.16; 11; 13-14); (*c*) The Story of David's rise (I 16.14–II 5; 8); the Story of David's Reign (II 9-20 and I Kings 1-2).

THE PROCESS OF COMPILATION

We must at this point attempt to assess the general implications of the work just reviewed. If a documentary theory is held and if the documents are thought to extend throughout the Books of Samuel, the last stage in the compilation of the book was the collation of these documents and the conflation of their contents. We are then entitled to ask on what principles this conflation was carried out. Whatever reply is given to this, it ought not to be readily assumed that it was an arbitrary and unintelligent process. If the final process was a conflation of documents, the task was literary and editorial and it would seem to have been partly a scissors-and-paste operation in the sense that a strip of one document was followed by a strip of another, so that, to some extent, the two (or three) documents have been formed into a composite narrative.

Now the result of this kind of activity (if this in fact was how the final product was constructed) does not conform to our canons of a finished and unified literary work, but we ought not to put too much trust in our criteria in approaching this ancient book. Its compiler may have had scant regard for canons of compactness and inner consistency. It is reasonable to suppose that his use of two or more strands with

[13] A. Weiser, *Introduction to the Old Testament* (ET of the 4th German edition), 1961, pp. 160-62.

variant accounts of the same events and episodes was a deliberate and artistic decision and this can only mean that his standards of literary craftsmanship were different from ours. It is therefore unwise to look too hard for a strong logical connection between all parts of the book or to be so obsessed with discrepancies as to be oblivious to the unity which has been superimposed on the work, despite the diversity of its material and the disconnectedness of some of its parts.

These general considerations would still hold, if the compiler's work is thought of as the bringing together of independent and self-contained literary traditions rather than as a conflation of documents. They would equally hold if it were believed that the interweaving of the narrative strands had already been effected at the stage of oral tradition. It would still be true that an oriental story-teller practises his craft in what seems to us to be a clumsy and unskilful way, but we have to ask ourselves whether we have any right to expect him to conform to our aesthetic canons. His audience or readers (in the case of a written work) were apparently not annoyed by the features which irritate us. The double and discrepant accounts of the same events would not perplex them, because they did not listen with that kind of critical interest. They wanted as comprehensive a story as possible and they expected the story-teller or author to include all the detail which he knew, even if different strands of tradition did not agree in their account of the same events. The striking feature of the final compilation of the Books of Samuel is its catholicity; it can thus accommodate two accounts of the inauguration of the monarchy, where the one is in ideological conflict with the other. The significance of this is not reduced by the circumstance that the later account may have been inserted at an earlier stage of the compilation as a deliberate attempt to correct the earlier one and to counteract what was scandalous in it to later theological thought.[14] In any case the earlier narrative was not suppressed either at an earlier or at the final

[14] So Eissfeldt, *Einleitung*, p. 308; Bentzen, *Introduction* II, p. 95, quoting R. H. Pfeiffer, *Introduction to the Old Testament*, 1941, p. 364.

stage of compilation and we simply do not know whether or not the final compiler or compilers were dogmatically committed to the later account. When we look outside the account of the inauguration of the monarchy at the other doublets, we see this striving after comprehensiveness—a concern to include in the work all the information which was available and a disregard of a harmonious composition.

In his account of the compilation of the Books of Samuel Bentzen[15] begins with the Narrative of Succession and he holds that the other parts of the book are formed around this nucleus. Two strands of narrative I 1–II 8 lead up to a description of David's life as king in Jerusalem and the culmination of these introductory strata is the designation of Solomon as heir to the throne (II 12.24). II Sam. 13-20 and I Kings 1-2 is the Narrative of Succession proper, and II 9-12 is introductory to it, although these chapters are sometimes reckoned as part of the Narrative.

The whole of this introduction is later than the Narrative of Succession, although old material has been incorporated into it (e.g. the two funeral dirges of David in II 1 and 3 and the various lists in I 14.49-51; II 3.2-5; 5.13-15; 8.16-18 and 20.23-26). S. R. Driver[16] had earlier suggested that the lists at I 14.47-51; II 8.16-18 and 20.23-26 marked the end of what were self-contained narratives and so throw some light on the history of the compilation of the Books of Samuel. With regard to II 21-24 Driver[17] observes that, since these chapters interrupt the Narrative of Succession, they must have been added at a date subsequent to the separation of the Books of Samuel and those of Kings. Besides the lists and the dirges Bentzen believes that other material in the introductory strata has also been taken over in written form, such as the stories of the ark (I 4-6 and II 6), the account of David's relations with Ishbaal etc. (II 2-5; 8), the song of Hannah (I 2.1-10)—a royal psalm which has no connection with Hannah and her

[15] Bentzen, *Introduction* II, pp. 93 f.
[16] Driver, *Introduction*, p. 173.
[17] Driver, *Introduction*, p. 183.

situation—and perhaps something of a Saul-Samuel complex (I 10-12; 15). II 21-24 contains a thanksgiving psalm (II 22; Ps. 18)—a royal psalm which cannot date from David's time —and a prophetic oracle formed on a pattern well-known from the wisdom literature (II 23.1-7). It should be noted that II 21-24 display a principle of arrangement. The complex opens with an account of a famine (21.1-14) and closes with an account of a pestilence (24). Between these are two narratives of heroes and their exploits (21.15-22 and 23.8-39) and between these two in turn a psalm and an oracle (22 and 23.1-7).

Weiser's[18] account of the compilation of the Books of Samuel is even further removed from the idea of a conflation of documents than that of Bentzen. There are, he holds, six stages to the process:

1. The individual traditions, both popular and courtly, to which belong the stories of the wars in the time of Saul in I 11, 13 f. and David's war against the Ammonites (II 10 f.). The popular narrative of the beginning of the monarchy is in I 9 f. Also among these traditions are the narrative of the ark (I 4-6; II 6), Nathan's earlier prophecy in II 7, the various lists and annals and David's dirges.
2. This is the stage of comprehensive accounts based on existing traditions and is the classical period of historical writing. Examples are the stories of the rise of Saul in I 9 f., 11 and 13 f.; and the account of David's rise in I 16.14–II 8. Also the court-history in II 9-20 and I Kings 1-2.
3. The collection and combination of the narratives mentioned in (2) and the welding of them into one comprehensive tradition, chronologically arranged, with the accretion of parallel and later traditions, probably in connection with the practical, cultic use of this material.
4. The prophetic reshaping of the tradition into a complete history reinterpreted theologically (e.g. I 1-3; 7; 8; 10.17 f.; 12; 15; 16.1-13; 28).

[18] Weiser, *Introduction*, pp. 162-70.

5. The Deuteronomic revision of the Books of Samuel.
6. Later expansions by the insertion of poetic pieces of cultic origin in I 2.1-10; II 22; 23.1-7 and also additions in I 17 and 18.

DEUTERONOMIC REDACTION

Something must now be said about the extent of the Deuteronomic editing or the Deuteronomic framework of the Books of Samuel. Bentzen[19] holds that the later account of the inauguration of the monarchy is closely related to the Deuteronomist work of history, but his view is that the Deuteronomist editing in Samuel is not so conspicuous as in Judges and Kings. It is then even less conspicuous if the more commonly held view that this later account is pre-Deuteronomic is asserted. S. R. Driver assigns it to E, as also does Eissfeldt, and Weiser associates it with stage four of the process of compilation—the prophetic reshaping of the tradition. It thus precedes the Deuteronomic revision which is stage five.

S. R. Driver,[20] however, although he thinks that the later narrative about the beginnings of kingship is pre-Deuteronomic, supposes that it has been expanded in parts by a later editor (especially in I 12. 9 f.) whose style and point of view were similar to those of Deuteronomy and the compiler of the Book of Judges. Similarly he says that I 7.2 f., which is homogeneous in style and content with the later narrative of the institution of the monarchy, may be regarded as forming with it the conclusion to the history of the 'Judges' contained in Judg. 2.6-16. (See Commentary on I 7.) In both the general point of view is similar; Israel's apostasy and obedience are contrasted in similar terms and the task of delivering Israel from the Philistines begun by Samson is continued under Samuel. Other passages reckoned by Driver as the latest in the book with some affinities in thought and expression to

[19] Bentzen, *Introduction* II, p. 95.
[20] Driver, *Introduction*, pp. 178, 183.

Deuteronomy are I 2.27-36; 15; II 7. Driver, nevertheless, agrees that the evidence of a Deuteronomic redaction is decidedly less marked than in the Books of Kings.

Bentzen[21] calls attention to certain framework notes which he believes are Deuteronomic (I 4.18b; 13.1; II 2.10a and 11; 5.4-5) and thinks that II 7, which he describes as later theological literature, may have had Deuteronomic additions. It is notable that there are so few attempts at harmonization in the Books of Samuel which would tend to support the conclusion that it has not been subjected to anything worthy of the name of a Deuteronomic redaction. Bentzen suggests that I 6.15 and 7.3, 14, 15 may be redactional devices, but he would assign 6.15 to P rather than D. He also holds that I 10.25b-27 and 11.12-14 are attempts to reconcile the two conflicting accounts of the inauguration of the monarchy.[22] Driver[23] suggests that I 10.8 and 13.7b-15a are insertions whose intention is to give the impression that the meeting of Samuel and Saul in 13. 7b-15a is the first after 10.8. These insertions, however, in Driver's opinion, only achieve their end if they are not interrupted by 11.14, and so they are assumed by Driver to be earlier than the fusion of the two accounts of Saul's elevation to the throne.

THE BOOK AS A UNITY

The Narrative of Succession is the centre of the Book of Samuel and the other parts, however heterogeneous in origin, cluster around this nucleus. The topic of the Narrative of Succession is the finding of a successor to David and its long-term concern is the stability of the Davidic dynasty. It shows how Amnon, Absalom and Adonijah each in turn failed to grasp the throne because Solomon was Yahweh's nominee.

[21] Bentzen, *loc. cit.*
[22] Cp. H. P. Smith, *Samuel* (International Critical Commentary), 1899, p. xxii.
[23] S. R. Driver, *Introduction*, p. 176.

The theme of the earlier part of the book is David himself, the anointed of Yahweh, who is destined to be king of Israel, although, for a time, appearances are all to the contrary and he lives the life of a fugitive relentlessly hunted and harried by Saul. Yet he endures in weakness and survives in danger, until at length Yahweh brings him to the throne.

The conflict here centres on David and Saul, the one chosen of Yahweh and the other rejected by him. It is this which makes the outcome of the conflict certain, even when the scales seem to be heavily tipped against David. Another aspect of David's strength is his alliance with a legitimate priesthood, for in the ordering of his affairs he relies on priestly guidance. Saul seals his doom by the massacre of the priests at Nob, for subsequently he has neither priestly nor prophetic guidance, so that in his desperation he tries to raise the ghost of the dead prophet Samuel. David, on the other hand, now has Abiathar and the oracle (see Commentary on I 22 f.; 28; II 5). And, after he becomes king he exercises his rule in conjunction with the priestly house (the Zadokite priesthood according to I 2.35; see Commentary *in loc.*), while the theology of kingship finds its supreme expression in the place occupied by the Davidic king in the Jerusalem cult.[24] (See Commentary on II 7; 21.17; 22; 23.1-7.) It is with this belief in the sacral king that we should connect the doctrine of the inviolability of the anointed (see Commentary on I 24; 26), while the ark stories, which culminate in David's bringing of the ark to Jerusalem, should probably be related to a concern to establish the legitimacy of that sanctuary to which the theology of Davidic kingship was indissolubly joined (see Commentary on II 6).

There are, of course, other topics which cannot be so satisfactorily related to the main theme. There is a strain of piety which refuses to put any reliance in military resources or

[24] See especially A. Bentzen, *JBL* 67, 1948, p. 51, and *Introduction* II, pp. 94 f., where it is suggested that much material in the book of Samuel is only secondarily 'history' and that prior to its 'historification' it was cultic recitation or 'myth' whose function was to provide a commentary on ritual. Also Weiser, *Introduction*, p. 165.

skills and which urges trust in Yahweh alone, in spirit and not flesh (I 7.10-11; 17 [see Commentary]; II 5.24). Strangely contrasting with this is the recognition of the validity of a purely empirical political wisdom which is seen especially in the portrayal of Ahithophel (see Commentary on II 15 f., and especially on 16.23) and in the just appreciation of the statesmanship of Joab (see Commentary on II 11; 14; 19; 24).

DATE AND AUTHORSHIP

Questions of date and authorship are not now thought to be so important as they were once deemed in this kind of enquiry. Part of the reason for this with respect to the book of Samuel is certainly that the history of its compilation is now seen to be a complicated and long drawn-out process. Where it is believed that an early source or document (J?) is co-extensive with the book, Abiathar, Ahimaaz and Zadok have all in turn been suggested as its author. Rost,[25] on the other hand, believes that Abiathar was the author of an introduction to the Narrative of Succession which contained the account of David's persecution by Saul and his victory. With regard to date the common view is that the Narrative of Succession is a contemporary or near-contemporary document and that the other parts of the book, excluding a small amount of old material, originated at a later date. S. R. Driver[26] holds that there is little in the book later than *c.* 700 BC.

A NOTE ON METHOD

Finally there is one particular exegetical problem which confronts the commentator on the Books of Samuel and on which something ought to be said. This problem stems from

[25] L. Rost, 'Die Überlieferung von der Thronnachfolge Davids', pp. 128, 133 f.
[26] S. R. Driver, *Introduction*, p. 183.

the nature of the book—a whole compounded of discrete parts. The assumption which I have made is that a part should always be seen in relation to its setting within the whole, because it has acquired a new significance in virtue of its context and it is the duty of the commentator to say what he believes this new significance—this super-addition of meaning—to be. This can be illustrated most simply in relation to the Narrative of Succession itself. The commentator is far more aware of propagandist traits or 'tendency' in the introductory narrative than he is when he reaches the Narrative of Succession, for here he encounters a remarkably frank and factual story (see especially the Commentary on II 19). In the David and Saul story the composition is regulated and even dominated by certain dogmatic convictions. There is antipathy to Saul and a partisan espousing of the cause of David (see Commentary on I 15.28; 16; 18; 19; 22; 23; 28). It would be misleading to say that the Narrative of Succession has no point of view, but it is more difficult to detect this theological orientation. Indeed we detect it only because the Narrative does not stand by itself, but is preceded by a fully elaborated theology of kingship, and so the struggle for succession is seen to be more than a political struggle. It possesses another dimension and its significance has to be assessed against the background of Nathan's promise to David (II 7) that he is to be the founder of an enduring dynasty. Nothing less is at stake than the fulfilment of Yahweh's purposes for Israel, since these are to be achieved through the enduring dynasty of David and, in the short term, the first crisis which has to be resolved is the securing of a worthy successor to his throne.

SAMUEL AND ELI

I 1-3

CHAPTER 1: THE BIRTH OF SAMUEL

ELKANAH AND HIS HOUSEHOLD

1.1-8

3. year by year Literally: 'from days to days', a phrase which elsewhere refers to a statutory annual religious observance (Ex. 13.10). Elkanah and his household were accustomed (the verb is frequentative) to make the annual pilgrimage to the central sanctuary of the Israelite tribes at Shiloh.

4. portions i.e. the portions of flesh eaten at the sacrificial meal.[1]

5. And although he loved Hannah . . . The point of this is that the annual distribution of the portions was a moment which aggravated the reproach of Hannah's childlessness. She counted only for one, whereas Peninah and her children each counted for one. MT is difficult and G should probably be followed. Thus: 'And to Hannah he gave one portion; nevertheless he loved Hannah, but Yahweh had shut her womb', i.e., Elkanah was not deliberately hurting Hannah; it was not his intention to discriminate against her, but it was inevitable that the occasion of the distribution should call attention to her barrenness. Peninah, on the other hand, makes the most of this occasion when she has so clear an advantage over Hannah. She taunts her with her barrenness and wages a campaign to put her out of spirits.

7. So it went on This translation is doubtful. Possibly we should emend and read: 'And thus she (Peninah) used to do year by year'. In any case the point is that Hannah's wound was reopened annually on the occasion of the sacrificial meal at Shiloh.

[1] W. R. Smith, *ROS* pp. 222, 237, 254.

HANNAH'S INTERVIEW WITH ELI AT SHILOH

1.9-18

9. Now Eli, the priest . . . This tends to support G in v. 3, where Eli is mentioned along with his two sons. Here G reads: 'And, after they had eaten at Shiloh, she rose and took up her stance before the Lord.' Eli was available for consultation, seated on a 'throne' at the doorpost of the temple.

11. and no razor shall touch his head i.e., he would be a Nazarite (Num. 6.5). Since a Nazarite could be released from his vows (Num. 6.13 f.), the words ALL THE DAYS OF HIS LIFE have an added significance.

16. a base woman Another understanding of the phrase is 'a disordered (or, confused) woman'.[2]

THE END OF HANNAH'S BARRENNESS

1.19-20

20. and in due time Hannah conceived and bore a son DUE TIME means that, after her intercourse with Elkanah, her pregnancy followed a normal course. The translation DUE TIME is, however, improbable. 'At the turn of the year'[3] is a more correct rendering, and, since a similar phrase is used in Ex. 34.22 in connection with the Feast of Tabernacles, there can be little doubt that the time reference is the same in both instances. The importance of this is that, since Hannah's son is born just as Elkanah is about to make the annual pilgrimage to Shiloh, the time of this festival is seen to coincide with that of the Feast of Tabernacles. The precise time reference of 'at the turn of the year' is more difficult to determine, whether, 'at the end of the year' or 'at the beginning of the new year'. If the latter is correct both the festival at Shiloh and the Feast of Tabernacles were new year festivals.

[2] G. R. Driver, *ZAW* 52, 1934, pp. 52 f.
[3] A. R. Johnson, *Sacral Kingship in Ancient Israel*, p. 49.

and she called his name Samuel The announcement of the name is followed by the clause, FOR SHE SAID, 'I HAVE ASKED HIM OF THE LORD'. The verb used here puns with 'Saul' and not with 'Samuel' and this has led some scholars to conclude that this is originally a birth story not of Samuel but of Saul; cp. 2.20.

ANOTHER PILGRIMAGE TO SHILOH
1.21-28

23. may the Lord establish his word This cannot refer to Hannah's hope of a son which has already been fulfilled. G and S read 'thy word' which gives better sense; i.e., 'May he enable you to implement your proposals', referring to her intention to proceed to Shiloh after the child was weaned in order to honour her vow.

25. they slew The subject is evidently the temple attendants and similarly with THEY BROUGHT. G, however, makes Hannah subject in both cases.

The chapter is important for the light it throws on religious observance in the pre-monarchic period. The annual pilgrimage 'at the turn of the year' to the central sanctuary of the twelve Israelite tribes at Shiloh (Groll. p. 162) would serve to nourish their common faith in Yahweh, especially at a time when the areas settled by them were not contiguous. It is possible that the tribes were officially represented at this gathering, but it is clear from the case of Elkanah that individual Israelites also attended. The name given to a confederation of tribes around a central sanctuary is amphictyony and so we may speak here of an amphictyonic festival.

It is not certain that this association of Israelite tribes had its focus in the cult of the central sanctuary, if 'cult' is narrowly defined, although the ark, which was the symbol of Yahweh's presence, was in the custody of the priestly family of Eli, and it is clear from the story of Elkanah that sacrifices did have a place in the festival. But it would seem that, when the central sanctuary of the amphictyony was elsewhere—at

Shechem, Bethel or Gilgal—the ark, for the time, was entrusted to the local priesthoods of these sanctuaries. It is not therefore certain that amphictyonic authority was embodied in the central sanctuary or that the high priest was the chief executive of the amphictyony. The cement of the amphictyony may rather have been the common acceptance by the constituent member tribes of certain historical traditions and of a Law originating in a covenant between them and Yahweh. In this case the cohesive power would lie in Law rather than the cult and this view is in accord with the fact that the only amphictyonic office mentioned in the oldest tradition is not priestly but judicial. The functions of the so-called 'minor judges' were probably the interpretation and development of the Covenant Law (Judg. 10.1-5; 12.7-15).

At the annual festival the emphasis would probably fall on the recalling of those traditions which all the tribes claimed as a heritage from the past: the Promise to the Patriarchs, the Deliverance from Egypt, the Covenant and Law-giving at Sinai. Having participated through worship in these mighty acts of God, the congregation would reaffirm its faith in Yahweh and bind itself anew to the Covenant Law. It was thus a festival of the renewal of the Covenant—the only authority to which the several tribes would subscribe in common[4] (Josh. 24).

CHAPTER 2

THE SONG OF HANNAH

2.1-10

1. my strength Literally. 'my horn'. The horn of an animal is the symbol of its majesty and strength, and the picture suggested is that of an animal with its head proudly erect.

[4] This account follows, for the most part, M. Noth, *Das System der Zwölf Stämme Israels*; *The History of Israel*, pp. 85-138. For the view that the cult of the central sanctuary and the office of high priest had an intrinsic connection with the structure of the amphictyony see J. Bright, *A History of Israel*, pp. 128-160.

my mouth derides my enemies Literally: 'my mouth is wide over my enemies', i.e., with derisory taunts.

2. there is no rock like our God G: 'There is no righteous one like our God.' The 'for' of 2b does not introduce a clause which is a proper sequel to 2a. In G 2b of MT appears as 2c. Since the second person of 2b is inappropriate, and, since it disturbs the parallelism between 2a and 2c, it should perhaps be deleted. With regard to the designation of God as ROCK it should be remembered that the terrain of the Holy Land is such that it was in rocky and mountainous tracts that a man might expect to find asylum when pursued by his enemies.[1] Cp. Judg. 20.47, I Sam. 13.6.

4. The bows of the mighty . . . The strength which is a characteristic of the warrior (hence the phrase 'man of valour') will become the property of the stumbler (i.e., he who stumbles for want of strength and so the weakling) and he will gird it on as a warrior does his armour.

5. have ceased to hunger CEASED is absolute in MT, followed by the phrase 'even the barren woman bears seven'. The theme, however, of vv. 5-10 is that of reversal of circumstances through the action of Yahweh and 5b needs emendation to bring it into line with this. An emendation which does this and restores the parallelism between 5a and 5b is 'and the hungry have ceased from toil' (cp. RSV). RSV FORLORN in 5d is strictly 'decays' or 'withers'.

9. cut off The meaning is rather 'reduced to silence or oblivion'. Verse 9c takes up again the idea of v. 4; a man will not be a mighty warrior by virtue of his physical endowment.

10. against them he will thunder in heaven Or: 'The Most High will thunder in heaven.'[2]

and exalt the power of his anointed MT: 'so that he may exalt' . . . A small emendation produces the reading of RSV. It has been pointed out that this reference to the anointed king presupposes the existence of the institution of the

[1] J. Begrich, *ZAW* 46, 1928, pp. 254 f.
[2] C. H. Gordon, *UM* p. 304, No. 1402. G. R. Driver, *CML* p. 142 n. 1.

monarchy so that the song cannot be a pre-monarchic composition.

CORRUPTION AT SHILOH

2.11-26

12. worthless men See Commentary on 1.16.

13. custom The meaning cannot be 'correct practice', but only what had become customary although it was an abuse.

12-17. These verses deal with two abuses. (a) The priests wrongfully appropriated boiled meat which should have been made available for the worshippers' sacrificial meal. (b) They wanted choice roast meat and so they demanded it raw with the fat which should have furnished a burnt-offering.[3]

19. the yearly sacrifice See Commentary on 1.20.

20. The Lord give you children G: 'The Lord compensate you with children from this woman in exchange for the request which you made of the Lord.' The closing words of the verse are difficult and a small emendation yields 'in exchange for the request which was made of the Lord', i.e., a circumlocution for Samuel. The Hebrew verb here again points to an original Saul birth story rather than a Samuel birth story. (See Commentary on 1.20.)

22. and how they lay . . . tent of meeting All of this is absent from G, but this may not be textually significant. Considerations of propriety may have operated here to expurgate the sins of Eli's sons. On a similar tendency in the Targum see S. R. Driver.

24. spreading abroad This verb might mean either 'spreading' or 'causing to transgress'. In the latter case the pronoun 'you' would have to be supplied. BH emends 'causing the people of Yahweh to do', i.e., coercing the people of Yahweh. The meaning 'spreading' is, however, the more probable.

[3] On the different vessels mentioned in v. 14 see A. M. Honeyman, *PEQ*, 1939, pp. 80 f., 87, 90 and fig. 11.

'For the report which I hear the people of Yahweh propagating is not a good one.'

25. If a man sins . . . If a man wrongs his fellow God may arbitrate through his representative (the judge), but if a man sins against Yahweh there is no machinery for arbitration. There may be the further implication that, since the priest performs judicial functions in Yahweh's community, he cannot be judge in his own cause and so his sin cannot be adjusted before a priestly tribunal, but can be dealt with only by the personal intervention of Yahweh. (So Driver, *Notes*, but this is to read a good deal into the text.) The theological explanation given of the heedlessness of Eli's sons is that it was Yahweh's pleasure to destroy them and the implication of this is that he disposes of men as he wills and no questions can be asked. The intention, however, is not to relieve them of responsibility for their actions and the question how this theological account can be compatible with moral accountability is not really raised.

A PROPHECY OF DOOM

2.27-36

27. I revealed myself to the house of your father RSV follows G. MT, 'Did I indeed reveal myself . . . ?'; i.e., in view of the behaviour of your sons, the fact seems incredible.

29. Why then look with greedy eye . . . ? RSV is based on G, but MT can stand. It has usually been translated, 'Why do you kick at my sacrifices and offerings?' i.e., perhaps 'why do you treat them with contempt?' The verb, however, is attested in Arabic with the meaning 'to exceed'. So the correct rendering may be 'Why do you take more than your share of my sacrifices and offerings which I have commanded in my house?' 'in my house' rests on an emended text.

32. Then in distress you will look with envious eye . . . This again is difficult. RSV follows MT with one emendation (cp. BH). MT has been differently emended to read 'And you will look at the adversity of my house in all wherein (Yahweh) bestows well-being on Israel,' i.e., the sanctuary at Shiloh will fall on evil days at a time when Israel is enjoying general prosperity. This interpretation, however, is forced. The words AND THERE SHALL NOT BE AN OLD MAN IN YOUR HOUSE FOR EVER predict the death of Eli's sons.

33. The man of you whom I shall not cut off . . . RSV follows G. MT: 'But there is one man whom I will not cut off from my altar to consume thine eyes (with tears) and to bring wasting on thy life, and all the increase of thy house will die as men.' This is obscure but the second person singular refers to Eli in a representative capacity, i.e., standing for the priestly house which bears his name. 'The man' then is Abiathar who survived the massacre of the priests at Nob (I Sam. 22.17-20) to the end that, through his ultimate downfall, the fate of the house of Eli might be sealed in a more terrible climax ('in order to consume thine eyes with tears and bring wasting on thy life'). G followed by RSV reads the third person and so the reference is to Abiathar himself.

shall die by the sword of men Following G. MT, 'shall die as men' is obscure but may mean 'shall die when they have reached mature manhood'.

35. my anointed This, like the reference in 2.10, presupposes the existence of the monarchy. The faithful priest is Zadok and priesthood and monarchy are represented as twin pillars of Yahweh's community.

36. for a piece of silver or a loaf of bread . . . i.e., for some menial tasks to perform, for which payment will be made in money or in kind. The priestly descendants of Eli will thus be dependent on the crumbs which the Zadokites throw to them. Verses 35 f. are a *vaticinium ex eventu* hinting at the circumstances of the Deuteronomic reform, and Eissfeldt[4] sees in v. 36 a reference to the degradation of the country priests at the time of the centralization of the cult.

[4] O. Eissfeldt, *Einleitung*, p. 316.

With regard to critical problems there is general agreement that the so-called Song of Hannah has been incorporated into the Books of Samuel at a late stage of their compilation. It is moreover not particularly related to Hannah's experience of Yahweh's favour, and its character as a royal psalm is seen from the reference to the key role of the king in the community in v. 10. Its 'place in life' is the Jerusalem cult. Verses 27-36 have been regarded as one of the passages in Samuel where a Deuteronomic working-over can be most clearly discerned (Kennedy, Eissfeldt, Weiser).

However composite the chapter may be it has a certain unity because of the theological affinity of its parts. The explanation of Eli's downfall rests on a theodicy which strongly resembles that expounded in the Song of Hannah. Yahweh enforces justice among men. He imposed an initial order on the world as creator (v. 8) and this order he effectively preserves; he will not fail either in his insight into human action (v. 3) or in his ability to intervene in order to redress wrongs. The main theme of the Song is the reversal of circumstances brought about by Yahweh's intervention (vv. 4-10). In this he acts to vindicate righteousness and piety and breaks his adversaries in pieces (vv. 9 f.). Similarly the argument of vv. 12-36 is that the wickedness of Eli's sons (made up of bad priestly practice and sexual immorality) brought them inevitably under the judgment of Yahweh, and this theological affinity between vv. 1-10 and the remainder of the chapter is enhanced by the fact that the function of the monarchy is conceived in the same way in v. 10 and v. 35. To the (Davidic) king Yahweh delegates power and responsibility not only to rule his own community but to judge the ends of the earth, and in v. 35 the claims of the priesthood are advanced along with those of the monarchy.

The prophecy of vv. 27-36 is obviously *post eventum.* It is a tendentious interpretation of history in so far as it makes propaganda for the priestly house of Zadok. Verses 12-36 could be described as a priestly legend which is both aetiological and propagandist: aetiological because it explains why the house of Eli was eclipsed and propagandist because it is concerned to establish the legitimacy of the house of Zadok, and to represent that the chief priest and the Davidic monarch are the chief officers of Yahweh's community. The king (the anointed) no less than the priest is a charismatic person.

CHAPTER 3

THE CALL OF SAMUEL

3.1-9

1. there was no frequent vision MT cannot be so translated. It has been emended to read 'no vision was disseminated'. Without emendation it can be rendered 'no vision was ordained'.[1]

2. in his own place This may mean 'official station'. The Arabic cognate certainly has this sense; i.e., there was a place appointed in the temple for Eli to sleep and similarly also for Samuel (v. 9).

3. the lamp of God had not yet gone out The lamp burned through the night and was extinguished in the morning. It must therefore be distinguished from the lamp which was never allowed to go out, mentioned in Ex. 27.20 and Lev. 24.2.

7. Now Samuel did not yet know the Lord These words are further defined by the remainder of the verse, THE WORD OF THE LORD HAD NOT YET BEEN REVEALED TO HIM, i.e., Samuel had had no experience of direct communication from God such as this chapter describes. This is what is meant here by 'knowledge of Yahweh'.

8. Then Eli perceived i.e. discerned or grasped, suggesting a moment of insight. The implication of this is that Samuel's experience was not novel, but belonged to a pattern which Eli eventually identified. That he was slow in doing so may perhaps be attributed to his physical disability (v. 2), but more

[1] G. R. Driver, *JTS* 32, 1930-31, p. 365.

probably it is to be understood in the light of what is related in v. 1. This kind of occurrence was rare at the time. It is possible that v. 1 refers specifically to 'revelation' imparted in the same circumstances in which Samuel heard the voice of Yahweh, and the intention may be to represent that a sanctuary was the recognized place for hearing the word of Yahweh, and even that the hours of night were the time for such communications.

9. Go lie down . . . Eli knows what is the correct procedure to be followed and his words give further point to the rendering 'station' in vv. 2 and 9. Moreover in v. 10 Yahweh, prior to addressing Samuel, comes and takes up his station. There is a recognized response which Eli divulges to Samuel. 'If he (or 'one') calls, you are to say: "Speak, Lord, for your servant is attentive."'

THE LORD SPEAKS TO SAMUEL

3.10-14

10. as at other times i.e., according to normal practice. This refers not to the previous occasions in the chapter when Yahweh had called Samuel, but rather to the established procedure for Yahweh's imparting of his word, namely, the twofold pronunciation of the recipient's name. Hence v. 4 should be emended to read SAMUEL, SAMUEL, in agreement with G.

13. And I tell him RSV follows MT, which, however, should probably be emended. There are two possibilities: (*a*) 'and I shall divulge to you'. (*b*) 'and you are to divulge to him'. (*b*) is the better. In the following part of the verse 'God' of G should be read instead of 'to them' of MT (so RSV).

14. be expiated The question here is whether the basic meaning of this verb is 'cover' or 'wipe', and the evidence of the cognate languages suggests that 'wipe' is primary and 'cover' secondary.[2] We have in English the same figurative

[2] G. R. Driver, *JTS* 34, 1933, pp. 34-38.

usage as that associated with this verb in Hebrew. We speak of wiping out a deficit. Yahweh tells Samuel that the wrong-doing of Eli and his sons has created a deficit of guilt which cannot be wiped out by any sacrificial offering, and that the holy office and Yahweh himself have been brought into disrepute. *zebaḥ* is an animal sacrifice and *minḥā* a present or gift. The latter word is used in the sense of an offering made to Yahweh, whether animal or cereal.

SAMUEL PROPHESIES TO ELI

3.15-18

17. Do not hide it from me Samuel was afraid to disclose his vision to Eli, but was subsequently obliged to tell everything. Eli threatens him with a curse in the event of his concealing any part of Yahweh's word. Despite the fate which hangs over him the old man is still his instructor, and this is a lesson which Samuel has to learn. It is his duty to transmit Yahweh's word to those to whom it is addressed. This was an aspect of prophetic responsibility with which the major prophets were greatly concerned. Cp. I Cor. 9.16.

SAMUEL AN ACCREDITED PROPHET

3.19-21

19. let none of his words fall to the ground The presupposition of this phrase is that prophecy has chiefly to do with prediction, and that a prophet is known to be genuine when his forecasts are correct. This is the same concept of prophecy as appears in Deut. 18.22. Whatever prophecies about the future were made by Samuel were validated by subsequent events. It is to this circumstance that the phrase in v. 20 refers, 'Samuel was accredited as a prophet of Yahweh'.

20. from Dan to Beersheba This is used here and elsewhere to denote the entire territory of Israel. Dan is in the extreme north-east and Beersheba marks the south-west limit.

The phrase is associated with the boundaries of the united kingdom under David (I Chron. 21.2) and Solomon (I Kings 4.25), but its earlier significance may be religious rather than political. It is a way of designating the area settled by the tribes of the Israelite amphictyony (so here and Judg. 20.1). Evidence that this earlier usage persisted into the period of the divided kingdoms is found in II Chron. 30.5. Political division and the use of 'Israel' for the northern kingdom did not obliterate the awareness of a prior 'Israel', a confederation of tribes settled over an area conveniently described as 'from Dan to Beer-sheba' (cp. II Sam. 17.11).

21. And the Lord appeared again at Shiloh This tends to confirm the interpretation offered in v. 8. It is the rarity of the word of Yahweh at Shiloh which is the special concern of the writer and so he observes that through Samuel communication with Yahweh has been restored. It is common to emend the remainder of the verse by inserting the opening words of 4.1 before the closing words of 3.21. The verse, with one small emendation, then reads: 'And Yahweh appeared again at Shiloh, for Yahweh revealed himself to Samuel at Shiloh; and the word of Samuel came to all Israel according to the word of Yahweh'.

This chapter is a unity with the possible exception of vv. 12-14 which contain a second prediction of the downfall of the house of Eli (cp. 2.27-36).

The chapter has several interesting features. In the first place it represents Samuel as both a prophetic and priestly figure and it assumes that prophecy is normally associated with the sanctuary and so with the priesthood. Samuel elsewhere (7.9 f.) performs sacrificial functions which are recognizably priestly, but he is also a prophet in his possession of the knowledge of Yahweh (v. 7). The central sanctuary at Shiloh was, in the writer's view, the place where such intimate converse with Yahweh should have taken place, but, at this period, the word of Yahweh was rare and no vision was appointed (v. 1). It was then that Samuel, being yet a youth, heard the voice of

Yahweh and this marked the inauguration of a new prophetic era (v. 21). This is the principal theme of the chapter.

Then there is the lack of precision in the vocabulary employed to describe the prophetic endowment. The setting of the scene at night in the Shiloh sanctuary might seem to indicate that revelation from Yahweh was not by word but by dream-vision. This impression is strengthened by the use of the words VISION in v. 1 and 'appearance' in v. 15 (the latter from the verb 'to see'). On the other hand, side by side with VISION in v. 1, there is the reference to the word of Yahweh which presupposes revelation by hearing. This is the more important concept in the chapter, for Samuel is not represented as seeing a vision in sleep, but as hearing the voice of Yahweh when awake. Hence Eli's instructions to him are to answer Yahweh when he hears his voice: 'Speak, Yahweh, for your servant is attentive' (v. 9). Yet, although the notion of revelation by dream-vision is not influential in shaping the narrative, the thought of it does appear in some of the vocabulary employed and in the night-setting at Shiloh.

Finally there is the high drama which is created by the nature of Yahweh's word to Samuel. Eli had already been warned of the impending downfall of his priestly house, but, in virtue of Yahweh's word, Samuel had incurred the special responsibility of reinforcing this prophecy of disaster. He was thus already setting a pattern for his great successors who were also charged to speak hard words of judgment and woe (cp. Ezek. 2.10). Samuel, in this situation, was sandwiched between the demands of modesty (he was still a boy) and those of prophetic responsibility, but he was extricated from this dilemma by Eli who acted with insight and delicate sympathy. Samuel was still the apprentice and was instructed in a first principle of prophetic responsibility by the old man over whose house the shadows were lengthening. The bearing of Eli in a painful moment compels admiration. He remembers his responsibility to a prophet in the making, and he accepts the judgment of Yahweh with composure: IT IS YAHWEH, LET HIM DO WHAT SEEMS GOOD TO HIM.

CONCERNING THE ARK

I 4.1–7.1

CHAPTER 4

ISRAEL DEFEATED BY THE PHILISTINES

4.1-2

1. And the word of Samuel . . . RSV follows MT. G has a longer text: 'And it came to pass in those days the Philistines were mobilized for war against Israel and Israel went out to meet them . . .'

2. and when the battle spread Or, deriving the verb differently, 'and the battle was clashed together'.[1] A free rendering would be: 'And there was the din of battle'.

A COUNCIL OF WAR AFTER DEFEAT

4.3-4

3. the ark of the covenant of the Lord The same phrase occurs in v. 5 and also (with the substitution of LORD OF HOSTS for 'Lord') in v. 4a. Verse 4b has THE ARK OF THE COVENANT OF GOD. In G^B 'covenant' is missing in all these passages: v. 3 reads 'the ark of our God', v. 4a 'the ark of the Lord', v. 4b 'the ark', v. 5 'the ark of the Lord'. It has been assumed that COVENANT is a later addition to MT.

Why has the Lord put us to rout . . .? Either 'permitted us to be routed' or 'actively participated in routing us'. The fetching of the ark would seem to be inconsistent with the latter alternative, since it points to the conclusion that the Israelites attributed their defeat not to Yahweh's intervention

[1] G. R. Driver, *JTS* 34, 1933, p. 379.

against them, but to their failure to harness his power effectively.

4. were there THERE is omitted by G and its absence removes the ambiguity of MT. The meaning cannot be that Hophni and Phinehas were at Shiloh with the ark, but that they accompanied it to the field of battle.

THE CAPTURE OF THE ARK

4.5-11

5. gave a mighty shout Cp. the formulae with which the ark was greeted on its exit and return (Num. 10. 35 f.). This was probably a beneficent incantation. Here, by means of the war-cry, expression is given to the new inspiration and strength which is felt in the presence of the ark. Hence v. 6 describes the adverse effect which the 'war-cry' and the discovery of its cause had on the Philistines.

7. The gods have come into the camp It is difficult to decide whether it is the writer's intention to make the Philistines speak polytheistic language or whether the plural is the normal Hebrew plural form for 'God'. It is arguable that the writer would not be interested in this kind of realism, that is, in making Philistines speak like Philistines, and that their references to Israel's God are in the language which Israelites would use. The polytheistic language seems out of place in v. 8, where 'This is the God WHO SMOTE THE EGYPTIANS WITH EVERY KIND OF PLAGUE' is more likely than THESE ARE THE GODS WHO SMOTE . . .

THE BRINGING OF THE NEWS TO SHILOH

4.12-18

13. on his seat by the road watching This presupposes a slight emendation of MT. BH follows G, 'on his seat beside the gate watching the road'.

15. and his eyes were set i.e., were fixed in a sightless stare.

17. He who brought the tidings The strict meaning of the root used here is 'to bring good news',[2] but the usage here is wider and less exact, and, in this case, the news is bad.

slaughter 'rout' is a better translation.

THE BIRTH OF A SON TO PHINEHAS

4.19-22

19. for her pains came upon her Literally: 'and her labour pains turned on her', i.e., came on her suddenly as a consequence of the shock she received on hearing the news of the disaster.

21. Ichabod It has been held that the meaning 'Inglorious' or 'Empty of glory' rests on a popular and false etymology. Moreover the originality of this form of the name has been called in question. Yet the meaning 'Empty of glory' suits the context well, so that, if the form is secondary, it was doubtless suggested by the words which follow it.

The two principal topics of the chapter are the loss of the ark and the consummation of Yahweh's judgment on Eli and his two sons, and it is the author's intention to establish a connection between them. That the house of Eli is ripe for judgment has been underlined by two predictions of Yahweh's impending action against it (ch. 2 and 3) and the fulfilment of these is sketched now in three bold strokes; in the death of Hophni and Phinehas on the battlefield; in that of Eli just as the full implications of a terrible disaster are grasped by him, and in that of the wife of Phinehas, in a moment of agony, when she finds no joy in the birth of a son, but sees in him a sign of Israel's shame and despair.

Eli collapses and dies at the mention of the loss of the ark.

[2] See however, C. H. Gordon, *UM* p. 249, No. 372, *pace* G. R. Driver, *CML* p. 164.

It is as though we are meant to understand that he could endure his private sorrow, but could not bear to entertain its implications for Israel. It was the public aspect of the failure of his sons which was unendurable. They had carried the ark with unclean hands and now the ark had been taken away, not only from them, but from all Israel.

It is the presence of Hophni and Phinehas which explains the disastrous fortunes of Israel in war. Otherwise the course of events is inexplicable. After deliberation the Israelites trace their first defeat to a failure to exploit effectively the power of Yahweh, and this power, concentrated in the ark, is transported from Shiloh to the camp, where the army greets its arrival with a great shout of confidence. A new power has entered into them; they have fresh appetite for the fight, and it seems that the scene is being set for a resounding Israelite victory.

This impression is confirmed by the picture given of dismay in the Philistine camp. Israel's God has arrived at the scene of battle, the God who battered Egypt—a major power—into submission. How then, with the scales tipped so heavily against them, is effective resistance possible? But they exhort one another to fight resolutely, for their existence as free men is at stake. But now, contrary to expectations, when the battle is joined, it issues in a Philistine victory, and the clue to this puzzling result is to be found in v. 11: AND THE ARK OF GOD WAS CAPTURED, AND THE TWO SONS OF ELI, HOPHNI AND PHINEHAS, WERE SLAIN. Their presence, as custodians of the ark, brought disaster on the whole army. Because Yahweh's judgment fell upon them at a moment when they were performing a critical public duty, all Israel was involved in their ruin; and the ark, with which the Israelite army should have advanced to victory as an irresistible force, was wrested from the custody of Hophni and Phinehas and fell into the hands of the Philistines.

CHAPTER 5

THE ARK AT ASHDOD

5.1-8

1. Ashdod Groll. p. 143; Ekron, p. 148 and Gath p. 150.

2. Dagon An old Accadian deity worshipped throughout the Euphrates valley as far back as the middle of the third millennium BC. In the Ugaritic literature Baal is represented as the son of Dagon, a corn god, and *dgn* has the meaning 'corn' there as it has in Hebrew. Here Dagon is the god of Ashdod where he has a temple as also at Gaza (Judg. 16.23).[1]

and set it up beside Dagon i.e., it was their intention that it should be permanently situated there. In placing it beside Dagon their intention may have been to bring it under his influence, so that they could control it and count on its support.

3. And when the people of Ashdod . . . RSV follows MT. G has a longer text: 'And the inhabitants of Ashdod rose early the next day and came to the house of Dagon and looked and behold . . .'

face downward on the ground This presupposes an emended text. Without emending we might translate: 'And behold, Dagon had fallen before it to the ground, (that is), before the ark of Yahweh'. This, however, is strained. The same phrase recurs in v. 4.

4. threshold The meaning 'podium' has been suggested, that is, the base or pedestal on which the god rested.[2]

only the trunk of Dagon was left to him This is based on G. MT has 'Only Dagon was left to him', which makes no sense. An earlier emendation which required no more than the assumption that one consonant had been written twice

[1] Albright, *ARI* p. 74.
[2] H. Winckler, *Altorientalische Forschungen*, 3. 2, 1905, p. 381.

(dittography) was: 'Only the fishy part was left to him'. This, however, presupposes that Dagon was a fish-god and it now seems clear that this was not so.

5. do not tread on the threshold of Dagon The tense is frequentative. 'Do not make a practice of walking on the podium of Dagon', presumably because the podium had become 'holy' through its contact with the parts of the god. Winckler[3] assumes that we have here an aetiological tale which offers an explanation of a peculiarity of cultic practice at Ashdod.

6. and he terrified and afflicted them Literally: 'And he made them desolate and struck them down', 'made them desolate' perhaps referring to the injurious effects of the plague on their morale as well as on their health.

tumours Or 'boils' or 'piles'. Just as Yahweh had chastised the Egyptians with plagues of every kind, so the ark of Yahweh had brought plague with it to Ashdod (cp. 4.8).

both Ashdod and its territory This is MT. Instead of these words G has 'and the jumping-mice came up into the midst of its territory'. TERRITORY refers to the rural area outside the city walls which was within the political jurisdiction of the 'metropolis' and subject to its economic control.

AT GATH

5.9

broke out upon them The verb is difficult and two derivations have been suggested, but the result in both cases is approximately the same. The primary idea of the one root is 'demolish' or 'dissolve'[4] and of the other 'to loose'.[5] A derivation from the second necessitates an alteration of the Masoretic vocalization.

[3] *Ibid.*, p. 382.

[4] S. R. Driver, *Notes, in loc.*; G. R. Driver, *Aramaic Documents of the Fifth Century BC*, 1957, p. 76 n. 1.

[5] E. Nestle, *ZAW* 29, 1909, p. 232; cp. S. R. Driver, *Notes*, p. 52 n. 2.

AT EKRON

5.10-12

11. deathly panic According to normal English usage this would mean 'panic as silent as death' which is almost a contradiction, since panic is normally associated with noise and frenzied activity. A better translation of the Hebrew 'panic of death' would be 'deadly panic' or 'fatal panic'.

The Philistines, victorious in battle, carry off the ark in triumph and install it in the temple of Dagon at Ashdod. But the ark is not their prisoner and it is soon evident that they have introduced a dangerous power into their midst. Before it Dagon cannot stand and, when they prop him up, he falls again and is broken. It is already clear that the ark is a power which they cannot control or exploit by according it the rank of a subordinate deity in Dagon's temple; for the ark is sovereign and unfriendly and capable of humiliating Dagon in his own house. This, however, is but the beginning of sorrows, a symbol of their defencelessness before the ark, for they may not look to Dagon for support.

As Yahweh inflicted the Egyptians with plagues, so his power, concentrated in the ark, inflicts plague on the citizens of Ashdod, and they speedily decide to have it removed to Gath. But plague accompanies it to Gath and travels with it to Ekron. Thus, in its circuit of Philistine territory, it has everywhere brought panic and disease in its train. The Philistines have got more than they bargained for and it may be, as has been suggested, that the author is making his point, here and elsewhere in the stories about the ark, with more than a touch of humour. The Philistines have exposed themselves to the power of Yahweh and he is no better disposed towards them than he was towards the Egyptians. This reinforces the point made in ch. 4 that the Israelites did not lose the battle because they were mistaken in the potency which they attributed to the ark. That the power of Yahweh is concentrated in the ark is now unmistakably demonstrated and the reason for defeat must therefore be sought in the persons of Hophni and Phinehas.

CHAPTER 6

THE ADVICE OF THE DIVINERS

6.1-9

1. seven months After these words G adds: 'and their land swarmed with jumping-mice'.

2. the priests and the diviners Or perhaps in this context, in view of the meaning of the Arabic cognate, 'soothsayers and diviners'. At any rate, the reference is to those who knew how to obtain authoritative answers by oracular procedures and techniques, e.g. the inspection of the entrails of animals; or by the observation and interpretation of certain phenomena, e.g. movements of birds, dispositions of stars, the material of dreams. In this instance the question posed to them was: 'WHAT SHALL WE DO WITH THE ARK OF YAHWEH?' The intention of the question is clarified by the words which follow: TELL US WITH WHAT (or, 'in what manner') we are to despatch it TO ITS PLACE, i.e., to Israelite territory or even, perhaps, to Shiloh from where it had come to the field of battle. Hence the Philistines have made up their minds to get rid of the ark and they now ask the diviners what is the correct way to implement this decision. The answer given (v. 3) is that the ark should not be returned without an accompanying guilt-offering which will compensate for the wrong done by the Philistines to the ark in the act of carrying it into their territory.

3. then you will be healed and it will be known to you This is the natural way to translate these words, but the statement does not agree with the following verses. For, from what follows, it appears that the diviners do not claim that they are prescribing a certain cure; they are merely conducting an experiment (cp. v. 9). It would be more in accord with the context if we could translate: 'Then, if you are healed, it will be known to you'. This, however, is not the plain sense of the Hebrew.

4. and five golden mice These words do not appear in G^B. The significance of the number five is that the Philistines were organized into five city-states each with its ruler (cp. v. 17).[1]

was upon all of you MT: 'All of them'. The emended text followed by RSV has the support of T.

6. Why should you harden your hearts? Literally: 'make your heart heavy or cumbersome', i.e., unresponsive. 'Why are you so slow in the uptake'?

made sport of them Köh. 'dealt severely with them'. The RSV translation is preferable; the idea of 'diversion' is prominent in the Arabic usages of the root.

8. box Köh. 'saddle-bag'.

THE CONDUCTING OF THE EXPERIMENT

6.10-13

12. Beth Shemesh Groll. p. 145, Beth Shemesh (1).

13. valley A 'deepening', i.e. a broad depression between hills.

THE ARK ARRIVES AT BETH SHEMESH

6.14-18

17. Gaza Groll. p. 150 and Ashkelon, p. 143.

18. according to the number of all the cities There is a discrepancy between this and v. 4 which reads: FIVE GOLDEN MICE ACCORDING TO THE NUMBER OF THE LORDS OF THE PHILISTINES. Here the number five is applied to the golden tumours or

[1] See Noth, *History*, pp. 35 f.

boils, one for each of the five cities, but the number of mice is said to be equal to the total of Philistine settlements, both fortified towns and open villages. It has been assumed that the words, 'These are . . . unwalled villages', are not part of the original narrative.

the great stone beside which This presupposes an emendation of MT, but it has the support of G and T and is demanded by the sense. 'upon which' is perhaps better than BESIDE WHICH. The intention is probably that the great stone should serve as an altar.

is a witness to this day This reading depends on a revocalized MT. Another possibility is: 'is still to this day'.

THE ARK WREAKS HAVOC AT BETH SHEMESH

6.19-20

19. And he slew some of the men of Beth Shemesh RSV follows MT. G: 'And the sons of Jeconiah did not rejoice among the men of Beth Shemesh'. S. R. Driver[2] thinks that the Greek verb is a very free rendering of its Hebrew original, which conveyed the idea of not going unpunished, not coming off guiltless. Thus: 'The sons of Jeconiah did not get away without punishment among the men of Beth Shemesh'. He thinks this is superior to MT.

because they looked into Rather: 'because they gazed (or, 'gaped') at'. They were punished for their inordinate and profane curiosity.

he slew seventy men of them After this figure 'fifty thousand' appears in both MT and G. This looks like a later exaggeration.

THE ARK FINDS A HOME AT KIRIATH-JEARIM

7.1

Kiriath-jearim Groll. p. 155.

[2] S. R. Driver, *Notes*, *in loc.*

This is a difficult chapter because it has more than one thread, but its main thread can be followed with comparative ease and assurance. The plague would appear to have consisted of mice and boils. It is true that there is no mention of mice in MT of ch. 5.6, but they are mentioned in G and again in 6.1 of G. Moreover it is reasonable to explain the making of the golden images of mice by the assumption that they were part of the plague. Whether there was a causal relationship between the mice and the boils, so that the intention is to represent the mice as carriers of the epidemic, must remain uncertain.

In their predicament the Philistines consult their soothsayers(?) and diviners and they are advised that an experiment should be carried out with a view to clearing up the obscurities of the situation. The procedure which they advise should be followed is symbolic, the guiding principle being that of sympathetic magic. The uncertainty which has to be resolved is whether the ark is the primary cause of the epidemic. Thus the ark is taken away and with it images of the mice and the boils. That is to say the presumed cause of the plague together with its manifestations are sent away. The crucial test is to be the route taken by the cows. If they make straight for Israelite territory it is to be assumed that the plague was on account of the ark, and it can be safely concluded that the elements of the plague have now been removed from Philistine terrain. The significance of the two cows in milk is not easy to decide. The intention may be to provide sacrificial animals in connection with the return of the ark to the Israelites, and, if so, it is to be noted that the motif of the animals offering themselves voluntarily for sacrifice may also be present,[3] the altar being the great stone; cp. Gen. 22.13.

But the ark, by reason of the power of Yahweh which is concentrated in it, is as dangerous to inexperienced Israelite laymen as it was to the Philistines and, in this thought, we perhaps encounter a distinctively Israelite and priestly point of view. The ark is 'holy' and it must be handled and cared

[3] W. R. Smith, *ROS* p. 309 n. 1.

for by someone who has been made 'holy'. It thus requires a priest as its custodian and so it finds a suitable lodging in the house of Abinadab at Kiriath-jearim who consecrates his son Eleazar as its guardian. There are other verses in the chapter which also seem to be written from this priestly point of view. Thus the objects which accompany the ark are described as a guilt offering (vv. 3 f.), although their form (golden images of boils and mice) suggests a therapeutic rather than a theological function. The concern of the Philistines is said to be to return the ark to its place (v. 2). PLACE may simply be equated with Israelite terrain or, in view of vv. 19-21, which describe the dangers to which even lay Israelites are exposed in the presence of the ark, it may mean an accredited sanctuary; cp. 7.1. There is nothing, however, distinctively Israelite in the association of 'holiness' and danger.[4]

If then this priestly point of view is present in the chapter, (it certainly seems to be present in v. 15 where the handling of the ark and the box is reserved for the Levites[5]) it appears to represent that the Philistines, when they return the ark, make restitution for the wrong done to it during its stay in Philistine territory. With this thought may be connected the words, THEN YOU WILL BE HEALED AND IT WILL BE KNOWN TO YOU WHY HIS HAND IS NOT AVERTED FROM YOU (6.3), i.e. having made this guilt offering and secured relief, you will realize that it was your offence against Yahweh in appropriating the ark which was the source of your trouble. This is a different idea from that of v. 9, which makes the procedure more of an experiment than a guilt offering. GUILT OFFERING implies that the cause of the plague is already known and that a remedy can be authoritatively prescribed, but v. 9 implies that the object of the experiment is to discover the source of the plague and that the answer only becomes clear when the cows make a bee-line for Israelite terrain.

[4] For an analysis of the primitive Semitic concept of 'holiness' see W. R. Smith, *ROS* pp. 140-64, especially p. 162.

[5] A Bentzen, *Introduction* II, p. 95, attributes this verse to P.

SAMUEL AND SAUL

I 7-15

CHAPTER 7

SAMUEL'S COUNSEL TO ISRAEL

7.2-4

2. lamented Or: 'And all the house of Israel followed after Yahweh'.[1] This, however, is contradicted by vv. 3 f.

3. direct Literally: 'make firm or steadfast', 'establish', i.e. follow Yahweh with unwavering purpose.

Ashtaroth The Syrian Astarte (Babylonian Ishtar) was a goddess who had chiefly to do with sex and fertility. Thus 'the Ashtaroth of the sheep' in Deut. 7.13 refers to the produce of the flock or to sheep breeding. Whether the phrase means more than this is doubtful, but it has been held that in one of her types Astarte was a sheep-goddess.[2] At any rate she was a mother goddess and also the patron of a cult involving sacred prostitution. In the west Semitic area she is mentioned frequently in Phoenician inscriptions and appears in the Ugaritic literature.[3] The forms ASHTAROTH and BAALIM (v. 4) are both plural and they presumably refer either to images of these deities or, more probably, to local manifestations of them. Thus in Phoenician inscriptions there is a Baal of Sidon, of Tyre and of Lebanon; and in the Old Testament such specifications of Baal occur as Berith (the Baal who invigilates over covenants, Judg. 8.33; 9.4); Zebub (Lord of Flies, the god of Ekron, II Kings 1.2 f.); Peor (Lord of Peor, Num. 25.3, 5; Deut. 4.3, Hosea 9.10). A commonly held view that the baalim of the Old Testament were local deities on whom the fertility of the soil was thought to depend has been contested in more

[1] G. R. Driver, *JTS* 34, 1933, p. 377.
[2] W. R. Smith, *ROS* p. 310.
[3] Albright, *ARI* pp. 74-77.

recent times, largely on the evidence of the Ugaritic literature, and the character of Baal as a god of cosmic power has been stressed. Baal is equated with the ancient Semitic storm god, Hadad, but he acquired the status of king of the gods not later than the fifteenth century BC.[4] On the other hand Robertson Smith's argument that the baalim are primarily gods of underground springs and only secondarily rain gods has not, so far as I can judge, been discredited.[5]

ISRAEL ASSEMBLES AT MIZPAH

7.5-11

5. Mizpah Groll. p. 157. Mizpah (1).

6. and poured it out G has the additional words 'to the ground'. The accompanying fast and confession make it clear that the ritual had a penitential significance. As the water was cast upon the ground so Israel was to cast away her sins.

and Samuel judged That this refers to the giving of legal decisions is confirmed by vv. 15-17, where the same expression is used in this sense. Otherwise JUDGED in v. 6 might have been understood as political and military leadership—a well-established meaning of the Hebrew word.

8. Do not cease to cry Literally: 'Do not be silent (or 'deaf') (turning) away from us so as not to cry'. The cry for help is indicative of the urgency of their intercession. It is to Yahweh that Israel looks for deliverance from the Philistines.

9. So Samuel took a sucking lamb Samuel is here represented as exercising priestly functions and this is in agreement with the account of his apprenticeship to Eli in the opening chapters. WHOLE BURNT OFFERING means that the entire sacrifice was burned and that the worshippers did not share in any part of it. The Philistine defeat is attributed to the fact that

[4] Albright, *ARI* pp. 73 f., 84-90.
[5] W. R. Smith, *ROS* pp. 93-108.

Yahweh answered Samuel's prayer on behalf of Israel. It is Yahweh's mighty voice thundering against the Philistines which produces demoralization and rout, (v. 10) and only subsequently do we hear of military activity by the Israelites against the fleeing Philistines (v. 11). Israel has been saved by Yahweh through Samuel's mediation.

11. Beth-Car The site is unknown. A conjectural emendation is Beth-Horon (Groll. p. 145).

THE PHILISTINES SUBDUED

7.12-14

12. between Mizpah and Jeshanah 'Jeshanah' is an emendation to which G and S have been thought to point. MT: 'Between Mizpah and the crag'. The site of Ebenezer is unknown.

13. And the hand of the Lord This underlines the representation of vv. 9-12. It is Yahweh who has helped Israel in association with a priestly intercessor (ALL THE DAYS OF SAMUEL) and the Philistines are so completely subject to him that the entire area occupied by them (FROM EKRON TO GATH) is restored to Israelite control.

SAMUEL JUDGES ISRAEL

7.15-17

15. Samuel judged Israel This apparently refers to the giving of legal decisions and this judicial activity is associated with the sanctuaries of Bethel, Gilgal and Mizpah where he held court in turn. That this interpretation is correct is strengthened by the notice in v. 17 that in the resident centre of justice, Ramah, Samuel built an altar to Yahweh. That is, he was a priestly judge, one whose decisions were given at a sanctuary. This concept of judging as a sacred activity where the hard decisions are left to Yahweh appears in Ex. 18.15 f. and 22.7 f. Cp. the palm of Deborah, a sacred tree which was the locus of her judicial activity (Judg. 4.5). This may have some connection with the idea of trial by ordeal which appears in Num. 5.11 ff. in relation to the woman suspected of infidelity towards her husband who is made to drink holy water mixed with the dust of the sanctuary and administered with a curse which brings dropsy and wasting in the event of her guilt. Cp. 'spring of judgment', i.e., the holy waters which elicit the right decision (Gen. 14.7); similarly 'the waters of litigation (Meribah) of Kadesh' (Num. 20.13-14; 27.14 and elsewhere). For Bethel see Groll. p. 145 and for Gilgal, p. 150, Gilgal (1). Gilgal means 'a (sacred stone) circle'. Cp. Josh. 4.20.

16. in all these places It is very dubious whether MT can be so translated. A possible rendering is: 'And Samuel judged Israel (even) all these places'. It has been suggested that 'Israel' should be regarded as a late gloss whose intention is to widen the sphere of Samuel's judicial activities beyond the three centres mentioned.

This is of a piece theologically with the account of the institution of the monarchy which views that institution with disfavour. It is ascribed by Noth[6] (also by Kennedy) to the Deuteronomist and by Eissfeldt to the Elohist. S. R. Driver[7] has called attention to its theological affinity to the framework of the Book of Judges. The point of view of this school of thought is that Israel's subjection to the Philistines follows from her dalliance with foreign gods and that she will be delivered when she gives Yahweh her unshared devotion. Hence at Mizpah there is a corporate act of penitence, and Samuel plays the part of a priestly intercessor between Yahweh and Israel. It is because Yahweh hears his prayer that the Philistines are routed, and so the dramatic turn in Israel's fortunes is traced to her change of heart and to the effectiveness of Samuel as a priestly mediator.

The subsequent period of Israelite dominance over the Philistines is described in the same terms. It derives from

[6] M. Noth, *History*, p. 172 n. 2.
[7] S. R. Driver, *Introduction*, pp. 174, 176.

Yahweh's action against them and from Samuel's ability as a ruler (v. 13). The military potential of Israel is not thought to be important; her well-being does not hang upon her political or military organization, but on the correctness of her religious posture and on the leadership of Samuel.

The question may be raised how far this picture corresponds to historical realities. The account of the fate of the ark in 4–7.1 may be a reflection of the first large-scale military clash between Israelites and Philistines, but the remove from historicity appears to be even further in this present chapter which has the aspect of a late reconstruction guided by dogmatic considerations. On the other hand the portrayal may not be late in all respects. If Albright[8] is correct in supposing that the high priest was a key figure in the amphictyonic community, the influence attributed here to Samuel *qua* priest may reflect early usage. There is a certain amount of difficulty, however, in the assumption that Samuel was high priest. He was not apparently so regarded, since the office is said to have remained in the line of Eli during his period of leadership (I Sam. 14.3; 22.20). But he may have been high priest *de facto* and in a period of great national emergency may have been the inspiration of Israelite resistance to Philistine pressure. Shiloh had been destroyed by the Philistines *c.* 1050 BC,[9] and Samuel, we are told, made his home in Ramah, where his parents had lived (I Sam. 1.19) and built an altar there. It would, however, be unwise to conclude that Ramah had, for the time, become the central sanctuary of the tribes, for it is mentioned along with Bethel, Gilgal and Mizpah, not in connection with an amphictyonic festival, but as a place where Samuel administered justice to Israel. Only Mizpah in this chapter features as a place of assembly for Israel.

There is one aspect of this description of Samuel's judicial duties which does seem to conform to authentic amphictyonic practice. Noth[10] has argued that the so-called 'minor judges'

[8] Albright, *ARI*, pp 107-110, followed by Bright, *History*, pp. 128-60.
[9] H. Kjaer, *JPOS*, 1930, pp. 87-174; Albright, *ARI*, pp. 103 f.
[10] Noth, *History*, p. 102.

were legal officers of the amphictyonic organization responsible for the administration of the Covenant Law. It is interesting that the expression, 'And Samuel judged Israel' (vv. 6, 16, 17) corresponds exactly to the formula employed in the lists of 'minor judges' in Judg. 10.1-5; 12.7-15. Of these lists Noth says that they contain 'the only exact and obviously authentic chronological information . . . which the Old Testament contains for the period before the founding of the Kingdom'. He further holds that the office of 'minor judge' was central in the twelve-tribe society of Israel in which the Covenant Law played a decisive role. It is worthy of note that the other meaning of 'judge', namely to exercise political and military leadership (cp. Deborah and Gideon, Judg. 4-8), does not appear in this chapter, although this is the role which Samuel is occupying at Mizpah. It seems safe to conclude that this aspect of the portrait of Samuel corresponds to the model of the 'minor judge' in Judg. 10.1-5 and 12.7-15.

CHAPTER 8

THE SONS OF SAMUEL PERVERT JUSTICE

8.1-3

1. History repeats itself in so far as Samuel's sons like those of Eli are unworthy of their father, but, whereas Hophni and Phinehas misbehave in a priestly context (2.12 ff., 22 f.), Joel and Abijah fail in the judicial trust which has been reposed in them. They are judges at Beersheba (Groll. p. 144), but they are carried away by greed and are amenable to bribery, so that they cease to administer and defend justice (vv. 2 f.).

A CONFERENCE AT RAMAH

8.4-9

5. to govern us like all the nations Here the same Hebrew word 'judge' is used with the sense of political and military leadership and the RSV translation brings this out. LIKE ALL THE NATIONS is not, however, a legitimate translation; it should be 'among all the nations'. 'To judge us among all the nations' means to provide us with effective leadership in a hostile world, with the implication that other nations have political structures which have their centre in a king, and that Israel must acquire the enhanced solidarity and coordination of resources made possible by this institution; cp. v. 20.

7. they have rejected me Samuel is given explicit instructions what attitude he is to adopt. He is not to take this demand for a king as reflecting the failure of his leadership. The issue is a fundamental one, but it is not between Samuel and Israel; it is between Yahweh and Israel. It has nothing to do with Samuel's performance as a 'judge' nor to the lack of integrity in his sons, although the elders make this the immediate occasion of their demand (v. 5). What is ultimately implied in this request for a king is that Israel prefers to rely on a monarchy of a worldly pattern rather than on the kingship of Yahweh. This is the logical outcome of a long record of rebelliousness and idolatry (v. 8). In the face of this demand Samuel is to advise against the institution of a worldly monarchy, but, if the elders persist in their demand, he is to let them have their way (vv. 8 f.).

SAMUEL DESCRIBES THE CHARACTER OF THE MONARCHY

8.10-18

11. These will be the ways of the king Or: 'This will be the practice of the king' (similarly in v. 9). Samuel then describes the various exactions associated with the pattern of a despotic monarchy. These include conscription for military service (vv. 11 f.), for agricultural work and the making of arms (v. 12) and for domestic service (v. 13). Moreover the king will expropriate the best fields, vineyards and olive orchards along with domestic servants and the pick of domestic animals

(vv. 14 and 16). He will tax all fields, vineyards and flocks to the tune of a tenth (vv. 15 and 17) and will deprive Israelites of their liberty (v. 17). If you get your king, he will be more than you have bargained for (v. 18). You will cry out to Yahweh for relief from his tyranny, but he will not answer you.

13. perfumers The word has the secondary sense of 'concubines' in Accadian, but, since the context is that of domestic service, PERFUMERS is probably preferable.

14. his servants SERVANTS is a technical term for royal officials and it refers (also v. 15) to the bureaucracy which was part of the pattern of monarchy in the ancient Near East.[1] The king will resort to confiscation and taxation in order to support this royal establishment.

15. officers Literally: 'the one at the head of the king'. The word has the specialized meaning of eunuch, since these were frequently employed in the palace especially in connection with the harem (cp. Esth. 2, 3, 14 f.; 4.4 f.).

16. cattle RSV follows G. This gives better sense than MT 'youths'.

SAMUEL'S ADVICE REFUSED

8.19-22

20. that we also may be like all the nations Cp. v. 5. Here the elders say exactly why they want a king. They expect him to exercise leadership, so that Israel will not be at a disadvantage in relation to the other nations which possess kings.

There are no particular difficulties about the unity of this chapter, although Kennedy assumes that v. 10 and v. 22b are redactional adjustments connected with the intertwining of the two different narratives of the institution of the monarchy. Otherwise the chapter is assigned by Kennedy to the Deuteronomist (D) and by Eissfeldt to the Elohist (E). It is generally

[1] Albright, *ARI* p. 138.

agreed that it belongs to the narrative strand which is unfavourably disposed towards the monarchy.

The two senses of 'judge' are present in this chapter; the judicial sense in vv. 1-3 and the political sense in vv. 5, 6, 20. Thus 'judge' in the latter sense is equivalent to 'reign' in vv. 9, 11. The link between the two is supplied by vv. 4-5, where the elders related their demand for a king to the corrupt legal practices of the sons of Samuel. This, however, is rather an unsatisfactory and unconvincing link, for the demand for a king as it is subsequently formulated is seen to have nothing to do with the judicial dishonesty of Samuel's sons, but to be related to an urgent political situation. It may be the intention of the writer to convey that the elders were disingenuous in the reason which they gave. The corruptness of Samuel's sons was an excuse rather than a reason and Yahweh divulges to Samuel the true significance of their demand for a king. At any rate, what they now say to Samuel is that Israel is confronting the Philistine menace and must organize herself for survival. Such survival is thought to hinge on effective leadership and it is believed that only a king can supply such leadership. Thus the demand of the elders is the expression of a practical, political judgment.

Samuel is still the intercessor as he was in ch. 7. It is he who carries the request of the elders to Yahweh and ascertains his attitude to the demand. He traces it to a long process of apostasy. Israel has forsaken him for strange gods (a Deuteronomic phrase) and now she sees her salvation not in his kingship, but in a compact political structure comparable to that of her neighbours and with a king at its head. This latest gesture of defection is related to a long history of rebellion and Samuel is not to conclude that it is an indictment of his rule. He must advise against the step, but, if his advice is disregarded, he is not to obstruct the elders in their resolve.

With regard to vv. 8-18 it is hard to resist the conclusion that, in its present form, this section is late. It reproduces with such detail the particular features of Solomon's despotism that it would seem to depend on the experience of Israel in this reign. This does not mean, however, that the later redactional elements are so overpowering that they have reduced to the point of extinction the traditional basis of the narrative. The newer point of view is well represented by Pedersen[2] who observes that the detailed account of the pattern of despotic monarchy in vv. 8-18 has the appearance of a *post eventum* prophecy based on the kind of tyranny which developed under David and Solomon, but who argues that there is nothing improbable in the assumption that Samuel may have foreseen in some measure the pattern which monarchy would assume in Israel, since she was surrounded by well developed monarchies. His conclusions would thus have had an empirical basis in his observation of the trends and effects of monarchy outside Israel. From this point of view vv. 8-18 are not just the pure invention of a late writer finding support for a priestly theory in the malpractices of Solomon's reign, but the expression of a fear native to Samuel that kingship in Israel would go the same way as kingship elsewhere, elaborated and made more precise by a late writer.

It should be noted that the attitude to kingship here resembles that implied by the so-called law of the king in Deut 17.14-20. In this passage the monarchy is tolerated, but it is insisted that it should not be assimilated to the general pattern of kingship in the countries surrounding Israel. The stipulation that the king should be one among his brethren is a riposte to the words which are put into the mouth of the people: 'I will set a king over me like all the nations that are round about me' (v. 14). The subsequent verses describe a king without horses or harem or treasury (vv. 16 f.); one who writes out a copy of the Law and shows his fear of Yahweh in the keeping of it; one who does not give himself airs, but who is answerable to the demands of the Law like any other Israelite (vv. 18-20).

The main intention of the chapter (as with chapter 7) is to inculcate the lesson that Israel ought to have looked for security in the kingship of Yahweh and relied on him to

[2] J. Pedersen, *Israel* III-IV, 1940, p. 99.

defend her by direct intervention (cp. 7.10), rather than seeking it in the efficient functioning of a monarchy conceived on the lines of neighbouring states, for in so doing she put her trust in the arm of flesh and not in Yahweh.

CHAPTER 9

THE ANCESTRY OF SAUL

9.1-2

1. a Benjaminite MT: 'son of a Benjaminite' which is perhaps the error of a scribe who anticipated the continuance of the genealogy.

a man of wealth The same Hebrew phrase can also mean 'a man of valour', 'a warrior of renown', but the meaning here is no doubt that Kish was a man of property and substance and so had a certain standing in the community. Cp. v. 21, where Saul's statement about the obscurity of his family is to be understood as an exaggerated humility.

2. From his shoulders upward . . . This corresponds roughly to our idiom: 'He was head and shoulders above any of the people.' Note the emphasis on Saul's physical attractiveness and superb physique.

SAUL SEEKS HIS FATHER'S ASSES

9.3-14

4. Shalisha Groll. p. 162. The site of Shaalim is unknown. The emendation Shaalbim, which is north-north-west of Aijalon (Groll. Map 17, p. 81), has been suggested.

6. a man of God in this city The city in question is Ramah, already mentioned as the home of Samuel (7.17). The qualities which make Samuel a man of God appear in the course of the chapter.

the journey on which we have set out The Hebrew is a

little obscure, but, if we are guided by the context, 'Perhaps he will tell us our way on which we have come' (which is MT literally translated) must mean 'Perhaps he will tell us how to reach the goal of our journey.'

7. present The meaning is dubious. The alteration of one Hebrew consonant would give the sense: 'There is nothing to bring to the man of God by way of exchange' (sc. for his advice).

9. Formerly in Israel . . . This is an interesting gloss which purports to explain the archaic nomenclature used in the story. Its writer therefore regards these events as lying in the distant past and this is an indication of its lateness. His purpose is to inform us that the offices of seer and prophet are identical and that the difference is simply one of terminology, the term seer having been superseded by that of prophet.

12. Make haste RSV follows MT. G: 'Behold he is ahead of you, now, just at this moment, he has arrived in the city.' It has been argued that this is an improvement on MT and that there is no point in the injunction to make haste. The point, however, may be that they should catch Samuel before he sets out for the high place; cp. v. 13. Notice that the question in v. 11, 'IS THE SEER HERE?', implies that Samuel was a well-known local figure with an established reputation; cp. v. 18. In addition to his powers of prediction (v. 6) and his special access to Yahweh (vv. 15 f.) he also wields priestly authority and must be present to bless the sacrificial meal at the high place before the invited company can begin to eat.

13. As soon as you enter the city you will find him The meaning of this sentence (cp. v. 12) seems to me rather to be: 'You are to find him as soon as you enter the city, before he goes up to the high place to eat.' Since meat could only be eaten at a sacrificial meal, animals had to be slaughtered at the altar of the local sanctuary. The meal was therefore religious in character, but it had an important social aspect in that those who furnished the animals were presumably responsible for inviting the guests. We should perhaps think of it as a family (clan) occasion.[1]

SAUL MEETS SAMUEL

9.15-27

16. to-morrow about this time It is doubtful whether the Hebrew can yield this sense. The most it can mean is, 'When to-morrow has come.'

and you shall anoint him to be prince . . . The ceremony of anointing became specially associated later with the office of kingship in the Davidic line. The anointing was symbolic of the special endowment which the king received in virtue of his office. This is the primary meaning of Messiah (Anointed). This was the basis of the later developments in Messianic theology. The usual Hebrew word for king is not used here, but the word employed is also applied to David (II Sam. 6.21; 7.8 and elsewhere) and can be translated 'leader'. Noth holds that it occurs in the Old Testament only with reference to a king-designate, but it is used of David in the passages cited above after he had become king. Noth believes that it points primarily to a man called by Yahweh to undertake a military action.[2]

I have seen the affliction of my people RSV follows G. MT: 'I have seen my people.'

17. who shall rule over Literally: 'who will keep in bounds', i.e. discipline, control.

21. And is not my family . . . ? FAMILY is not the small family, but a kin group consisting of a number of families (in our restricted sense of the word) and so a clan within the tribe.

22. hall According to Köh. a hall whose fourth side is

[1] W. R. Smith, *ROS*, p. 239.
[2] Noth, *History*, p. 169 n. 1.

open towards a court and along the three sides of which are rows of stone benches, where those taking part in the sacrificial meal eat.[3]

24. and the upper portion Another understanding of MT is the translation of AV, 'and that which was upon it'. An attractive emendation which requires no alteration of the Hebrew consonantal text is: 'So the cook took up the leg and the fat tail,' i.e. the choice parts of the animal.[4]

See, what was kept . . . From this point on the verse is difficult. MT: 'Behold, what is left over is set before you. Eat, since it has been kept for you to the appointed time saying: "I have invited the people."' The text is corrupt and has been conjecturally emended to read: 'See, what has been kept is set before you, for they have reserved it for you to the appointed time that you might eat with those who are invited' (cp. RSV).

25-26. A bed was spread for Saul . . . RSV follows G, which gives a better sense than MT. The latter reads: 'And they came down from the high place to the city and he (Samuel) conversed with Saul on the housetop. And they rose early in the morning, and, when dawn was coming up, Samuel called to Saul on the housetop, saying . . .' It is difficult to make sense of this sequence of events and G is easier to follow. Thus: 'And a bed was spread for Saul on the housetop and he lay down; and, when dawn came up, Samuel called to Saul on the housetop, saying . . .'

27. and when he has passed on RSV follows MT. The phrase is not represented in G and MT is smoother without it.

In this chapter a routine and tiresome occurrence, like the straying of animals, is subsequently seen as a meaningful direction of Saul's life and the contriving of a situation in

[3] Cp. W. R. Smith, *ROS* p. 254.

[4] But AV is most probably correct. See G. R. Driver, *CML* p. 131 n. 5; Gordon, *UM* p. 47 n. 1 (the loin and the-upon-it = the loin and the sirloin).

which he confronts his destiny. The search for the asses is real and the attitudes of Saul and the servant are in accord with the tedious nature of their task, but the significance of the episode lies beyond the lost asses.

In this providential ordering of the affair the servant has an important part to play, for, when Saul reaches the point of exasperation and perceives that his father will become more concerned about their welfare than that of the asses, if they do not make tracks for home, it is the servant who suggests a visit to Samuel. He urges Saul in effect not to give up yet, but to consult this seer of repute; perhaps he will indicate to them how they can bring their search to success. Even then Saul raises an objection to the proposal—he has nothing to offer the seer in exchange for his information—but this too is overcome, when the youth produces a piece of silver. Thus it is the persuasiveness of one of his father's workers which directs him towards Samuel and towards the deeper purpose of his journey. At this point Yahweh has taken into his plan an anonymous and ordinary employee of Kish.

After the two have met, Samuel makes it clear to Saul that there is more to their meeting than the whereabouts of strayed asses. Saul's assessment of his journey at this point is that it has been frustrating and fruitless, but Samuel tells him that, all the while, Yahweh has been directing his steps and bringing about this meeting between his prophet and the king-designate of Israel. 'Your asses were found three days ago,' he tells him, 'and you are not to worry about them. You are rather to consider the prospect of your great preferment' (v. 20). And so Samuel bids him send his servant on ahead, while he discloses the momentous word revealed to him by Yahweh concerning Saul (vv. 15-17, 27).

Samuel is again represented as enjoying priestly authority and performing priestly duties. In this chapter, however, his status as a mediator between Yahweh and Israel depends especially on his gifts as a seer. He has extraordinary access to the knowledge of Yahweh and receives special revelations from him (vv. 15-17). According to the servant lad he employs his special gifts to clear up mundane perplexities, so that one can apply to him for help in the matter of lost asses (v. 6).

There can be no doubt that, contrary to 7-8, the attitude to kingship in this chapter is favourable and that its institution is traced to the word of Yahweh communicated through Samuel to the nominee Saul. Moreover Saul's appointment is made with direct reference to the Philistine menace. He is to be anointed leader over Israel and is to save her from the hand of the Philistines (v. 16). Thus the attitude which in chs. 7-8 was characterized as sinful and as a slur on Yahweh and a repudiation of his kingship is here seen as originating in a word of God (v. 27) spoken to Saul. It is Yahweh's will that Israel should have strong political and military leadership in the face of Philistine pressure, and Saul, with his good looks and magnificent physique, is the kind of man who will organize and inspire Israel in the struggle for survival.

CHAPTER 10

SAMUEL INSTRUCTS SAUL

10.1-8

1. Then Samuel took . . . RSV follows G which has a longer text than MT. The latter reads: 'And Samuel took the vial of oil and poured it on his head and kissed him and said: "Has not the Lord anointed you over his inheritance as a leader?"' The shorter text of MT may be the result of a copyist's error, i.e., the movement of the eye from 'The Lord anointed you' at the beginning of the verse to 'The Lord has anointed you' at the end. In Hebrew the two phrases are identical.

3. going up to God at Bethel Proceeding to the sanctuary to hold a sacrificial feast. Hence the provisions.

5. Gibeathelohim i.e. Gibeah of Saul (Groll. p. 150, Gibeah, 2).

a garrison of the Philistines The word translated 'garrison' might also mean 'pillar', that is, a pillar erected as a mark of Philistine domination. A further possibility is 'officer'.

6. come mightily upon you Or: 'Be effective in you.'

7. do whatever your hand finds to do i.e., 'Act immediately and resolutely as the need arises.'

8. peace offerings More probably 'sacrifices which are made to honour or discharge a vow'.

SAUL PROPHESIES AT GIBEAH

10.9-13

12. And who is their father? There are at least two interpretations of this. (*a*) It means that Saul is as well-entitled to be an ecstatic prophet as any other man, since prophetic inspiration is not a hereditary possession. The use of the verb ANSWERED might seem to favour this understanding of the verse, since it might be thought to imply that the MAN OF THE PLACE was offering a riposte to those who said: WHAT HAS COME OVER THE SON OF KISH? IS SAUL ALSO AMONG THE PROPHETS? In other words, to those who felt the strong incongruity of Saul's behaviour and felt that he was acting out of character this MAN OF THE PLACE retorted 'Why not?' (*b*) It means that Saul had good family connections, and ought to have no dealings with an ecstatic rabble. In behaving like a dervish he was falling out of the accepted patterns of behaviour of his social station and was associating himself with the outlandish and bizarre. Hence the question, WHO IS THEIR FATHER? is not a retort to the PROVERB, 'IS SAUL ALSO AMONG THE PROPHETS?', but a further explication of it. The second interpretation seems to me to be the correct one. This particular PROVERB illustrates appositely what this Hebrew word translated PROVERB means. Primarily it signifies the generalized application of what in the first place is strikingly particular. Thus the incongruity attaches in the first instance to a particular person, Saul, in connection with a particular incident, his dancing with ecstatic prophets (cp. however I Sam. 19.23 f.), but it becomes a paradigm and acquires general significance, so that, whenever a person is acting out of character, his behaviour is commented on by resort to the PROVERB, 'IS SAUL ALSO AMONG THE PROPHETS?' The cognate Aramaic word is behind the Greek translated 'parable' in the Gospels and the basic meaning of parable is the same, i.e., the intuiting of a general truth in a particular set of circumstances. This usually involves the employment of pictures and figures. Thus the imagery is representative and the general truth is intuited in the concrete imagery.

13. he came to the high place G: 'He came to Gibeah.' BH conjectures 'to the house'. The difficulty here is that the conversation recorded with his uncle in vv. 14 f. is of a kind that might more naturally have taken place at home than at the high place.

SAUL INTERROGATED BY HIS UNCLE

10.14-16

16. But about the matter of the kingdom . . . Apparently Saul did not judge the time to be ripe for disclosure and considered himself particularly vulnerable to denigration and misunderstanding among his kinsfolk. He did not want to be thought a megalomaniac (cp. Gen. 37.5 f.). The words OF WHICH SAMUEL HAD SPOKEN do not appear in G.

SAUL CHOSEN BY LOT AS KING AT MIZPAH

10.17-27

19. by your thousands Or, more probably, 'by your clans'.

21. Finally he brought the family of the Matrites near, man by man RSV follows G. The words are not present in MT, but are needed to complete the sense of the verse.

22. Did the man come hither? RSV follows G. MT: 'Is there yet a man to come hither? ' G is the smoother reading.

25. the rights and duties of the kingship Literally 'the practice of kingship'. The word translated 'practice' is the same as that used pejoratively in 8.9, 11, in the description of the excesses of despotic monarchy, and it has been argued that the meaning is the same here. When Samuel's gloomy forecast of the consequences of kingship have been fulfilled, this book, laid up before Yahweh (i.e., in a sanctuary of Yahweh), will testify against those who canvassed for its inauguration. It is doubtful, however, whether v. 25 can be understood in this way. It seems to mean rather that, having yielded to the demand for a king, Samuel insisted that the monarchy should be constitutional and not absolute, and sought to write in such safeguards as he could for the structure of the old Israelite community (cp. Deut. 17. 14-20).

26. men of valour RSV follows G. MT: 'The army'.

27. worthless fellows Or, 'confused fellows', cp. 1.16.

But he held his peace Literally: 'He was as a man who keeps silent.' RSV follows MT. Probably the phrase should be attached, with G, to 11.1. Thus: 'And it came to pass after about a month Nahash, the Ammonite, went up . . .' This requires the alteration of one Hebrew consonant.

Chapter 10.1-16 is a unity, although v. 8 has been taken by Kennedy as a redactional insertion which prepares the way for 13.7b-15a. It will be more convenient to deal with this in connection with ch. 13. Verses 1-16 continue the narrative of ch. 9. Samuel anoints Saul king over Israel, and, as a confirmation that he is acting in good faith and does possess the gifts of a seer, describes certain events and experiences in which Saul is shortly to be involved. In virtue of these 'signs' Saul will know that the ceremony of anointing did have the significance attached to it by Samuel and that the seer was acting on knowledge specially revealed to him by Yahweh.

The most important of these 'signs' will be the onset of

prophetic ecstasy after which Saul will prophesy in the company of a band of prophets. However, even prior to this, at the very moment of his turning away from Samuel, he knows that the ceremony of anointing has been matched by an inner change. He has been charismatically endowed; God has given to him ANOTHER HEART. This portrait of the spirit-filled leader would seem to owe something to the descriptions of the 'judges' who were similarly possessed and acted in a fury of inspiration (Othniel, Judg. 3.10; Gideon, 6.34; Jephthah, 11.29; Samson, 13.25; 14.6; 15.14).

The description of Saul's association with a band of ecstatic prophets and his inspiration in this particular context draws attention to the existence of such prophetic guilds in Israel at that time. Whether we are to suppose that Samuel was in some way connected with them, perhaps as their superior, and that they were regular cultic personnel is hard to decide. Certainly they are described as coming down from the high place at Gibeah which shows that they had associations with a sanctuary, but the adverse estimate of them implied in the 'proverb' (v. 12) is perhaps hardly consistent with their status as cultic officials. Apparently they were not regarded as belonging to the more worthwhile and solid sections of the community, and there was thought to be something extravagant and disreputable in their ecstatic exercises.

The other half of the chapter presents more difficulties. It is not continuous with vv. 1-16, but rather takes up again the point of view of chs. 7-8. Thus Samuel reappears as one who convenes the assembly of Israel (not as a seer, as in 9–10.16), and the attitude to kingship in vv. 17-19 is demonstrably unfavourable. Yahweh reminds Israel of his mighty acts for her in the past and charges her with rejecting his kingship and clamouring for an earthly king. 'NO, BUT SET A KING OVER US' in 10.19 echoes 8.19, 'No, but we will have a king over us'— the phrase by which the people affirm their unwillingness to accept Samuel's advice. Moreover, whereas Saul is Israel's saviour in 9.16, this is seen as the historic role of Yahweh in 10.19.

Verses 20-25 appear to represent the same attitude as vv. 17-19, although here the position is not so clear. Samuel, his advice refused, takes steps to implement the will of Israel as Yahweh had required of him (8.7-9, 22) and assembles the tribes at Mizpah (cp. ch. 7, where the place of assembly is also Mizpah) in order to choose a king by lot. It is, of course, arguable that the choosing of the king by lot should be regarded as the human or democratic aspect of Saul's election, and, as such, not incompatible with the prior account of his election by Yahweh at the hands of Samuel in the earlier part of the chapter. In support of this it could be further argued that Samuel's words in 10.24, 'DO YOU SEE WHOM YAHWEH HAS CHOSEN?' presuppose a favourable and not an unfavourable attitude to the monarchy. On balance, however, it seems to be more probable that the choosing of Saul by lot is connected with the narrative of 7-8, the attitude of which is that, while disapproving of the innovation of kingship, Yahweh instructs Samuel to accede to the demand, if it is persisted in. All that 10.24 can mean on this view is that Yahweh has given Israel what she was determined to have—in that sense only has he chosen Saul.

Verse 25 is another echo of 8 (vv. 9, 11), but it is a distorted echo, for the connotation of the key word 'practice' or 'usage' has been changed. In 8.9, 11 it refers to the malpractices and abuses of despotic monarchy, but here it refers to a 'law of the king', the hedging of the monarchy with constitutional safeguards. It is thus a similar concept to that of Deut. 17.14-20. This does not necessarily mean, however, that 10.25 is late. On the contrary it may reflect an early if unsuccessful attempt to preserve the social values of amphictyony by limiting the monarchy, so that 'the law of the king' imposed on Josiah (II Kings 23.3) may represent the reimposition of old demands whose aim was the entrenching of amphictyonic values.

Verses 26 f. cannot be associated with vv. 20-25, because they are manifestly favourable towards Saul. His supporters are men of valour whose hearts God has touched (i.e. they are spirit-filled as Saul is) and the opposition comes from worthless (or, confused) men. Moreover Saul is at Gibeah in vv. 1-16 and again in 11.4, which would indicate that 11.1 f. was originally continuous with 10.1-16. If this is so GIBEAH in 10.26 looks like a bridge between 10.20-25 and 11.1 f. 10.26-27 should therefore be regarded as an editorial link joining 10.20-25 to 11.1 f. Eissfeldt assigns 10.17-21a to E and 21b-27 to L, Kennedy assigns 10.17-27 to D.

CHAPTER 11

NAHASH BESIEGES JABESH-GILEAD

11.1-4

1. Jabesh-gilead Groll. p. 153.

Make a treaty with us Literally: 'Cut a covenant with us'. This idiom may be derived from the sacrificial procedure associated with the making of a covenant, where the victim is divided into two pieces between which the two parties to the covenant pass. The ritual is explained as an imprecation, those making the covenant swearing to each other that, if they prove unfaithful, they may similarly be cut in pieces[1] (cp. Gen. 15; Jer. 34.18). Here it is a political treaty that is in question; the inhabitants of Jabesh ask for terms and indicate their willingness to accept political subjection.

2. and thus put disgrace upon all Israel The point is that the humiliation will not be that of Jabesh alone, since the intention of Nahash is that all Israel should be involved in the disgrace occasioned by the disfigurement of the men of Jabesh. It is because the outrageous terms imposed on Jabesh have this representative significance that the inhabitants of Gibeah are so moved when they hear of them (v. 4).

[1] Cp. W. R. Smith, *ROS* pp. 480 f.

SAUL DEFEATS NAHASH

11.5-11

6. And the spirit of God came mightily upon Saul The same expression as 10.6. Here as in ch. 10 Saul acts spontaneously in the heat of inspiration, after the manner of the earlier 'Judges'.

7. He took a yoke of oxen i.e., a pair of oxen. Noth[2] argues that this action of Saul can only be understood against the background of the amphictyonic organization of the tribes. In particular, he observes that the details of this episode are strongly reminiscent of the account of Judg. 19.29 f. which he describes as the joint action of the member tribes of the amphictyony against an offending member. The phrase which is common to both accounts ('throughout all the territory of Israel') denoted, according to Noth, the joint sphere of the old Israelite amphictyony. Saul summoned the tribes according to the time-honoured amphictyonic usage by cutting up a pair of oxen and despatching the pieces along with a curse which would operate in the case of non-compliance. In so doing he constituted himself charismatic leader of the Israelite tribes.

8. Bezek Groll. p. 145. While the numbers mentioned here are very high and are no doubt unreliable, it is interesting that Israel's numbers preponderate over those of Judah in the ratio of ten to one. This may be significant in so far as it can be taken as an indication of the view of the author that the more powerful components of the amphictyony were in the north. Since this agrees with the historical facts, it tends to confirm the earliness of this notice.

THE VOICE OF DISSENT

11.12-15

12. Shall Saul reign over us? Notice that the objection

[2] Noth, *Das System der zwölf Stämme Israels*, pp. 109 f.

alluded to is specifically associated with Saul's assumption of kingship as if the writer were aware of the objections which had been raised to the institution of the monarchy. Verses 12-15 seem to take into account the theological scruples expressed in chs. 7-8 and in 10.17-25, namely, that the appointment of a king was a renunciation of the kingship of Yahweh. In the face of this challenge Saul acts with generosity and displays theological acumen. In disclaiming credit for the victory and ascribing salvation to Yahweh (v. 13) he is perhaps seeking a formula for reconciliation, since opposition to kingship had been based on the assertion that it implied a loss of faith in the power of Yahweh to deliver Israel (cp. 7.3; 10.18), and the substitution of reliance in an earthly king, i.e., not Yahweh as a saviour but a king (cp. 9.16; 10.27). There is a certain similarity between 10.26 f. and 11.12-15. According to 10.26 f. the supporters of Saul are men of valour whose hearts have been touched by God and the opposition to him comes from worthless characters. Nevertheless this opposition is apparently related to the theocratic objections to kingship, since the key word of the controversy is employed: 'How can this man *save* us?' These opponents refuse to bring him presents in token of their allegiance, but in the face of this provocation Saul acts with restraint and dignity. (Following MT, but perhaps v. 27b should be attached to ch. 11 with G.)

14. renew the kingdom This is a puzzling expression and it may be suspected that 'renew' is a redactional adjustment made in view of the acount of Saul's election by lot at Mizpah in 10.20-24. BH's emendation, which requires the alteration of one Hebrew consonant, is attractive: 'Come let us go to Gilgal and there sanctify (consecrate) the kingdom.'

15. peace-offerings See Commentary on 10.8.

Eissfeldt assigns ch. 11 to L and Bentzen[3] thinks that it may be a special tradition, describing Saul after the pattern of the 'judges'. The chapter, however, has commonly been

[3] Bentzen, *Introduction* II, p. 93.

regarded as a continuation of 9–10.16 and Saul is acting in full concert with Samuel and enjoys his support (11.7, 12). In his action against Nahash he is carrying out the order of Samuel that he should do whatever his hand finds to do (see Commentary on 10.7) and he is represented as a spirit-filled leader on the model of the earlier ‘judges’. The possible significance of vv. 12-15 has already been discussed. The assembly at Gilgal and Saul's coronation there connect with Samuel's instructions to Saul in 10.8, although the latter makes no reference to Saul's coronation, but makes the purpose of the assembly at Gilgal the fulfilment of sacrificial rites over which Samuel is to preside.

With regard to the historical value of the material in this chapter, it reflects the impotence to which the Israelite tribes had been reduced as a result of Philistine dominance, so that even a small nation like Ammon can inflict humiliating terms on Jabesh with impunity. When the men of Jabesh ask for seven days' respite in order to sue for help from the other Israelite tribes, it is granted to them in the confidence that none of them is in a position to offer effective help.

This condition of extreme weakness and ineffectiveness forms the background to the elevation of Saul to the office of king. It was a move to give to the tribes a political organization and a durable military leadership which would equip them more adequately in their struggle for survival against the threat of Philistine expansion. The choice of Gilgal as the place of assembly may also be related to similar historical factors. After the destruction of Shiloh it was a suitable centre for several reasons. It was an ancient and celebrated shrine on the borders of Ephraim and Benjamin much frequented by the tribes of central Palestine, and, in all probability, it was outside the area of Philistine dominance and not subject to their control.

CHAPTER 12

SAMUEL DEFENDS HIS RULE

12.1-5

2. my sons are with you All that is probably intended is that his sons are grown men and that he is advanced in years, although there may be the suggestion that the sons could have succeeded to their father's rule had Israel so chosen. This, however, would conflict with 8.3 f. and should perhaps be discounted.

3. and before his anointed Similarly in v. 5. It is odd that Samuel should swear by Yahweh's anointed (i.e. the king), since this seems to imply the recognition that the king has been endowed by Yahweh for his high office and has such pre-eminence in the community that one swears by Yahweh and his anointed. This in turn presupposes a belief in the sacral character of the monarchy and in the importance of the king's religious role in the community, and all this is odd in a chapter which represents the innovation of kingship as a fundamental betrayal of Yahweh.

Have I taken a bribe to blind my eyes with it? G: 'Or from whose hand have I taken a bribe and sandals?' This is the reading presupposed by Ecclus. 46.19; cp. Amos 2.6; 8.6.

5. And they said RSV follows G. MT: 'And he said'.

A SUMMARY OF YAHWEH'S DEALINGS WITH ISRAEL

12.6-12

6. The Lord is witness RSV follows G. In MT 'witness' is not present, but some such word is required to complete the sense.

7. Now therefore stand still This can be well translated by our idiom, 'Stand by', i.e., a warning that an important message is about to be delivered. RSV follows MT. A small insertion from G would make the grammar easier. Thus: 'But now stand by that I may state my case to you before Yahweh, *and declare to you* all Yahweh's acts of justice which he wrought for you and your fathers.' 'Acts of justice' are acts through which Yahweh has vindicated the right and maintained his rule of righteousness.

8. When Jacob RSV follows MT. G has the additional words 'and his sons'.

and made them dwell According to MT, followed by RSV, it was Moses and Aaron who settled Israel in Canaan. According to G it was Yahweh and this is probably the correct reading, since the other statement does not agree with what is recorded elsewhere of the circumstances of the settlement in Canaan.

9. and he sold them This expression is used in Deut. 32.30 and also in those parts of the Book of Judges usually attributed to a Deuteronomic redactor (e.g. 2.14; 3.8; 4.2; 10.7) and commonly described as the framework of the book. There are affinities of style between I Sam. 7; 8; 10.17-19; 12, and the 'framework' of the Book of Judges.

11. Barak RSV follows G. MT: 'Bedan' for which 'Abdon' (Judg. 12.13) has been conjectured. Where MT has SAMUEL G^L and S read 'Samson'. Driver[1] explains MT as the lapse of a writer who forgot momentarily that he was putting his words into the mouth of Samuel.

12. No, but a king shall reign over us This is an echo of the words first spoken in 8.19; cp. also 10.19.

SAMUEL EXHORTS ISRAEL

12.13-15

13. for whom you have asked RSV follows MT. The

[1] S. R. Driver, *Notes, in loc.*

words are not present in G[B]. Note that according to this verse the king has been chosen by Israel and Yahweh's action in setting a king over them is consequent on this choice. Cp. Commentary on 10.20-25.

15. and your king RSV follows G which is better than MT, 'and your fathers'.

SAMUEL WORKS A SIGN

12.16-18

16. and see this great thing The purpose of the sign (cp. 9.20; 10.1, 7) is to demonstrate the complete accord which exists between Samuel and Yahweh, so that, when he condemns Israel's choice of a king, he speaks with the full approval of Yahweh. It is therefore a proof of his claim that he knows and speaks the will of Yahweh in connection with the innovation of kingship. The miracle of what he does consists in his producing thunder and rain at a season when they would never in the normal course of nature occur, namely, at the season of the wheat harvest (v. 17). The effect of the sign was to convince the people that Yahweh and Samuel were unanimous in their condemnation of the monarchy, so that ALL THE PEOPLE GREATLY FEARED YAHWEH AND SAMUEL (v. 18).

ENCOURAGEMENT AND WARNING

12.19-25

19. Pray for your servants The people, convinced by the sign, confess that to all their previous sins they have added this crowning evil of asking for a king (cp. 8.7-9). They plead with Samuel not to resign from his role as an intercessor (cp. 7.8; 8.6 f.), and he promises that he will continue to pray for them and instruct them in the right way (v. 23).

21. and do not turn aside after vain things The word translated VAIN THINGS means formlessness, confusion, unreality. Here it must refer to idols as in Isa. 41.29 and it therefore recalls the Deuteronomic warning against following after other gods (Deut. 6.14; 11.28; 28.14 etc.; also Judg. 2.12, 17, 19.)

22. for his great name's sake This has been understood to mean, 'for the sake of his great reputation'. It may, however, mean more than that. Yahweh brought Israel out of Egypt (v. 6) and chose her as his people and he will not now, not even in the face of this great provocation, abandon his initiative and permit the undoing of what he purposed in Israel's election. He will punish Israel for her sin, but he will never permit that she cause his ultimate purposes for her to miscarry, because Yahweh has resolved to make Israel a people for himself.

24. Only fear Yahweh . . . The last two verses continue the pattern of exhortation and threat which is characteristic of vv. 20 f. The monarchy is viewed as a *fait accompli* and both people and king are warned of the consequences of forsaking Yahweh and committing evil.

This chapter, in form partly political speech and partly sermon, maintains the same attitude to kingship as that of 7-8 and 10.17-25. Samuel defends his record as a ruler as if he were conscious of being on trial and felt that the institution of kingship was in some way a vote of no confidence in his administration (cp. 8.7-9).

Verses 6-12 are a historical retrospect in which, in agreement with the theocratic character of the related chapters noted above, the effectiveness of Yahweh's kingship in the past is demonstrated. The key word is 'acts of justice' (v. 7), and these acts have a double-sided character, since through them Yahweh both saves and punishes, but always he acts to maintain his rule of righteousness. To do this he saves Israel from her enemies through Moses and Aaron (v. 6), Jerubbaal, Barak, Jephthah and Samson (v. 11), and, when she sins and goes after other gods, he asserts his righteousness by delivering her into the hand of her enemies. This is the same interpretation of Israel's history as that which appears in the Book of Judges.

Although SAMUEL is probably not original in v. 11, there can be no doubt that the point of view of the chapter is that Samuel is in the line of the 'judges', a charismatic leader comparable in stature to those previously used by Yahweh to save Israel. Thus Yahweh is depicted as a king who has always governed his people with justice and who saved them in their distress, when they cried to him in penitence (v.10). Why then should Israel have been so presumptuous as to demand another king? What reason have they to believe that he will rule more effectively or justly than Yahweh? The historical background to the demand for a king is misrepresented in v. 12, where it is connected with the emergency created by the demands of Nahash on Jabesh-gilead. It is clear that the political background was in fact the Philistine menace and that monarchy was envisaged by its supporters as an institution which would mobilize and unify the resources of Israel so as to meet this peril (cp. 9.16).

In his exhortations and threats to Israel Samuel accepts the monarchy as an accomplished fact. Kingship has arrived, but the king must be subject to Yahweh; he is no more exempt from this demand than are the people (vv. 14 f., 25). The sign (vv. 16-18) has already been commented on. In vv. 19 f. the people are represented as being anxious to retain Samuel who has so spectacularly proved his authority as their intercessor and instructor. He has not therefore, according to this account, suffered the fate of redundancy, but has demonstrated that, even with a king, Israel cannot dispense with his services.

The main problem of interpretation in the chapter is constituted by the phrase BEFORE YAHWEH AND HIS ANOINTED (vv. 3, 5). HIS ANOINTED reflects a situation where the king is an important religious personage, and it seems likely that the origin of this in Israel was the key role of the Davidic king in the Jerusalem cult. (See Commentary on II Sam. 7.) It is true that Saul bears this title (I Sam. 24.6, 10; 26.9, 16; II Sam. 1.14), but it is probable that here too, in this portrait of the inviolability of Saul's person, the concept of sacral kingship is intruding into an earlier period. Here Samuel says: TESTIFY

AGAINST ME BEFORE YAHWEH AND HIS ANOINTED, as if this were an established legal formula for giving evidence on oath. Now this would seem to presuppose a period when the theology of Davidic kingship had been in existence for such a long time that one could use a legal formula incorporating it without realizing that it represented a theology directly at variance with the anti-monarchical polemic of the rest of the chapter. This is therefore a mark of the lateness of this chapter.

CHAPTER 13

ISRAEL IN REVOLT AGAINST THE PHILISTINES

13.1-7

1. Saul was . . . years old This is a type of notice, giving the king's age and the duration of his reign, common in the Books of Kings (cp. I Kings 14.21). The verse is not present in G. In MT the king's age is omitted, perhaps because it was not known. Of the further statement that he reigned two years Noth says that it is 'incontestable on textual grounds and probable historically too'.[1] It has, however, been customary to emend TWO YEARS to 'twenty-two years'.

2. Michmash Groll. p. 157. For Geba see Groll. p. 150 and for Gibeah p. 150, Gibeah (2). It has been suggested that Gibeah in this verse should be emended to Geba, while in v. 3 Gibeah should be read instead of Geba with G and T, but Noth[2] comments on the difficulty of deciding between these two names, since they so closely resemble each other and since the places are fairly close to each other.

3. garrison See Commentary on 10.5.

Let the Hebrews hear RSV follows MT. If this is the correct text, the meaning must be: 'Let them hear the news and

[1] Noth, *History*, p. 176 with n. 1 and p. 177 n. 1.
[2] Noth, *ibid.*, p. 173 n. 1.

the summons to the standard of Saul which is implied by it.' G, instead of LET THE HEBREWS HEAR, reads: 'The Hebrews have rebelled' and also shows a different order of words from MT. Thus: 'Jonathan defeated the garrison of the Philistines which was at Gibeah and the Philistines heard and said: "The Hebrews have rebelled"; and Saul blew his trumpet in all the land' (i.e., he summoned Israel to war).

5. thirty thousand chariots RSV follows MT. G: 'three thousand'.

Beth-aven Meaning 'house of vanity' and used by the prophets (e.g. Hos. 4.15) as a derogatory corruption of Bethel. This Beth-aven, however, is sited by Driver[3] near Ai.

7. or crossed the fords of the Jordan RSV follows G. MT: 'And Hebrews crossed the Jordan'. Another reading which is conjectured is: 'And a large body of people crossed the Jordan'.

followed him trembling i.e., the Philistines were massing against Israel (v. 5) and morale among the Israelites was low (vv. 6 f.). To follow the account in more detail is difficult. Verse 7 appears to say that ALL THE PEOPLE were still with Saul at Gilgal, although they were in poor shape, but v. 6 states that some of his army had gone into concealment, while others had run away across the Jordan to Gad and Gilead. An emendation, based on G^L, reads: 'And all the people deserted him in terror,' and this agrees better with v. 6.

SAUL AND SAMUEL AT GILGAL

13.8-15

11. within the days appointed Or: 'when the time-limit had expired.'

12. entreated the favour of the Lord Literally: 'stroked the face of Yahweh.' The idea is that of soothing or putting

[3] S. R. Driver, *Notes, in loc.*

in a good humour, so conciliating or propitiating, i.e., preparing the ground for a petition, so that it may be entertained with favour.

so I forced myself This translation is rather misleading. The idea is well conveyed by the idiom 'to pull oneself together'. 'So I pulled myself together,' i.e., Saul had to brace himself in order to bring himself to exercise priestly functions, but he was convinced that the emergency justified such extraordinary measures.

13. you have not kept RSV follows MT. Without any change in the Hebrew consonantal text the verse can be read: 'Would that you had kept the commandment of Yahweh your God which he commanded you, for in that case Yahweh would have established your kingdom over Israel for ever.'

15. and went up from Gilgal to Gibeah of Benjamin RSV follows MT. After 'Gilgal' G continues: 'and he (Samuel) went on his way; and the remainder of the people went up after Saul to meet the soldiery, and they came from Gilgal to Gibeah of Benjamin.' This longer text relieves a difficulty in so far as it mentions the movement of Saul from Gilgal to Gibeah and so prepares the way for v. 16. Note, however, that v. 16 locates Saul at Geba and it may be suspected that the longer text of G represents an attempt to link v. 15 to what follows.

PHILISTINE MANOEUVRES

13.16-18

17. Ophrah Groll. p. 158, Ophrah (1). For Valley of Zeboim (Valley of Hyenas) see Groll. p. 165, Zeboim (2). The exact site of the land of Shual is not known.

18. border RSV follows MT. Driver,[4] on the basis of G, suggests 'hill'.

[4] S. R. Driver, *Notes, in loc.*

ISRAEL DEPRIVED OF THE SINEWS OF WAR

13.19-23

20. or his sickle RSV follows G. MT repeats the word for plough-share. G should be followed, but the translation is 'goad' rather than 'sickle', a translation which RSV adopts in v. 21.

21. and the charge was a pim . . . RSV rests on an emended text.[5] The verse has been translated without emendation as follows: 'And the charge[6] was a pim[7] for plough-shares and mattocks and three-pronged forks and axes, and for the setting of goads.' The Israelites were forced to go to the Philistines for the maintenance of their agricultural implements, because it was Philistine policy to prevent them from acquiring the art of the smith and so from arming themselves effectively. By this 'economic warfare' Israel was kept in a state of disarmament (v. 22).

The difficulties of this chapter are so considerable that it is not easy to frame a concise account of them. The least objectionable course is to take vv. 15b-23 as a continuation of vv. 1-7a (minus 4b or minus 'Gilgal' in 4b; the mention of 'Gilgal' represents an attempt to link vv. 1-7a to vv. 7b f.). Kennedy[8] holds that the account of Saul's rejection in vv. 7b-15a is inferior historically to the parallel account in 15 and that 10.8 is a late insertion whose purpose was to prepare the way for 13.7b-15a. The view that 10.8 and 13.7b-15a are secondary is rejected by Eissfeldt[9] who assigns 13.3ba, 4b-5, 7b-15a to J, while vv. 1-3a are given to L. Smith[10] holds that the account of Saul's rejection in 13.7b-15a is earlier than the parallel account in 15.

The opening section gives a credible and connected account of hostilities between Israel and the Philistines. Jonathan

[5] J. Bewer, *JBL* 61, 1942, p. 45.
[6] G. R. Driver, *Archiv für Orientforschung* 15, 1945-51, p. 68.
[7] E. A. Speiser, BASOR 77, 1940, p. 19. A *pim*=two-thirds of a shekel.
[8] A. R. S. Kennedy, *Samuel* (Century Bible), *in loc.*
[9] Eissfeldt, *Einleitung*, p. 310.
[10] H. P. Smith, *ICC*, p. xxi.

defeated the Philistines at Geba and this act of rebellion put Israel in bad odour with the Philistines (vv. 3 f.). It also served as a signal for general mobilization in Israel, it having been noted in v. 2 that Saul had demobilized his militia, retaining three thousand men under arms. When the Philistines mustered at Michmash, Saul withdrew to Geba and joined forces with Jonathan (v. 16, cp. v. 2). The Philistines began to probe with patrols and occupied a forward position in the Pass of Michmash (vv. 17 f., 23). The Israelites were greatly hampered by lack of armament as a consequence of the economic warfare waged by the Philistines (vv. 20-22).

It is doubtful whether vv. 7b-15a should be understood as late priestly propaganda (cp. Kennedy), representing a kind of clerical, closed-shop attitude. If this is the intention of the passage, it is a clumsy and ineffective piece of work, for its effect is to enlist sympathy for Saul rather than for Samuel. It is perhaps no more than a rather flimsy and unconvincing pretext for charging Saul with disobedience to Yahweh and so preparing the way for the emergence of David. Its main concern is apparently to make propaganda for the Davidic dynasty (v. 14, cp. II Sam. 22.51; 23.5). Saul has been rejected because he disobeyed the commandment of Yahweh, but David's house will be established for ever, since he is a man after Yahweh's own heart. The account may, however, as Noth[11] suggests, also reflect tensions which were early felt between the monarchy and the structure of the old amphictyony.

An attempt has been made to link vv. 1-7a to vv. 7b f., but the link is obviously artificial. Thus, although v. 4b locates Saul and his army at Gilgal, vv. 5 f. presuppose a different location, for had they been at Gilgal, they would not have felt the pressure of a Philistine build-up at Michmash. The implication of vv. 5 f. is that they were in close touch with the enemy and the correct assumption may be that, under Philistine pressure, Saul withdrew from Michmash (v. 2) and joined Jonathan at Geba (cp. v. 16). Again in the longer text

[11] Noth. *History*, pp. 175 f.

of G in v. 15 Saul is represented as journeying from Gilgal to Gibeah (Geba?) and this looks like an attempt to create an impression of continuity between v. 15 and vv. 16 f. Note also that in v. 15 of G Saul is said to have gone up to Gibeah to meet the soldiery—a confirmation that the location of the Israelite army was really at Gibeah or Geba.

Further, 13.8 refers back to 10.8, but it is hard to resist the conclusion that this connection is artificial. In 10.8 Saul is commanded to go down to Gilgal, but his subsequent actions do not conform to this command. Even if 11.15, which tells of Saul's coronation by Samuel at Gilgal, be discounted as belonging to another narrative strand (according to Eissfeldt 11 belongs to L), 10.10 f. seem to show that he went to Gibeah and not to Gilgal. Since 9.1–10.16 are also assigned by Eissfeldt[12] to J, we have to assume in order to make sense of his argument that in 10.10 f. Saul was simply passing through Gibeah on his way from Ramah to Gilgal. In 11.5 f., however, Saul is engaged in agricultural duties at Gibeah and this is a pointer to 11.1 f. being a continuation of 10.16. If this is so, there can be no real continuity between 10.8 and 13.7b f. and 10.8 must be regarded as a secondary and superficial attempt to supply a link between 10 and 13 and to set the stage for Saul's forthcoming disobedience and rejection.

CHAPTER 14

JONATHAN'S EXPLOIT AGAINST THE PHILISTINES

14.1-15

2. Migron Groll. p. 157. But Migron is near Michmash and not IN THE OUTSKIRTS OF GIBEAH (or, Geba) and so the emendation 'at the threshing-floor' has been suggested.

3. Ahijah . . . wearing an ephod Cp. 4.21. The 'ephod'

[12] Eissfeldt, *Einleitung*, p. 310.

in this chapter is some kind of receptacle from which the lots are drawn. See Commentary on v. 18.

6. Nothing can hinder i.e., no restrictions can be placed on his activity.

7. Do all that your mind inclines to RSV follows G. MT: 'Do all that is in your mind; reach out (sc. your hand in action).'

13. And they fell before Jonathan . . . RSV follows MT. G: 'And they turned before Jonathan and he struck them down and his armour-bearer was wreaking slaughter behind him.'

14. half a furrow's length The word translated 'furrow' means literally 'the point where the plough turns' and then 'the distance between the two turning points', hence the length of the furrow. Apparently the writer expects his readers to visualize a furrow of a specific length once he has indicated the area of the field which he has in mind.

15. the raiders Literally: 'the destroyer'. The same term is used in 13.17 of the forward patrols of the Philistines and the reference must be the same here.

REPERCUSSIONS IN THE ISRAELITE CAMP

14.16-23

16. the multitude was surging hither and thither RSV, for the most part, follows G, but 'multitude' is MT. Here G reads 'camp'. The phrase refers to the panic and confusion which was evident in the Philistine lines.

18. Bring hither the ark RSV follows MT. G: 'ephod', which must be correct.

for the ark of God . . . RSV follows MT, but the grammar of the Hebrew is obscure. G should again be followed: 'for he wore the ephod at that time before the children of Israel.'

19. Withdraw your hand i.e., the hand which was in the

ephod to draw out the lot. The opportunity offered by the panic in the Philistine camp was so great that Saul decided to act with extreme speed and not to await the verdict of the oracle.

21. Now the Hebrews . . . RSV follows G and the Versions. MT is obscure.

SAUL'S OATH

14.24-30

24. And the men of Israel were distressed . . . RSV follows MT. G shows a longer text: 'And all the people were with Saul, about ten thousand men, and the fighting was dispersed throughout the whole city in the mountain of Ephraim, and Saul acted in ignorance on that day; for Saul laid an oath . . .' G is superior, since there is no obvious connection between the men of Israel being hard pressed (which would refer to Philistine pressure) and Saul involving them in an oath. It has been suggested that 'acted in ignorance' needs emending, since it is out of keeping with the otherwise sympathetic attitude to Saul maintained in this chapter. 'Imposed a great abstinence' or 'made a great vow' has been suggested. There does not seem, however, to be anything objectionable about the statement that he acted in ignorance and its intention is probably not pejorative. It simply means that he did not foresee all the consequences of his action and certainly not that Jonathan's life would become forfeit as a result of it.

25. And all the people came into the forest . . . The word translated FOREST may here mean 'honeycomb'. Verses 25 and 26 have the appearance of doublets in both MT and G, and the following is a conjectural reconstruction based on G: 'And there was a honeycomb on the face of the field and the people came to the honeycomb and lo! the bees had left it, but no man . . .'

29. My father has troubled the land Perhaps rather: 'My father has made the earth taboo.' MY FATHER HAS TROUBLED

THE LAND implies an adverse estimate of Saul or even downright disloyalty to him, and the words are not in keeping with the portrayal of Jonathan in the remainder of the chapter. He is no political agitator. On the other hand 'my father has made the earth taboo' is a statement with real point, since the honey was there for the taking 'on the face of the field' (v. 25). Jonathan observes that it seems unreasonable that food which has been put under his nose should not be eaten.

30. has not been great RSV follows MT. NOT is absent in G. Thus: 'for in that case the slaughter among the Philistines would have been great.'

SAUL BUILDS AN ALTAR

14.31-35

31. Aijalon Groll. p. 141, Aijalon (1).

32. and the people ate them with the blood Cp. Lev. 17.14 f.; 19.26; Ezek. 33.25. The great stone which Saul ordered to be rolled to him was to serve as an altar in order that the people might slay the sheep and cattle at it and not eat the flesh with the blood. The shedding of the blood on the altar consecrated the slaughter and made it a legitimate sacrifice, and Saul officiated as a priest (cp. v. 35).

33. You have dealt treacherously This is strange in the context. A conjectural emendation would give the reading: 'And he said to those who brought the news roll . . .'

THE VERDICT OF THE LOT

14.36-42

38. how this sin has arisen RSV follows MT. V: 'by whom this sin has arisen.'

39. though it be in Jonathan RSV follows MT. G points to the reading: 'though one were to testify against (or, indict) Jonathan.'

41. Therefore Saul said . . . RSV follows the longer text of G. MT: 'And Saul said to Yahweh: "O God of Israel give a perfect one" and Jonathan was taken (sc. by the lot) and Saul and the people escaped.' The obscurity of MT may be due to a copyist's error. ISRAEL occurs before WHY NOT and before GIVE THUMMIM and the copyist's eye has strayed from the one occurrence to the other. (Note there is a third occurrence of ISRAEL before GIVE URIM.) 'A perfect one' represents a corruption of Thummim.

42. my son Jonathan After these words G adds: 'Whoever Yahweh takes will die. And the people said to Saul: "Let not this matter be so ordered." But Saul prevailed over the people and cast the lot between himself and Jonathan, his son. And Jonathan was taken.'

JONATHAN RANSOMED

14.43-46

45. ransomed How they ransomed him is not disclosed. Such ransom or redemption could be effected either by the substitution of another human life or that of an animal or by a money payment.

46. went up from pursuing i.e., gave up the pursuit.

SAUL FIGHTS AGAINST THE ENEMIES OF ISRAEL

14.47-48

47. Zobah A small Aramaean state. Groll. p. 165.

he put them to the worse This is an attempt to translate MT, which, however, would more usually mean 'he condemned them', in a legal sense. G: 'he was victorious.'

SAUL'S ESTABLISHMENT

14.49-52

51. was the son of RSV follows MT, but 'sons of' rather

than 'son of' is desiderated. Thus: 'Kish, the father of Saul, and Ner, the father of Abner, were the sons of Abiel.'

52. any strong man or any valiant man i.e., he was building up a nucleus of picked troops and attaching them to his establishment.[1] See Commentary on 9.1.

Jonathan steals the thunder in this chapter as it is the intention of the author that he should. He is portrayed as both brave and modest with a suggestion of thoughtlessness in his make-up deriving from his modesty and *sang froid*. He tells no one in the camp that he is about to risk his life on a dangerous mission and so his father has to call the roll in order to discover who it is that has introduced confusion into the Philistine camp. And he is impatient with protocol and taboos. He is unaware that Saul has involved the army in a solemn oath and he can see little military sense in the fast to which the soldiers have been bound. In particular he cannot see why they should not have made use of the rations which have been put under their noses, and he is convinced that they would have better pressed home their advantage had they been pursuing the Philistines on full stomachs. The author creates a strong impression of his popularity with the army. Saul expresses his determination to accept the verdict of Urim and Thummim, even if the lot should fall on Jonathan, but at the point when the decision lies between Saul and his son, the people urge that the oracular procedure should be abandoned (v. 42 G). When the lot has fallen on Jonathan and Saul says: 'You shall surely die, Jonathan,' there is a clash between his will and that of the people. They have no intention of standing by while he dies for contravening an oath of whose existence he was not aware. Saul is inflexible but they are equally adamant and declare that not a hair of his head will be harmed, for it is he who has saved Israel (v. 45, cp. v. 23).

An interesting aspect of the chapter is the prominence

[1] On the archaeological evidence for the nature of Saul's establishment see W. F. Albright, *AASOR* 4, 1924, p. 51.

attached to the 'sign' (cp. ch. 10), and the decision of the oracle. Jonathan seeks a sign from Yahweh before committing himself to his audacious operation against the Philistines. He tells his armour-bearer that the sign will consist in the form of words used by the Philistine sentries when the two of them come into view. One form of words will indicate that the time is not propitious for the operation, while the other will show that Yahweh has delivered the Philistines into their hands (vv. 8-12). Again Saul, on the occasion of the confusion in the Philistine camp, consults the priest Ahijah who wears the ephod containing Urim and Thummim, but then, in view of the need to act with extreme speed, decides not to await the advice of the oracle. The exact procedure followed with Urim and Thummim is indicated by the longer text of G in v. 41: 'If this iniquity is in me or in Jonathan, my son, O Yahweh of Israel, give Urim, and, if this iniquity is in thy people Israel, give Thummim.' Another kind of procedure is evidently followed in vv. 36 f., but there is no hint as to what it is.

No impropriety is felt in the representation that Saul performed priestly functions (vv. 31-35). If the intention of 13.7b-15a is to represent that Saul had no right to assume priestly powers, this chapter knows nothing of these scruples. It is improbable, however, that this is the point of 13.7b-15a, although the passage has been understood in this way.[2]

CHAPTER 15

SAUL'S DISOBEDIENCE

15.1-9

2. Amalek Groll. p. 142.

3. and utterly destroy all that they have RSV follows MT, with a change from the second person singular ('Go thou and

[2] J. Wellhausen, *Prolegomena to the History of Israel*, ET 1885, pp. 257-60.

smite thou') to the second person plural ('and ye shall utterly destroy'). G: 'and thou shalt put to the ban both them and their property.' This is better since what follows implies that the destruction of property was also intended. RSV 'utterly destroy' is an inadequate rendering of the Hebrew. The command to wipe out the Amalekites and destroy their property had a religious significance; it was a putting under the ban, a devoting or consecrating to destruction; persons and property so consecrated were 'holy' to Yahweh[1] (also vv. 8, 9, 15, 18, 20, 21).

4. Telaim Groll. p. 164 (=Telem).

6. lest I destroy you with them The Hebrew idiom is 'Lest I gather you (sc. to death) with them'; cp. the phrase 'to gather to one's fathers' (II Kings 22.20). On the Kenites and their former friendly relations with the Israelites see Num. 10.29 f., Judg. 1.16.

7. Shur Groll. p. 162. The site of Havilah was presumably somewhere in Amalekite territory, although it has been suggested that we should emend to Telem.

9. fatlings RSV follows T. MT is obscure, but has been taken to refer to the second calf born to a cow which had the reputation of being superior to the first. The text should perhaps be emended to read: 'and the best of the sheep and the oxen, even the fatlings and the lambs.'

all that was despised and worthless RSV follows G and the Versions. MT: 'despised and melted away (mangy?).'

SAMUEL CHALLENGES SAUL

15.10-16

12. Carmel Groll. p. 146, Carmel (1).

monument Possibly to commemorate his victory over the Amalekites. G, 'has set up', followed by RSV, is preferable to MT, 'is setting up'.

[1] W. R. Smith, *ROS* pp. 453 f.

13. I have performed the commandment of the Lord Literally: 'I have caused the word of Yahweh to stand.' i.e., I have fulfilled it by destroying the Amalekites and have thereby shown that it was not an empty word but a word of power. The same idiom occurs in v. 11, where, however, Yahweh's estimate of Saul's performance contradicts his own. 'He has not caused my words to stand'; cp. vv. 23 and 26: Saul rejected Yahweh's word.

SAUL REJECTED AS KING

15.17-35

17. Though you are little in your own eyes are you not the head of the tribes of Israel? RSV follows MT. The meaning is: Self-depreciation cannot exonerate you. Yahweh appointed you king and you should have ruled the people (cp. vv. 15, 21); the authority and responsibility are yours.

18. until they are consumed RSV based on G, S and T ('until they are annihilated by you'). MT: 'until they consume them', which is not what the sense requires.

23. and stubbornness is as iniquity and idolatry RSV follows MT, which translated literally is: 'And evils and idols are insubordination.' 'Insubordination' rather than 'stubbornness' is suggested by Köh. Symmachus, 'the lawlessness of idols', may point to a Hebrew text, 'the iniquity of idols', i.e., 'the sin of divination is rebellion and the iniquity of idolatry insubordination.'

27. As Samuel turned to go away Saul laid hold upon the skirt of his robe and it tore. MT: 'As Samuel turned to go away he laid hold on the skirt of his robe and it tore.' HE is understood by RSV as referring to Saul. Three considerations weigh against this interpretation. (*a*) One would expect that a change of subject would be unambiguously indicated. (*b*) Samuel is the subject in v. 28 and this enhances the probability that he is the subject throughout v. 27. (*c*) Samuel's words in v. 28 have more force if they are the sequel to his symbolic tearing of Saul's robe. The interpretation of RSV[2] is no doubt influenced by the phrase AS SAMUEL TURNED TO GO AWAY, and the meaning is taken to be that, as Samuel made to go, Saul grabbed his robe in an effort to detain him. The balance of advantage, however, is with the other rendering for the reasons given above.

28. and has given it to a neighbour of yours An allusion to David; cp. 13.14.

29. will not lie or repent . . . In vv. 11 and 35 Yahweh repents that he has made Saul king. This verse may be regarded as a corrective administered by another writer who disliked this anthropopathism, or it may be that the writer of vv. 11 and 35 is telling us that he is perfectly aware that his anthropopathism should not be pushed too far.

32. cheerfully The only meaning that can be had from MT is something like 'voluptuously'. At least two emendations have been suggested. One produces 'tottering'[3] and the other 'reluctantly'.[4]

Surely the bitterness of death is past RSV follows MT, i.e., Surely Saul has already done all the killing that needs to be done and it is not to be resumed by Samuel. The Hebrew word translated 'is past' is absent from G and S.

It has been noted that the concept of the 'ban' occupies a prominent place in this chapter (see Commentary on v. 3). By sparing Agag and holding back from destruction the choice part of the spoil Saul disobeyed the demand of Yahweh that the 'ban' should operate absolutely. This is a second account of the circumstances surrounding Saul's act of disobedience in virtue of which he forfeited his right to be king in Israel (cp. 13). What is interesting is that the two accounts make the same point—that of Saul's disobedience. In 13 this consists in

[2] Also in H. P. Smith, *ICC, in loc.*
[3] S. R. Driver, *Notes, in loc.*
[4] Köhler.

his not awaiting the arrival of Samuel at Gilgal and here in his disregard of the 'ban'.

There are some details of Saul's behaviour whose interpretation is not obvious. Is it the intention of the author to portray him as disingenuous when he says in v. 13, 'I have caused the word of Yahweh to stand'? At any rate the statement is immediately challenged by Samuel. It is more certain that Saul is represented as a weak king—perhaps a king with an inferiority complex—who cannot exercise effective leadership and allows himself to be overruled by the people. (See Commentary on v. 17.) Hence it was the people who made the decision to keep back from the 'ban' the best of the sheep and the oxen in order to sacrifice them to Yahweh (vv. 15, 21), and Samuel's words in v. 17 are directed against this situation.

The emphasis on obedience as against sacrifice recalls prophetic utterances on the same theme, (Isa. 1.11-17, Micah 6.6-8, Amos 5.21-24) and Samuel's pronouncement to Saul on this subject has the form of a prophetic oracle (vv. 22 f.). Again Samuel reinforces his word about Saul's rejection by a piece of symbolism which recalls similar prophetic procedures, especially those of Ezekiel. The tearing of Saul's skirt symbolizes the tearing of kingship from his person, or, if it is understood as a type of sympathetic magic, actually deprives him of kingship (vv. 27-29).

This then is a conflict between a prophet and a king and the prophet armed with the authority of Yahweh is more than a match for the king. There is no place in Israel for a king who 'will not cause Yahweh's word to stand'. Samuel is master of the situation and tells Saul that there can be no question of his being forgiven and making a clean start (v. 26). He relents only to the extent of agreeing to accord to him the dignities of an office in which he has no future, and accompanying him to an act of worship (vv. 30 f.). In Yahweh's community the prophet as the bearer of his word can make and unmake a king and already the way is signposted to David (v. 28).

SAUL AND DAVID
I 16–II 1

CHAPTER 16

SAMUEL IN SEARCH OF A KING
16.1-5

2. How can I go? It is interesting that in a chapter, where Samuel is represented as about to make a new king after having deposed Saul, this reflection of political realities should be allowed. It is clear that Samuel is not after all the all-powerful figure we might have supposed from 15 and from this chapter, and also that Saul is not down and out. Samuel is afraid of Saul and is instructed by Yahweh to employ a subterfuge so that his suspicions may not be aroused. Yet Samuel is portrayed as vested with such awful authority by Yahweh that the elders of Bethlehem come out to meet him trembling (v. 4).

5. Consecrate yourselves i.e., by ceremonial washing; cp. Ex. 19.10, 14, 22. The basic meaning of this word is probably that of separation or withdrawal. Before coming into close contact with Yahweh and handling holy things men must take certain precautions, lest the holy be contaminated with what is profane or unclean. By ritual washing the intending worshippers are separated from the profane and prepared for their entrance into the domain of the holy.[1]

and come with me to the sacrifice RSV follows MT. G: 'and you are to rejoice with me to-day.'

DAVID ANOINTED KING
16.6-13

6. Surely the Lord's anointed is before him RSV follows

[1] W. R. Smith, *ROS* pp. 150 f.

MT. BH: 'Surely Yahweh's leader, (even) his anointed' involves no change of the Hebrew consonantal text. The word translated 'leader' is that used of Saul in 10.1.

7. for the Lord sees not as man sees RSV follows G. The words FOR THE LORD SEES are not in MT. The intention of the verse is clearly to make a comparison between Saul and David. Saul had a fine presence and was unusually tall (9.2), but Samuel is now told that these are not the attributes which weigh most with Yahweh, and Samuel is not to have regard to these things in his choice of a new king. These are the qualities which most impress men and Saul possessed them, but now he is rejected by Yahweh, and Samuel is instructed not to be so superficial in his assessment of the candidates about to be interviewed by him. He is to look below such externals and is to have regard to the 'heart' and, in so doing, he will be employing Yahweh's criteria. Cp. the cryptic reference to David in 13.14 as a man after Yahweh's own heart.

11. we will not sit down i.e., to the sacrificial meal. Or, as it has been explained by Köh., 'we shall not proceed (literally, go round) with the cultic procession.'

12. and had beautiful eyes RSV translates MT, but the Hebrew is unusual. A conjectural emendation reads: 'Now he was ruddy, a virile youth with fine eyes and good appearance.'

13. and the spirit of the Lord came mightily . . . Or: 'The spirit of Yahweh was effective in' . . . The same phrase is used of Saul in 10.6, 10 and there too it follows the ceremony of anointing. See Commentary on 9.16.

DAVID AT THE COURT OF SAUL

16.14-23

14. Now the spirit of the Lord departed . . . Note that David gains what Saul loses. The charismatic endowment reserved for the king of Israel passes from him to David and so Samuel's word on the rejection of Saul is fulfilled. Moreover the place vacated by the spirit of Yahweh is filled by an evil spirit which is also from Yahweh. Formerly Saul was chosen of Yahweh and now he is tormented by him.

16. Let our lord now command your servants who are before you . . . It is dubious whether MT can be so translated. It should rather be: 'Let our lord now command, your servants are before you and they will seek . . .' G: 'Let your servants now speak before you and let them seek . . .' SERVANTS in vv. 15 and 16 is again a technical term for the officers of Saul's establishment. Cp. Commentary on 8.14.

18. a man of valour David is not only a musician; he is also an accomplished warrior and a man judicious in his speech. His musical talents are then a kind of bonus and they can be usefully employed in soothing Saul's troubled spirit, but it is his military qualifications and his capacity as a counsellor which secure his election to Saul's establishment. See the Commentary on 14.52.

19. Send me David Saul, notwithstanding what has been said of his rejection and the departure of Yahweh's spirit from him, still issues orders and has the power to command obedience and respect. Here again political realities intrude into the narrative. Cp. Commentary on v. 2.

21. and entered his service This shows a correct understanding of the Hebrew which is literally: 'and stood before him'. Again in v. 22 LET DAVID REMAIN IN MY SERVICE might be rendered, 'Let David take up a royal appointment.' Saul is represented as having been so attracted to David as to confer on him the honour of a personal appointment, that of armour-bearer.

Another account of David's introduction to Saul occurs in 17.55 f. and moreover the unity of 16 has been questioned. Eissfeldt[2] holds that there are two accounts of David's intro-

[2] Eissfeldt, *Einleitung*, p. 309.

duction to Saul in 16. According to one (E) he is brought as a musician to soothe Saul's spirit and according to the other (L, vv. 18, 21) he joins Saul's establishment as a seasoned warrior. The other account of David's introduction to Saul in 17.55 f. is given by Eissfeldt to J.

There are two aspects of this chapter which are worthy of notice. On the one hand its principal concern is to enlist sympathy for David and to represent Saul as rejected and deprived of Yahweh's charisma. The charismatic endowment reserved for the king of Israel has passed to David, leaving Saul not merely impotent, but demented and ravelled, so that he needs the solace of music. The choice of Saul was a mistake and in making it Israel was too much influenced by his splendid physique and fine presence, but Yahweh's scrutiny goes deeper. He looks on the 'heart' (i.e., on qualities of mind and character) and David is chosen not because of his physical attractiveness, although he has this advantage (vv. 12, 18), but because he is a man after Yahweh's own heart (cp. 13.14). Samuel, as the bearer of Yahweh's word, makes and unmakes kings; his authority is so impressive that, at his approach, the elders of Bethlehem tremble.

On the other hand there are places in the chapter where, in spite of the author's 'tendency', it is plain that Saul is still a power in the land. It is because of his fear of Saul (v. 2) that Samuel misrepresents the purpose of his journey to Bethlehem and gives out that he is going there to discharge priestly functions. Hence he invites the elders along with Jesse and his sons to a sacrificial feast, but this merely provides the cover for the main purpose of his visit. Jesse's sons pass in review before him and David is chosen and anointed king. Moreover Saul is still in a position where his orders have to be obeyed and where men behave towards him as to a king (vv. 19 f.); and he is still adding to his establishment (see Commentary on 14.52), for, apart from his musical gifts, David is chosen as a skilful exponent of the military arts and for his qualities as a counsellor.

CHAPTER 17

GOLIATH'S CHALLENGE

17.1-11

1. Socoh Groll. p. 163, Socoh (2). For Azekah see Groll. p. 144, and for Ephes-dammim, p. 149.

2. the valley of Elah i.e., the valley of the terebinth. See Groll. Plate 179, p. 62. Here Saul and his army took up battle formation.

4. a champion i.e., one who would decide the issue by engaging in single combat with an opponent in the area between the two armies. Noth[1] is of the opinion that Goliath was one of a class of mercenary specialists employed by the Philistines, men who were granted land and who undertook to supply a body of mercenaries for military service.

six cubits and a span About ten feet.

5. a coat of mail Or: 'scaled armour'. The same Hebrew word is used of the scales of a fish.

6. greaves RSV follows the Versions. MT reads the singular.

between his shoulders Or, perhaps, 'among his weapons'.[2]

7. a weaver's beam According to S. R. Driver this is the weaver's shaft or leash-rod which was used for holding the threads of the warp apart, while the shuttle carrying the weft was passed between them.

his spear's head Literally: 'the flame of his spear'. Perhaps 'the blade of his spear' (Köh).

8. to draw up for the battle Or: 'to draw up in battle formation'. Goliath's proposal is that the issue of freedom or

[1] Noth, *History*, p. 164 n. 2.

[2] G. R. Driver, *CML* p. 145 n. 8. R. T. O'Callaghan, *Orientalia* 21, 1951, pp. 37-46.

subjection should be decided by single combat between himself and an Israelite nominee.

10. I defy the ranks of Israel Or: 'I throw abuse at the ranks of Israel'; i.e., I make such insulting remarks or behave so provocatively that Israel must accept my challenge for the sake of her honour. In Bentzen's[3] opinion there is an element of incantation in Goliath's words; he is hurling curses at his opponents before the fight.

11. were dismayed i.e., crushed (in spirit), demoralized.

DAVID ARRIVES AT THE BATTLEFIELD

17.12-25

12. of an Ephrathite MT (not in proper grammatical form): 'this Ephrathite'. The reading of MT represents, in all probability, an attempt to link 17 with 16 and to make out that there is a continuity between the two chapters. Thus 'this Ephrathite' is equivalent to 'the above-mentioned Ephrathite'. It is clear, however, that the two chapters are separate and inharmonious.

15. But David went back and forth . . . This verse may also be a late addition designed to explain why David is absent from the court of Saul after the account of 16.21 f.

18. See how your brothers fare i.e., look into their welfare, and bring back a token that you have fulfilled your mission and that they are well.

20. and took the provisions Perhaps rather, 'and lifted the provisions (sc. on to an ass)'.

25. and make his father's house free in Israel Pedersen[4] holds that in the Amarna letters the word translated 'free' means 'a land-owning freeman' and that in the Old Testament it is generally used less exactly simply to mean 'one who

[3] Bentzen, *Introduction* I, p. 140.
[4] J. Pedersen, *JPOS* 6, 1926, pp. 103-5.

is free'. In this passage, however, Pedersen takes the word to mean 'an aristocrat', one who is raised by the king above the people. Albright[5], on the other hand, holds that the word has the meaning of 'serf' in the Amarna letters and that it has undergone a change of meaning, being used in the Old Testament with the sense of 'free'. This change, according to Albright, corresponds to a difference between the structures of Canaanite and Israelite society; in the former the peasant was a serf, in the latter a free land-holder. This account, however, does not throw much light on this particular passage.

DAVID ACCEPTS THE CHALLENGE

17.26-40

26. that he should defy Rather: 'that he should have defied' (or, insulted, see Commentary on v. 10).

28. those few sheep A contemptuous reference to the flock for which David is responsible. David is charged by his eldest brother with idle curiosity and arrogance. His arrogance or presumption consists in his joining in conversation with other soldiers and particularly in his observation, FOR WHO IS THIS UNCIRCUMCISED PHILISTINE THAT HE SHOULD insult THE ARMIES OF THE LIVING GOD? (v. 26). Eliab is offended by the pretentiousness of David just as the brothers of Joseph were with their young brother (Gen. 37.5 f.).

the evil of your heart Eliab accuses David of mischievous intentions. A conjectural emendation gives the reading, 'the intention of your heart', i.e., what you purpose or intend.

29. Was it not but a word? Referring to David's words in v. 26, i.e., 'Is there any sin in making a remark?'

32. Let no man's heart fail RSV follows MT. G: 'Let not the heart of my master fail.'

39. he tried in vain to go RSV follows G. The meaning is

[5] W. F. Albright, *JPOS* 6, 1926, pp. 106-8.

that his movements were laboured. MT, which makes no sense, reads, 'he resolved to go.'

40. in his shepherd's bag, in his wallet RSV follows MT. G: 'in his shepherd's bag which served him as a wallet'.

DAVID DEFEATS GOLIATH

17.41-58

45. the Lord of Hosts David's reliance is in the name of Yahweh of Hosts. The title is further defined as 'God of the battalions of Israel'. There seems little doubt therefore that 'Yahweh of Hosts' here means 'Yahweh of the armies of Israel'. When the ark was brought to the battlefield, Yahweh was among his army (I Sam. 4.3 f.) and the war in which they engaged was a holy war. The word translated 'Hosts' is the plural of that used of the army of Israel in v. 55. It has been argued, however, that the phrase 'Yahweh of Hosts' originally meant 'Yahweh of the armies of heaven', that is, the commander of the heavenly bodies which move with the precision and order of well-drilled battalions.

46. the dead bodies of the host RSV follows MT. G: 'thy corpse and the corpses of the host'.

53. came back from chasing Literally: 'from burning after', i.e., from hot pursuit of the Philistines.

54. and brought it to Jerusalem An anachronism, since Jerusalem was still a Jebusite city.

It is plain that 16 and 17 contain separate and irreconcilable accounts, although the attempt has been made to establish a connection between the two narratives (see Commentary on 17.12, 15). In 16 David is a mature and accomplished warrior, while in 17 he is a youth ignorant of military technique and professing a distrust in reliance on professional excellence. Such experience as he possesses has been won in conflict with wild animals who attacked his flock and he ascribes his victories on these occasions to the power of Yahweh (v. 37).

Moreover, according to 17, he is unknown to Saul, who asks particulars about him from Abner (vv. 55-58), and this is incompatible with his position in 16, where he has been selected for Saul's cadre (16.21-23). Noth's[6] opinion that 17 is secondary as compared with 16.21-23 is reinforced by the consideration that the slaying of Goliath has probably been transferred from Elhanan (II Sam. 21.19) to David in accordance with the tendency to attach heroic acts to the one conceived as the heroic figure *par excellence*.

The question of the relationship of 16 to 17 has, however, to be considered in connection with the shorter text of G^B in 17. In G^B, 17.12-31, 41, 50, 55–18.5 are absent and the significance of this shorter text is a matter over which scholars have disagreed. On the one hand it has been held that MT is original and that these verses have been excised in order to reduce the disharmony between the accounts of 16 and 17; on the other hand the originality of the shorter Greek text has been maintained and it has been argued that the lack of continuity between vv. 11 and 12 and vv. 31 and 32 of MT supports this assumption. (There is an excellent summary of this debate in Kennedy.) The discovery of fragments of the Hebrew text of Samuel in Cave 4 at Qumran has some bearing on this debate, although it does not resolve the issue. These fragments have a text related more closely to the Hebrew that lies behind G than to the MT, and Cross therefore concludes that where G of Samuel diverges from MT the divergence is to be explained by the fact that the Greek translators had before them a different Hebrew text from that of MT. Cross continues: 'This does not mean that the LXX presents a text superior to MT, though this is not infrequently the case. It simply means that the LXX accurately reflects a Hebrew textual tradition at home in Egypt and perhaps in Palestine in the second century BC.'[7] We are therefore still left with the problem of deciding whether in the case of 17 MT or G preserves the better textual

[6] Noth, *History*, p. 180 n. 1.

[7] F. M. Cross Jr., *BASOR* 132, 1953, pp. 15-26; 141, 1956, pp. 11-12; *JBL* 74, 1955, pp. 165 f.

tradition, and there seem to me to be no adequate grounds for departing from MT.

The moral of the chapter is obvious. David is great not only in physical courage but also in faith in Yahweh, so that he both acts with bravery and supplies a theological commentary on his action. The Israelite army is invincible not because it is superbly equipped and professionally competent, but because it is the army of the living God, and it is this that makes Goliath's insolence insufferable (vv. 26, 36). David is inexperienced and unskilled in the military arts, but Yahweh of Hosts is with him (v. 37) and will deliver him from the hand of Goliath. But he will not fight Goliath in the orthodox way using the recognized tools of the soldier's trade in which he places little store, for the primitive character of his weapons, sling and pebbles, will emphasize that it is Yahweh who gives the victory. Goliath is the technical expert, endowed with skill and physique, but David says to him: YOU COME TO ME WITH A SWORD AND WITH A SPEAR AND WITH A JAVELIN; BUT I COME TO YOU IN THE NAME OF YAHWEH OF HOSTS, THE GOD OF THE ARMIES OF ISRAEL, WHOM YOU HAVE INSULTED. THIS DAY WILL YAHWEH DELIVER YOU INTO MY HANDS. (vv. 45-46). And he states the theological conclusion which ought to be drawn from this victory. It will demonstrate to all the earth that there is a God in Israel and to all those present that Yahweh does not save with sword and spear (v. 47).

Bentzen[8] has described this chapter as a devotional legend in which David is represented as a witness and confessor, one who testifies that faith in Yahweh counts more than armaments or technique. This is the same attitude as that evident in 7 (especially v. 10) and in 10.18, and also in 11.12 f., where Saul gives Yahweh the credit for his victory over the Philistines—Yahweh is the saviour of Israel.

[8] Bentzen, *Introduction* I, p. 240.

CHAPTER 18

DAVID JOINS SAUL'S ESTABLISHMENT

18.1-5

2. would not let him return Cp. 16.22. 18.1-5 is to be taken with 17 and together they form a parallel account to that of 16.14-23.

3. made a covenant See the note on 11.1.

4. And Jonathan stripped himself . . . In giving his garments and weapons to David Jonathan was giving part of himself. The clothes, armour and weapons are so much part of the man that they can serve as a vehicle of personal connection and by means of them Jonathan and David become one flesh.[1]

5. and was successful This Hebrew word is not easily rendered into English. It means that David was judicious, that he carefully weighed all his actions, and also that he possessed the technical competence to achieve the practical result which he had planned. Similarly in vv. 14, 15 and 30.

and this was good . . . It was not only the people who approved of David's promotion to a military command, but also Saul's officials. Hence it was not only a popular appointment, but one which had the assent of the professionals who appraised it critically.

SAUL BECOMES JEALOUS OF DAVID'S SUCCESS

18.6-30

6. as they were coming home More accurately: 'entering (sc. the city)'. 6a (up to 'Philistine') does not appear in G, which thereafter reads: 'And the dancing women came out to meet David from all the cities of Israel with timbrels . . .'

[1] W. R. Smith, *ROS* p. 335.

instruments of music Perhaps 'lutes' or 'triangles'.

7. And the women sang to one another as they made merry Or: 'And the revellers sang and said'.

8. and what more can he have . . . ? Literally: 'And there is still only the kingdom (sc. to give) to him.' This is an expression of Saul's suspicion that David is ambitious to supplant him and the chapter is a record of how that suspicion grows into an obsession. Hence v. 9 states that Saul kept an eye on him implying an attitude of ingrained distrust and the expectation of treasonable behaviour. RSV: 'Saul eyed David' does not quite bring out this meaning; 'kept an eye on David' is better; cp. v. 29.

10. rushed upon Saul This idiom, used here in connection with an evil spirit, is employed in relation to positive charismatic endowment in 10.6, 10 (Saul) and 16.13 (David). It means 'to be effective in'.

raved This is from the same root as the word for 'prophet', and would therefore seem to indicate that there was some association between prophecy and ecstatic behaviour. What is really being said here about Saul's state of wild excitement is that he is behaving like a prophet. Thus to go berserk is to play the prophet.

11. cast RSV follows MT. G^A and G^L: 'took up'.

13. he went out and came in . . . i.e., he was much in the public eye. It also has the implication that he was a popular idol and this is made explicit in v. 16.

18. my father's family This may be a gloss on the rare word translated 'kinsfolk' by RSV.

20. and the thing pleased him Literally: 'And the affair was straightforward in his eyes.' This corresponds to our different idiom: 'and it was plain sailing.' What is meant is that David's being in love with Michal fitted in very well with Saul's mood of enmity towards him, because it furnished him with a plan by which he hoped to lure David to his death.

We might paraphrase: 'And they told Saul and he saw the way opening up for him'; i.e., the matter of contriving David's death had been facilitated. The same phrase is used by David in v. 26 and the sense of the whole passage depends on the correct understanding of it. The point is that David cannot afford the bride-price which was the sum paid by the suitor to the father of the bride. This inability of David to find a sum worthy of a princess may be what is hinted at earlier in relation to Merab (v. 18). At any rate the entire narrative hinges on David's impecuniosity from v. 20 onwards. Thus Saul's officials, prompted by the king, tell him that he enjoys royal favour, is popular with all the king's entourage and is to become Saul's son-in-law (v. 22). When David protests that he is poor and of small reputation, what is in his mind is his inability to pay the bride-price (v. 23). It is this which Saul exploits and it is because of the disqualification which David suffers through his poverty that he rises to the bait. Hence the officials now say to David: 'The king desires no marriage present except one hundred foreskins of the Philistines'; i.e., 'If you really want to please the king, this is the marriage-present to make him.' The meaning of v. 26 therefore is not, 'it pleased David well to be the king's son-in-law' (RSV), but 'the affair was facilitated in David's eyes with respect to his becoming the king's son-in-law.' That is to say, there now seemed to be no obstacles in the way of his achieving the desire of his heart, since he could have his bride in exchange for military valour.

26. Before the time had expired These words are connected with 27 by RSV. This may be the correct meaning, namely, that David had performed the deed before the prescribed time-limit. The words are not present in G^B.

27. two hundred RSV follows MT; cp. v. 25; II Sam. 3.14. Perhaps this number is a later exaggeration. G^B and G^L: 'one hundred'.

which were given in full number Literally: 'and they filled (completed) them to the king,' i.e., counted them out in full.

28. and that all Israel loved him RSV follows G. MT: 'and Michal, daughter of Saul, loved him.' The reading of G has more point. It is David's stature as a great popular figure which is so galling to Saul.

30. David had more success . . . See Commentary on v. 5. David by sheer ability and courage became pre-eminent among Saul's band of picked soldiers.

Again in this chapter (see Commentary on 17) G^B has a shorter text than MT. The verses which do not appear in G are 1-5, 6a (as far as 'Philistine'), 8b ('and what more can he have . . . ?'), 10-11, 12b ('because the Lord was with him . . .'), 17-19, 21b ('Therefore Saul said to David . . .'), 26b ('Before the time had expired'), 29b-30 ('So Saul was David's enemy continually . . .'). It is a complex matter to decide what is the significance of this shorter text. S. R. Driver's[2] conclusion is that the longer text of MT is the result of additions whose purpose is to exaggerate the intensity of Saul's enmity. It is not possible here to enter into a full discussion of the problem, but the account which follows is based on the longer MT.

Chapter 18, like 16, is pro-David and anti-Saul. The spirit of Yahweh has passed from Saul to David, and Saul, deprived of his charismatic endowment, has been possessed by an evil spirit from God. While he is being soothed by David's music, he makes an attempt on his life (18.10-11; cp. 16.14-16, 23). Saul feels in his bones that he has been rejected as king and he knows that Yahweh is with David (v. 28); hence he acts with cunning and without scruple to remove the danger to his throne. Besides having Yahweh's blessing and endowment David also enjoys massive popular support. He belongs to the people and they take him to their hearts (v. 28b G, v. 30). The women, welcoming home their heroes with song and dance, and celebrating their exploits in battle, ascribe to David greater deeds than they do to Saul (v. 7). David himself makes reference to his lowly origins; he comes from an ordinary

[2] S. R. Driver, *Notes, in loc.*

home, and his promotion must therefore be attributed to sheer ability (vv. 18-23, cp. Eccles. 4.13-16). Not only is he a superb man of action, but he has intellectual gifts and a general competence (vv. 5, 14, 30; cp. 16.18).

Saul, with the connivance of his retainers, who leak the king's intentions to David (vv. 22 f., 24, 26), attempts to lure him to his death. Perhaps the intention is that we should understand that they too are jealous of David who outshines them in war (v. 30), although we have been told that they approved of his promotion to a military command (v. 5). David, who cannot afford the bride-price for a princess (vv. 18, 23), seizes on the opportunity to pay for Michal with the foreskins of Philistines, but the outcome is not that for which Saul has plotted, and David emerges from the exploit unscathed and wins his bride.

CHAPTER 19

JONATHAN MEDIATES BETWEEN SAUL AND DAVID

19.1-7

3. and stand beside my father . . . It is not clear why Jonathan should hold this conversation with Saul in the field where David is hiding. It has been suggested that the point of this was that David should overhear and know immediately the outcome of Jonathan's mediation, so that, if he had to flee for his life, he would be able to get away without delay.[1] This interpretation, however, requires the deletion of the final clause of the verse, AND, IF I LEARN ANYTHING, I WILL TELL YOU. It also conflicts with 7a, 'And Jonathan called David, and Jonathan divulged to him all these proceedings.'

4. Let not the king sin . . . Perhaps the translation ought not to be so theological. Rather, 'Let not the king do a wrong to David.' Jonathan's argument is that David has not done

[1] H. P. Smith, *ICC in loc.*

any wrong to Saul but has served him well and that he consequently deserves better than the malice which Saul is bearing towards him.

5. for he took his life in his hand An idiom which has passed into English. It means to place one's life in an exposed position, i.e., to expose oneself to great danger, to take big risks.

MICHAL SAVES DAVID'S LIFE

19.8-17

9. Then an evil spirit from the Lord came upon Saul Cp. 18.10 f. Perhaps the two are variant accounts of the same incident, but they are now represented as successive acts of violence separated by an interval of reconciliation (v. 7). Saul's malady therefore consists of periodic fits of violence and, since it is David's duty to soothe him with music when he is overtaken by this EVIL SPIRIT FROM YAHWEH, his life hangs by a thread, for just at the time when Saul is disposed to harm him he has a sitting bird for a target.

11. That night This is joined to v. 11 by RSV, following G. In MT the words stand at the end of v. 10. Thus: 'And David fled and escaped that night.' The full reading of G is: 'And it came to pass on that night Saul sent . . .'

that he might kill him RSV follows G, which is superior to MT. The latter reads: 'to guard him and to kill him in the morning.' This would mean that the messengers had orders to prevent David's escape during the night and to kill him in the morning, but the meaning obtained from G is more probable, namely, that the messenger's task was limited to preventing David's escape during the night and that Saul in person intended to put him to death in the morning.

13. Michal took an image The Hebrew word translated image is *teraphim* and it has been taken here to refer to a household god. It has been thought that there is significance in the fact that it is Michal, a daughter of Saul, whose name is mentioned in connection with this idol and that it is the intention of the author to indicate that the house of Saul, which he wants to discredit, was implicated in idolatry.[2] This seems to me to be rather a perverse piece of interpretation, for a plain reading of the passage would suggest that the intention of vv. 11-17 is to represent Michal in a favourable light—a devoted wife possessing courage and resourcefulness and ready to expose herself to danger in order to secure David's escape. Moreover the equation of *teraphim* with household god has been challenged by Albright,[3] who observes that no idols comparable in size to a man have been found in Palestinian excavations. Albright[4] suggests that the phrase translated THE PILLOW OF GOATS' HAIR should read instead 'an old he-goat', and he believes that a sick man could be effectively impersonated with the half-concealed head of such an animal. As for *teraphim* he suggests, on the basis of a cognate Canaanite root meaning 'to wear out', the meaning 'old rags'.

17. Let me go; why should I kill you? Michal, having contrived David's escape, has to defend herself against the anger of her father. She makes out that she acted under duress and that David in effect said to her: 'If you do not help me to escape, I will kill you.'

DAVID TAKES REFUGE WITH SAMUEL

19.18-24

20. and when they saw RSV follows G. MT: 'And he saw' is defective in sense.

company G translates this unusual Hebrew word 'assembly' and, on the basis of G, MT has been emended to 'congregation'. G. R. Driver[5] has explained MT with refer-

[2] So Hertzberg, *ATD in loc.*
[3] Albright, *ARI* p. 114.
[4] Albright, *ibid.*, p. 207 n. 63.
[5] G. R. Driver, *JTS* 29, 1928, p. 394.

ence to the usages of a cognate Ethiopic root. This gives the meaning, 'the elder-company (or, venerable band) of the prophets', i.e. referring to a group of seniors or superiors, 'the seigniory of the prophets'.

22. Then he himself went . . . RSV follows MT. Before these words G reads: 'And Saul's anger was roused.'

to the great well that is in Secu RSV follows MT, but the Hebrew is ungrammatical. G: 'The threshing floor which is on the height.'

23. And he went from there RSV follows G, which is better than MT, 'And he went there'.

24. Is Saul also among the prophets? See Commentary on 10.12. The meaning of the 'proverb' is the same in both passages; the saying points to behaviour which is thought to be incongruous and out of character. Note, however, that the implied estimate of the prophet as a class or profession is different in the two passages. The point of 10.11 is that Saul has respectable and solid family connections and that he ought not to behave like a scruffy ecstatic. That is, the 'proverb' hinges on a pejorative estimate of ecstatic prophecy. But in 19.24 the implication is that Saul is out of place in the ranks of Samuel's prophetic guild. He has been rejected as king over Israel by the word which Samuel spoke for Yahweh and it is incongruous that he should be doing ecstatic exercises among Samuel's disciples. He is not there as a true devotee, but has been made the prisoner of ecstasy; he is in Samuel's and therefore in Yahweh's power.

I have tried to interpret this chapter as a unity, although there are difficulties in such an enterprise and the common assumption has been that it is composite. Kennedy breaks it up into no less than four pieces and Eissfeldt[6] holds that it contains two parallel accounts of David's escape. The first in vv. 11-17 he assigns to L and the second in vv. 18-24, 20.1a

[6] Eissfeldt, *Einleitung*, p. 309.

he assigns to E. The J account of the same episode is, he believes, contained in 20.1b–21.1.

David, exposed to the insane violence of Saul, stands in great peril and, in this extremity of danger, is helped through his friendship with Jonathan and through the loyalty of his wife. By his advocacy Jonathan persuades his father to become reconciled to David (vv. 1-7) and, when this interlude is over and Saul resumes his designs on David's life (vv. 9-10), Michal's warning of imminent danger and her successful stratagem enables David to make good his escape (vv. 11-17). Yahweh presides over the destiny of his anointed and delivers him from the clutches of his enemy.

He thus rejoins Samuel, the prophet who in Yahweh's name has anointed him to be king of Israel, and there he is protected not by sword or spear but by the spiritual forces which Samuel deploys. The ecstasy of which Samuel and his disciples are practitioners is directed against the supporters of Saul, when they come to lay hands on David (v. 20). They are infected with it as with an epidemic[7]; they are imprisoned by this eruptive spiritual fury and are made incapable of carrying out Saul's orders. And, when Saul comes in person to deal with Samuel and David, the spirit of God falls on him too and he is consumed by a fever of ecstasy, prophesying before Samuel and lying naked ALL THAT DAY AND ALL THAT NIGHT (vv. 22-24).

The emphasis here has already been noticed more than once. Samuel is Yahweh's prophet and disposes of spiritual forces which are superior to the arm of flesh. The truth of this has been demonstrated in Samuel's victory over the Philistines (7.10 f.) and in David's defeat of Goliath (17. 41-50), and is now seen again in the powerlessness of Saul to enforce his will against that of Yahweh expressed through Samuel. Yahweh has rejected him from being king and has anointed David. Against this there is no appeal and to contest it is futile.

There is another aspect of this to which attention should

[7] So Bentzen, *Introduction* I, p. 193.

be drawn. Saul has ceased to be the anointed of Yahweh and the grace bestowed with the anointing has passed to David (16.13 f.). But, although Saul can no longer act effectively with the divine fury which he once possessed (10.9-13; 11.6), he is now demented with a hellish fury described as an evil spirit from Yahweh (16.14; 19.9) or an evil spirit from God (16.15 f., 23; 18.10), and, when subject to such fits of violence, he behaves like a prophet (see Commentary on 18.10). That is to say Saul is still possessed by spiritual forces, but this possession is now the evidence of his rejection. Hence it is futile for him to contest Yahweh's judgment; he cannot subdue Yahweh with physical force, for a superior force is being deployed against him and Yahweh has possessed him with an evil spirit. The evidence of Yahweh's mastery over him is his inner darkness and confusion. Ecstasy once made him free and able to do Yahweh's will, but now it evidences his derangement and slavery (19.22-24).

CHAPTER 20

DAVID CONFERS WITH JONATHAN

20.1-23

1. Then David fled from Naioth in Ramah This stitches 20 to 19 although there is no intrinsic connection between the two chapters. They are rather parallel but divergent accounts of the train of events which culminated in David's flight from Saul's court (see Commentary on 19). 19.2 would seem to presuppose a point in the narrative after 20.34, since at 19.2 Jonathan already knows that his father is resolved to kill David. 19.1-7 perhaps refers to an attempt at conciliation temporarily successful subsequent to the rebuff which Jonathan received in 20.28-34. 19.3 may be a brief and obscure allusion to the elaborate procedure described in full in 20.20-23.

3. There is but a step between me and death David's survival hinges on Jonathan's assumption that he enjoys his father's confidence in all matters and that he will therefore always be able to warn him, if Saul has designs on his life. David points out that this is a precarious assumption, since Saul knows of the friendship existing between the two men and may therefore, in this vital respect, withhold his confidence from Jonathan.

5. Behold to-morrow is the new moon and I should not fail to sit at table with the king RSV follows MT. S. R. Driver[1] argues that such a statement is inconsistent with the nature of David's proposal. David is not saying that the festival of the new moon obliges him especially to eat with the king, but, on the contrary, that it furnishes him with an excuse for being absent, since he was the regular companion of Saul at table and had a 'seat' allocated to him (vv. 18, 25, 27). Hence Driver follows G: 'Behold to-morrow is the new moon and I shall not be sitting with the king at meat.' Yet MT makes good sense. The festival of the new moon certainly furnishes David with his excuse—the annual sacrificial meal of his kinsmen at Bethel—but, by the same token, the meal with Saul which he was to miss must also have had a special religious significance (see Commentary on v. 26), and David ought to have been there. MT emphasizes and increases the conflict (see Commentary on v. 30), and is not inconsistent with David's proposal. On the contrary it makes the point which G misses and which is necessary for the correct understanding of v. 30, namely, that in the presence of a conflict of obligations David put his duty to his family before that to his king.

6. misses me Literally: 'takes note of me', i.e., of my absence.

7. that evil is determined by him i.e., it is his fixed and final determination to do me evil.

8. a sacred covenant Literally: 'a covenant of Yahweh'. This means a covenant to which Yahweh is a witness and in

[1] S. R. Driver, *Notes, in loc.*

which he is involved. Cp. 18.3. If David has been guilty of any wrong (sc. towards Saul), it is Jonathan's sacred duty as a covenant brother to carry out the sentence against him; if he should hand over David to Saul, he would betray the covenant.

guilt The basic meaning of this Hebrew word is usually given as 'crookedness', 'perverseness', and so 'iniquity', 'guilt'. A different explanation on the basis of a cognate Arabic root gives the meaning 'deviation from the right track' and so 'error'.[2]

9. Far be it from you Jonathan repeats the assurance of v. 2. He will in no circumstances hand David over to Saul and he will warn him of any danger from that quarter.

11. the field Cp. 19.3 and Commentary on 20.1.

12. about this time to-morrow Or: 'When to-morrow has come'. See Commentary on 9.16.

or the third day There is nothing in MT corresponding to the 'or'. THE THIRD DAY is probably a later correction of TO-MORROW bringing v. 12 into harmony with the time reference in vv. 19, 20(G), 35. Since the conversation between Jonathan and David takes place on the day before the new moon (v. 5), TO-MORROW of v. 12 is the first day of the new moon. Hence the gloss THE THIRD DAY does not mean the day after TO-MORROW of v. 12, but 'the third day of the new moon', i.e., two days after TO-MORROW of v. 12. Only if it is so understood does it harmonize with vv. 19, 20(G) and 35.

13. May the Lord be with you . . . The implication of this and also of the subsequent verses (vv. 14-17) is that Jonathan accepts the fact of his father's and so also of his own rejection (vv. 30 f.) from the throne of Israel and recognizes that David is destined to be king.

14. If I am still alive show me Or, translating MT with its

[2] S. R. Driver, *Notes*, p. 170 n. 2.

extant vocalization, 'And will you not, if I am still living, will you not show me . . . ?'

the loyal love of the Lord The love which unites two covenant brothers, and so we could render, 'the covenant love of Yahweh', since the covenant between the two was 'a covenant of Yahweh' (v. 8); cp. v. 15.

16. Let not the name of Jonathan . . . RSV follows G in attaching v. 15b to v. 16 and reads v. 16 with G. MT: 'and not when Yahweh cuts off the enemies of David, everyone, from the face of the earth. And Jonathan made (sc. a covenant) with the house of David and Yahweh will seek (sc. satisfaction) from David's enemies.' MT is obscure and unsatisfactory.

17. And Jonathan made David swear again RSV follows MT. G: 'And Jonathan again swore an oath with David because of his love for him, for he loved him as his own life'; i.e., he repeated the oath of v. 13 that he would inform David, if Saul purposed evil against him. However MT has more force, because it relates v. 17 directly to vv. 14-16. Jonathan has solemnly requested David to act towards him and his family according to covenant love after David has become king. He now binds David to this undertaking by an oath. Thus: 'And Jonathan again bound David by oath to love him, for he (Jonathan) loved him (David) as he loved his own life.'

18. you will be missed, because your seat will be empty More accurately: 'your (absence) will be noticed, because your (empty) place will be noticed.'

19. and on the third day you will be greatly missed RSV follows G. MT makes no sense: 'and on the third day you will go down exceedingly.' RSV margin 'quickly' is incorrect.

20. And I will shoot three arrows to the side of it RSV follows MT. G: 'And on the third day I will shoot to the side of it with arrows.' According to vv. 35 f. Jonathan shoots only one arrow, and, since David takes his cue from what

Jonathan does, it is proper to assume that Jonathan's procedure in vv. 35 f. would exactly follow the arrangements which were made here. Even G 'with arrows' does not surmount this difficulty. Jonathan communicates Saul's intentions to David by means of the instructions which he gives to his attendant. One set of instructions indicates that all is well, another that David must flee (vv. 21-22); cp. 14.9 f.

21. arrows RSV follows MT. G: 'arrow'. Also in v. 22.

take them RSV translating MT, which, however, cannot give this sense. MT must be translated either 'fetch it (the arrow)' or 'fetch him (David)', the former being obviously correct.

23. As for the matter . . . Referring back to vv. 14-16 and to the promise extracted on oath by Jonathan from David (v. 17).

JONATHAN DISCOVERS SAUL'S INTENTIONS

20.24-34

25. sat opposite RSV follows G. MT: 'rose up' does not give the required sense.

26. He is not clean Saul thinks that David may accidentally have overlooked the necessary process of 'consecration', and so disqualified himself from sharing in the meal which on the occasion of the new moon had special religious significance and so required extraordinary ritual preparation. Cp. Commentary on 16.5. Instead of the repetitive SURELY HE IS NOT CLEAN of MT, G reads, 'He is not clean, for he has not purified himself.'

29. And my brother has commanded me to be there RSV follows MT. G: 'And behold my brethren have ordered me (sc. to come).' 'Brethren'=clansmen. David's excuse for being absent is that he has been summoned to the annual sacrificial meal of his clan.[3] This was the most effective explanation that

[3] W. R. Smith, *ROS* p. 276 n. 1.

could have been concocted, since kin obligations were among the most primary and urgent.

30. You son of a perverse, rebellious woman This is an attempted translation of MT. G points to 'son of a rebellious girl' which S. R. Driver[4] understands as 'son of a runaway slave girl'. MT has also been translated 'son of a woman gone astray from discipline', that is, son of a prostitute.

you have chosen the son of Jesse RSV follows MT. G: 'you are the companion of the son of Jesse.' Saul is charging Jonathan with the neglect of a primary obligation, namely, that to his own kin, and the reason why he becomes so angry is that Jonathan has excused David on the ground that his duty to his kinsmen takes precedence over that to his king. This is too much for Saul and so he flays Jonathan for not applying this canon to the conflict of loyalties in which he is involved. If a kin obligation is primary for David, why should it not be so for Jonathan also and why does he put his friendship for David before the loyalty which he owes to his father? In so doing he is acting against his own interests, for David has fixed his sights on the throne which in the normal course of events would have come to Jonathan (v. 31). Since this is the gist of what Saul is saying, it is not to the point that he should be making derogatory remarks about Jonathan's mother and so none of the meanings suggested for the phrase discussed above is satisfactory. The real point is that Jonathan's covenant with David has made him disloyal to his own kin and so put his mother to shame ('TO THE SHAME OF YOUR MOTHER'S NAKEDNESS', i.e., she has incurred shame in bearing such a son).

33. cast 'took up' has been conjectured; i.e., 'But Saul brandished his spear at him.' Cp. 18.11.

[4] S. R. Driver, *Notes, in loc.*

JONATHAN COMMUNICATES WITH DAVID

20.35-42

38. Hurry, make haste, stay not *Double entendre*, ostensibly addressed to the boy, but really an instruction to David, although redundant in view of the previously arranged cue (v. 22). Also v. 37, IS NOT THE ARROW BEYOND YOU? Verses 40-42 are incompatible with the agreed procedure for the communicating of Saul's mind to David. The assumption of this arrangement was that it would be impossible for Jonathan and David to engage in conversation. Or, are we to assume, that Jonathan could not, at the last moment, let David go without taking a last farewell of him and felt compelled to take the risk? There is a similar difficulty in 19.3 (see Commentary).

41. until David recovered himself MT cannot be so translated. It can only mean 'until David exceeded', that is, showed greater emotion than Jonathan. The conjecture of BH, on the basis of G, 'excessively' is dubious Hebrew. 'And they kissed each other and wept together excessively.'

Jonathan occupies a central place in this chapter, although he acquires this importance not for his own sake, but because of the part which he plays as the agent of David's survival. This is achieved through the covenant existing between David and Jonathan which creates a brotherhood superseding the brotherhood of blood and constraining Jonathan to act against his own and his father's interests. In order to be loyal to this covenant and communion of souls Jonathan makes great sacrifices. He is prepared to save David's life, although in so doing he assists one nominated and anointed for the throne which might have been expected to come to himself (v. 31). He has such magnanimity of spirit that he can envisage David as king of Israel (v. 13) without any shadow falling across their friendship; he is uncorrupted by ambition and he asks in return a love which matches his own (v. 17). He is concerned that the fineness of their mutual devotion should be preserved and that it should not be coarsened or destroyed when David comes to power.

It was common practice for a king in the ancient Near East, acquiring power in the circumstances in which David did, to exterminate the previous royal family as an act of political expediency and self-preservation, and Jonathan's earnest appeal to David is perhaps to be understood against this background. Would David be corrupted by power or would his covenant love to Jonathan and his family survive unimpaired, when the tables were turned and David was king?

Jonathan's covenant of love with David and the obligations which it creates bring him into conflict with ancient obligations based on kinship. To Saul it is disloyalty amounting to treachery that any bond between Jonathan and David should come between father and son and prevent Jonathan from serving his father and the throne with undivided allegiance. Jonathan is thought to have failed his family, to have defected from an elementary duty and to have been an unnatural son and a fool (see Commentary on v. 30). He thus suffers affliction for the sake of a covenant of Yahweh (v. 8), for this covenant between David and Jonathan is the instrument chosen by Yahweh for the preservation of his anointed, and had it not been for Jonathan's costly fulfilment of his obligations under this covenant, David could not have escaped the clutches of Saul. (See Commentary on v. 3.)

CHAPTER 21

DAVID AT NOB

21.1-9

1. Nob Groll. p. 158.

2. Ahimelech, the priest Designated in vv. 4, 6 and 9 simply as 'the priest', that is, the Elide high priest presiding over the central sanctuary now at Nob.[1]

[1] Albright, *ARI* pp. 119 f.

I have made an appointment with the young men RSV follows G, which is superior to MT. The latter reads: 'I have directed the young men.' THE YOUNG MEN are a band of soldiers and David represents to Ahimelech that he has arranged to rendezvous with them at a certain place and needs rations.

3. What have you at hand? Or: 'What have you in stock?' G: 'If you have five loaves of bread in stock, give (them) to me.'

4. common bread i.e., unconsecrated bread. Consecrated bread is available but David's soldiers can have it only if they have been abstaining from sexual intercourse and so are in a state of holiness. See Commentary on 16.5.

5. women have been kept from us Because they were taboo to those who were about to engage in war which was a sacred occupation.[2] See Commentary on 17.45.

as always Or: 'as is customary'. David tells Ahimelech that even when his men are not on a specific warlike mission, they are in a state of holiness. Since on this occasion they have a military assignment, it can be concluded *a fortiori* that both they and all their equipment are in a state of holiness.

6. the bread of the presence i.e., bread set out in Yahweh's presence and originally envisaged as his food;[3] cp. Ex. 25.30; Lev. 24.8.

7. detained before the Lord i.e., prevented from entering the sanctuary to fulfil a religious obligation because of a ceremonial impurity.

the chief of Saul's herdsmen Literally: 'the mighty one of Saul's herdsmen'. This has been emended to read, 'the mightiest of Saul's runners', i.e., referring to a courier or royal escort; cp. 22.17. In any case Doeg was a 'servant' or

[2] W. R. Smith, *ROS* pp. 455 f.
[3] W. R. Smith, *ibid.*, pp. 241 f.

official of Saul and his mention here is doubtless connected with the part which he plays in 22.9 f.

9. the sword of Goliath Weapons were laid up in sanctuaries as offerings in fulfilment of vows.[4]

DAVID WITH ACHISH, KING OF GATH

21.10-15

11. David, the king of the land This can only be understood in terms of his nomination and anointing by Samuel. He was not in fact king. BH emends conjecturally so that the words apply to Saul: 'Is not this David servant of Saul, king of the land?'

Did they not sing? David's popular renown was his undoing. The song celebrating his military prowess had gone before him to Gath and now made his position untenable. The words

SAUL HAS SLAIN HIS THOUSANDS
AND DAVID HIS TEN THOUSANDS

had an ominous ring in the ears of Achish. David was a fugitive because of his designs on Saul's throne, and a leopard does not change its spots. David knew that this was how Achish would reason and, on this account, he WAS MUCH AFRAID (v. 12).

13. So he changed his behaviour Literally: 'he changed his taste'. The word translated 'taste' means basically taste which is experienced through the palate. Then like our English word it is used in the sense of 'discrimination'; but whereas we use 'taste' in an aesthetic context, the Hebrew word comes to mean rather 'composure', 'balanced behaviour', 'discretion', 'good judgment'. David was normally well-balanced and sagacious (cp. 16.18), but now, to save his life, he acted like a madman.

[4] W. R. Smith, *ibid.*, p. 460.

in their hands i.e., as they sought to restrain him.

and made marks RSV follows MT. G: 'and drummed on (literally, 'fell upon') the leaves of the gates'.

In 19.18 f. David is secure behind an inpenetrable screen of spiritual power, but in 20 and 21 Yahweh makes no such extraordinary provision for his safety. David knows that there is but a step between him and death (20.3) and he depends for survival not on a legion of angels but on the constancy of a friend. This flavour of earthiness is increased in 21, where David is thrown back on his own resources and has to engage in lying and subterfuge in order to keep himself alive. His quick thinking and brilliant improvisation save him at Gath in a moment of extreme danger, and this is a performance which we can applaud without feeling any ethical twinges, but it is otherwise with the deception which he practises on Ahimelech.

The writer, of course, is unembarrassed by any such scruples and all is written in praise of Yahweh's anointed who is tough and determined and resourceful in the fight for survival. Indeed, from one point of view, David's behaviour at Nob might have been criticized as impiety rather than immorality. He had represented that he and his soldiers were consecrated for war and so were entitled to the holy bread, when in fact he was a hungry fugitive from the court of Saul. On this aspect of impiety our Lord is reported as having spoken in defence of David's action in the course of a discussion on Sabbath observance (Matt. 12.3 f.; Mark 2.25 f.; Luke 6.3 f.). David had a proper sense of values and the urgency of his need abrogated the demand for ceremonial holiness.

But David's treatment of Ahimelech cannot but raise for us serious ethical questions. He deceived the priest of Nob and enlisted his sympathy by fundamentally misrepresenting the circumstances. Ahimelech had no reason to suspect that he was not acting as a loyal subject of Saul; on the contrary he believed that he was giving proof of his loyalty by supplying rations for David and his soldiers (22.14). He was unaware that he was assisting the escape of one whom Saul was determined to kill, and the price which he had to pay for his unwitting co-operation in David's escape was a terrible one (22.11-19). David's hands were red with the blood of Ahimelech and his house. This, however, is not the point of view of the narrative in which none of these scruples is felt. (See further the summing up of 22.)

CHAPTER 22

DAVID ON THE RUN FROM SAUL

22.1-5

1. Adullam Groll. p. 141.

they went down there to him This is an indication that David's family was inseparably involved with him and that in giving vent to his hostility Saul would regard not only David but also his family as a legitimate target. The same principle is implied in 17.25 where it is said that the preferment to be bestowed on the man who kills Goliath will extend to his father's house. The solidarity of the family was so real that it possessed a kind of corporate personality and was indivisible in preferment as in disgrace, sharing in the honour of one of its members and being liable to punishment, as if every member had committed the offence.

2. who was in debt Literally: 'everyone who had a creditor'. The point here again is that the individual had to keep his place in the family and in the larger social groupings in order to live a civilized life. If the normal social relationships were disturbed for one reason or another, the individual found himself cut off from society and denied the supports of communal life. Such were the disorientated individuals who made their way to David, some running away from undisclosed pressures, some who could not pay their debts, and some with a chip on their shoulder.

4. the stronghold Where was this stronghold? We are told that David, conscious of his precarious existence and uncertain how things would turn out, found asylum and protection for his father and mother in Moab. THE STRONGHOLD was apparently somewhere in the vicinity of Moab, since in v. 5 David is told by Gad, the prophet, to make his way from THE STRONGHOLD to the land of Judah. This would seem to preclude the assumption that THE STRONGHOLD of v. 4 can be equated with THE CAVE OF ADULLAM in v. 1, although it has been commonly suggested that v. 1 should be read 'the stronghold of Adullam'. It would appear then that David is being represented as constantly on the move, driven from pillar to post. First we find him at the cave of Adullam, from there he proceeds to MIZPEH OF MOAB and to THE STRONGHOLD of v. 4; then, on the instructions of Gad, he returns to Judah and seeks cover in THE FOREST OF HERETH (Groll. p. 152). Verses 3-5 are assigned by Eissfeldt to E.[1]

SAUL MASSACRES THE PRIESTS OF NOB

22.6-23

6. that David was discovered This is not the sense which seems to be demanded by what follows. Saul's indignation is caused by the uncommunicative habits of his officials and it is hard to see how the 'discovery' of David could spark off his harangue. Perhaps the small emendation of BH should be accepted: 'Now Saul heard that David and his men had joined up' (referring to the situation described in v. 2). David was no longer a solitary fugitive, but had gathered around him four hundred tough and desperate men.

on the height This may be correct, but 'at Ramah' is also a possible translation. If the latter is the correct translation, we have conflicting statements about Saul's location, since in the same verse he is said to be at Gibeah (where he had his establishment). The picture in v. 7 is that of Saul holding court

[1] Eissfeldt, *Einleitung*, p. 307; cp. H. P. Smith, *ICC* p. xxv.

and denouncing his officials as conspirators whose sympathies are with David and who withhold vital information as to his whereabouts from the king. He was kept in the dark about the special friendship between David and Jonathan—the friendship which enabled David to slip through his fingers in the first instance—and so he reminds his fellow-tribesmen on which side their bread is buttered. Land and military appointments are in his gift and he bestows these upon the men of his own tribe. If David becomes king, his patronage will be reserved for the tribe of Judah and they will find that he has no favours to spare for Benjamites.

8. is sorry for me Or: 'is sympathetic towards me'. RSV follows G. MT: 'is sick because of me'.

to lie in wait Literally: 'as an ambusher'. 'Stirred up' of RSV is not quite accurate. Render: 'none of you is sympathetic towards me or discloses to me that my son has set up my servant (sc. in opposition) to me as an ambusher.' 'As an ambusher' expresses Saul's conviction that David is waiting his chance to pounce and seize the throne.

13. and have enquired of God for him i.e., consulted the oracle and given him advice in relation to a particular problem.

14. and captain over your bodyguard RSV follows G. It is difficult to make sense of MT. RV: 'is taken into thy council' is a very dubious translation.

17. that he fled Rather, 'that he was on the run' or 'that he was a fugitive'.

18. You turn and fall upon the priests Or perhaps, 'You surround and despatch the priests.' (Similarly in v. 17.)

22. I have occasioned the death It is doubtful whether MT can be so translated. 'I am guilty of the death . . .' is an emendation on the basis of G and S. It has been suggested that MT without emendation should be translated, 'I have surrounded all the persons of your father's house ',[2] i.e., I have brought about the death of all the persons of your father's house (cp. vv. 17 f.). This is not very convincing.

Saul can find no Israelite official to inform against David and it is Doeg, an Edomite, who lays the information about the episode of David and Ahimelech at Nob. This may be an attempt to show that the sympathies of Saul's retinue were secretly engaged on the side of David, although the picture is different in ch. 18. More probably, however, the point here is that Saul imagines treachery and conspiracy in every face on which he looks, and it is this insane and ungovernable suspicion which is leading him towards the enormous crime which he commits in this chapter.

In his interview with Ahimelech Saul is unreasonable and bloodthirsty. Ahimelech has a good case and states it well and forcibly, but Saul is not in a judicial frame of mind, and is not willing to take time to sift the evidence. Ahimelech represents truthfully that he gave David only such assistance as loyalty to Saul seemed to demand, since he assumed that David was on the king's business and had no way of knowing that his circumstances had changed. David had lied about his situation, but he (Ahimelech) ought not to be held responsible for his deceit. Saul, overruled by his obsession that conspirators were everywhere, was immovably persuaded that Ahimelech had been hand in glove with David and had knowingly furthered his escape.

That David no less than Saul comes badly out of this is not a thing which our author pauses to consider. His horizon is filled with the poor figure cut by Saul. Already Saul has clashed with Samuel who has rejected him from being king over Israel and has anointed David as his successor. Now he seeks to extirpate the priestly house established by Yahweh in Israel, an institution indispensable for the support of the throne and the Israelite community. To his own royal escort it seemed an offence of such enormity to lay violent hands

[2] P. A. H. de Boer, *Oudtestamentische Studien* 6, 1949, p. 43.

on holy men that they refused to carry out his orders, and Saul had to turn to Doeg, the Edomite, in order to have the massacre executed.

Prophet, priest and king all had a place in Yahweh's community, but a king who had been rejected by a prophet and who was the murderer of the priestly family of Shiloh had no future in Israel. This is the point of view of our chapter. The massacre of the priests is another significant stage in Saul's degeneration. David, the nominee of Samuel and the anointed of Yahweh, is now joined by the only survivor of the purge at Nob, and our writer does not feel that, at the moment he confronts Abiathar, David has any cause to reproach himself or any need to answer for his actions. The sin is entirely Saul's, and David, in assuring Abiathar that he will place between the last Elide and the hatred of Saul the shield of his life, is all chivalry and valour. Abiathar's solidarity with David is a portent that the future lies with him, a king who will take his rightful place in Yahweh's community and will exercise his legitimate functions; who will value the contribution of the prophet (v. 5) and whose dynasty will have the support of a legitimate priesthood.

CHAPTER 23

DAVID DELIVERS KEILAH

23.1-5

1. Keilah Groll. p. 154. David's men questioned the wisdom of leaving the Forest of Hereth, where they were already in a state of fear, for a location where they would have less cover and be exposed to even greater dangers. In deference to their opinion David consulted the oracle a second time (v. 4), but he received the same answer as he had on the first occasion (v. 2) with the further assurance that Yahweh would deliver the Philistines into his hand.

SAUL TRIES TO TRAP DAVID AT KEILAH

23.6-14

6. When Abiathar, son of Ahimelech, fled to David at Keilah Or, more exactly: 'As Abiathar, son of Ahimelech was fleeing to David at Keilah'. This, however, does not agree with 22.20 f., according to which Abiathar joined David before he had gone to Keilah, presumably in the Forest of Hereth. Hence we should probably follow G^B: 'And it happened that in fleeing to David Abiathar, son of Ahimelech, went down with David to Keilah, having an ephod in his hand.' For the last phrase MT reads: 'the ephod came down in his hand', This cannot be rendered 'he came down with an ephod in his hand', (AV, RV, RSV) although this is the sense which is required and which is supplied by G.

7. God has given him This presupposes an emendation of MT, whose verb can only mean 'alienate', 'reject' and does not give the required sense. BH emends: 'God has sold him.'

9. Saul was plotting evil Or, preserving the Hebrew idiom, 'fabricating evil'; i.e., shaping it with the same skill and cunning as a craftsman exercises with his raw material. The noun of the same root means 'craftsman', 'artificer'.

11. the men of Keilah Literally: 'the owners of Keilah', i.e., the citizens of Keilah.

13. and they went wherever they could go The point of the idiom is that they had no safe destination for which they could make, but were continually on the move seeking to evade capture. It is the extremity of their insecurity which is emphasized.

14. the hill country i.e., the central hill country of Judah where Ziph was located (Groll. p. 165, Ziph [2]). There was another Ziph in the Negeb, south-west of the Dead Sea (Groll. p. 165, Ziph, [1]).

JONATHAN VISITS DAVID AT HORESH

23.15-18

15. Horesh Groll. p. 152.

and David was afraid This is no doubt correct since it seems to be demanded by what follows. It requires the alteration of the vocalization of MT, which as it stands reads 'and David saw'. Thus it was in order to boost David's morale and to revive his flagging spirits that Jonathan visited him at Horesh (v. 16). There he sought to persuade him that his cause would eventually triumph and assured him that he would be happy to serve as his right hand man when he became king. He further told David that, despite the vigour with which Saul was pursuing him, he too knew that David was destined to be king and that nothing could stave off the event (v. 17). The phrase 'strengthened his hand in God' is peculiar, but it seems to mean 'assured him of divine protection'; i.e., assured him that Saul's hand would not find him (v. 17).

18. made a covenant They renewed their covenant brotherhood before Yahweh—a relationship which took precedence over every other tie or claim. (See Commentary on 20.8, 30.)

THE ZIPHITES INFORM AGAINST DAVID

23.19-29

19. the hill of Hachilah According to Groll, p. 151, located between Ziph and Engedi.

Jeshimon Meaning 'wilderness' or 'desolation' and referring to some part of the wild and desolate wilderness of Judah.

20. according to all your heart's desire The Ziphites are in effect saying to Saul: 'We know that you are eager to lay your hands on David. Very well, come down and get him, for we know where he is.'

22. make yet more sure MT can hardly be so translated, although the general sense is correct. Rather: 'Prepare further' or 'Make further preparations' (so G); i.e., 'Make certain that your preparations are complete and foolproof and that, when I do come, the operation will go without a hitch.'

know and see the place where his haunt is Literally: 'Note and mark his place with respect to which his foot is'; i.e., 'Note and mark the place where his tracks are.'

and who has seen him there RSV follows MT, which, however, has no 'and'. Perhaps we should read with some support from G: 'Note and mark the place where his fleeting foot (tracks) may be.'

23. and come back to me with sure information MT cannot yield this sense. Rather: 'Be sure to come back' or 'Come back without fail.'[1]

all the thousands of Judah Or: 'All the clans of Judah'; cp. 10.19.

24. Maon Groll. p. 156.

25. which is in the wilderness of Maon RSV follows G. MT: 'and he resided in the wilderness of Maon.'

28. the Rock of Escape Driver[2] suggests 'the rock of divisions', in the sense that here the ways of Saul and David divided. Perhaps rather 'the rock of slitherings', referring to the scrambling among the rocks of pursuer and pursued (so Köh.).

29. Engedi Groll. p. 149.

There are no pressing critical difficulties in this chapter, but vv. 14b-18 have been assigned by Eissfeldt[3] to E and regarded as one of three parallel accounts of Saul's pursuit of David. The other two are in 24 (J) and 26 (L).

[1] S. R. Driver, *Notes, in loc.*
[2] S. R. Driver, *ibid, in loc.*
[3] Eissfeldt, *Einleitung*, p. 309

Saul is still able to rule effectively and the men of Keilah will not defy him in order to protect David, although they owe him a debt of gratitude. Similarly the Ziphites believe that it is more prudent to assist Saul than to preserve the secret of David's hiding-place; their conduct rests on the assumption that Saul will eventually triumph and that they had better be on the winning side. In this situation, where there is little inclination to put much reliance on his ultimate success and where every man's hand seems to be against him, David and his men are in constant danger and are continually on the run. When the strain of unrelieved insecurity begins to weigh on his spirits and he has doubts about his destiny, Jonathan visits him to cement the bond between them and to persuade him that he will yet be king; that Saul knows this, and that, when he does assume power, he can count on his friend's support. Thus at a time when David is oppressed by his loneliness, Saul's son swears again that he has not wavered in his allegiance and that he is closer to David in virtue of their covenant than he is to his father in virtue of blood.

The chapter is interesting for the references in it to David's resort to divine guidance and this should be connected with his acquisition of Abiathar and the ephod. In one respect he enjoys an advantageous position in relation to his adversary who, by the massacre of the priests at Nob, no longer has access to Yahweh's guidance (cp. 14.3, 18, 36 f., 40-42). David has the ephod and we are to infer that it is by this method that he discovers Yahweh's will in connection with the proposed relief of Keilah (vv. 2, 4). It is certainly explicitly stated that the ephod is used in order to ascertain the attitude of the men of Keilah (v. 9) and the procedure followed there points to Urim and Thummim, since it is the same as that of 14.40-42.[4] (See the summing-up of ch. 14.) The implications of Saul's break with the priesthood are thus being worked out in this chapter. However precarious may be David's position he now possesses the accredited means of discovering Yahweh's will in moments of fateful decision and is no longer entirely

[4] Bentzen, *Introduction* I, p. 186.

dependent on the sporadic word of a prophet (cp. 22.5). Saul, on the other hand, has neither prophet nor priestly oracle to advise him, and, in any case, he has ceased to show any concern for Yahweh's will, so that, despite all the power which is at his elbow, his policies are now senseless and self-destructive.

And, when every other means by which Yahweh preserves his anointed fails, and nothing it seems can save him from the blood-lust of his enemy, Yahweh so manipulates historical contingencies as to snatch him from the arms of his adversary. Saul has to turn aside from settling a vendetta in order to meet a new threat to his kingdom from the Philistines. The theme of the chapter therefore is that, even when exposed to terrible danger, David is not so defenceless as might appear, for he has Abiathar and the ephod, and, with this, access to the guidance of Yahweh; and, when all else fails, Yahweh's vigilance and resources are more than sufficient to shield him from the malice of Saul, for he watches over his anointed.

CHAPTER 24

DAVID SPARES SAUL'S LIFE

24.1-7

2. Wild-goats' Rocks Understood by RSV as the name of a particular place. Probably it simply means rocks where wild goats were found.

3. sheepfolds Low stone walls forming pens or enclosures for sheep.

7. persuaded Köh. 'chided'. G. R. Driver[1], 'summoned'.

DAVID'S ADDRESS TO SAUL

24.8-15

10. and some bade me kill you RSV follows MT, but the translation is dubious. The reference apparently is to the atti-

[1] G. R. Driver, *JTS* 28, 1927, pp. 285 f.

tude of his men when Saul was at his mercy in the cave (vv. 4, 7). G: 'and I refused to kill you.'

but I spared you RSV follows G and S. In MT the verb is third person feminine singular and 'eye' which appears in V should perhaps be understood, although it is not in the text; i.e., 'but my eye spared you'.

11. you hunt my life More accurately: 'lie in wait for my life.'

13. proverb The Hebrew word rendered 'proverb' has a weakened sense here as compared with the usage commented on in 10.12. It means no more than 'aphorism' or 'gnomic saying'.

15. and see to it and plead my cause . . . Or: 'that he may look into it and state my case and give me the verdict (and so deliver me) from your hand.'

SAUL BARGAINS WITH DAVID

24.16-22

18. And you have declared this day . . . David's case is that he has been misrepresented as having designs on Saul's life (v. 9), but that he has never at any time done Saul any wrong (v. 11). Saul now admits that his behaviour in the cave is convincing proof of his goodwill towards the king and cannot be reconciled with the suspicions which have been harboured by Saul against him. The emendation of BH is: 'you have magnified this day the good which you have done to me'; i.e., the splendid gesture of sparing my life when it was at your mercy is a spectacular enlargement of your former goodwill and forbearance during a period when your motives were misrepresented as base.

19. for what you have done to me this day This rendering is made possible by transposing 'this day' to the end of the verse. The literal translation of MT is: 'in return for this day with respect to which you have done to me.' This hardly makes sense and has been emended conjecturally to read: 'in return for this good which you have done to me.' Without emendation a rather forced translation of MT would be: 'in respect of what you have done for me.'

22. the stronghold According to S. R. Driver[2] the cave of Adullam.

The intention of this chapter is to write large the magnanimity of David and to exhibit him as the very soul of honour. He is a hunted man, driven to hiding with his men in the caves of the earth and he has been presented in an incredible way with an opportunity of settling with his implacable enemy. His desperate situation might be thought a sufficient justification of the deed, for, in the circumstances how could he be expected to exercise restraint and mercy? David's position is made even more difficult by the attitude of his men who are in no doubt as to what should be done and who supply him with theological reasons for assassinating the king. Yahweh has delivered Saul into David's hands and given him perfect freedom of action (v. 4). Thus it is represented to David that the killing of Saul is a religious duty from which he must not shrink.

Yet David resists all these pressures and refuses to take Saul's life; instead he uses the occasion in order to demonstrate to Saul that he has never at any time meditated evil against him. He cuts off the skirt of the king's robe and afterwards produces it in Saul's presence as evidence that he had him at his mercy. If this will not persuade Saul that his suspicions of David and his settled malice towards him are groundless, nothing will. As for David he is content to leave the verdict with Yahweh and is confident that he will be declared innocent and vindicated. What he is not prepared to do is to take the law into his own hands and execute judgment on Saul, not even when it might seem that Yahweh was calling him to this task (vv. 4, 10, 18). Saul, for his part, is over-

[2] S. R. Driver, *Notes, in loc.*

come by this singular token of David's generosity and chivalry and admits that he has persecuted David without cause and repaid good with evil. In saying that he and his royal house have no future in Israel and that the future lies with David, he repeats the statement of Jonathan (23.17); and, in asking clemency for the members of his house, he recalls to our mind the terms of Jonathan's plea to David. (See Commentary on 20.16.)

Such would appear to be the main impression which the author tries to create. It is a portrayal which would seem to be in contradiction with the realities of the situation. Saul has his three thousand picked troops (v. 2) and David is in hiding in a cave with a bunch of desperate men. David invites capture, but Saul proceeds to make an apology for his behaviour, to predict that the throne will pass to David and to ask a favour of the one destined to be king. Yet Saul has the power and keeps it and, at the end of the chapter, the man from whom he has been asking favours returns to his hide-out. He is still a hunted man. It is difficult to make sense of this, but our author's point may be that, notwithstanding all appearances to the contrary, David is Yahweh's choice for the throne, so that, however heavily the scales are tipped against him, nothing can obstruct his progress to that throne. David believes this and Saul knows it, but, for the moment, David remains the fugitive and Saul the king, although why he should now need to remain in hiding after Saul's professed change of heart is not clear (vv. 16-19): perhaps on the ground that, because of his madness, Saul's constancy of purpose could no longer be relied on and reconciliation might soon turn again to hatred (cp. 19.6, 9 f.).

Verses 4-7 (5-8 in MT) constitute a special problem. It has been held[3] that a rearrangement of these verses produces a more intelligible train of thought, and that 4b and 5 should follow 7a; i.e., 'Then David arose . . . because he had cut off Saul's skirt' to follow 'So David persuaded . . . to attack Saul.' The purpose of this rearrangement is to give to the cutting off

[3] S. R. Driver, *ibid.*, *in loc.* (4b and 5 in EVV=5b and 6 in MT).

of Saul's skirt the kind of interpretation which suits vv. 8 f. Thus David's men urge him to kill Saul, but he refuses to raise his hand against Yahweh's anointed (4a, 6), rebukes his men for meditating violence against Saul (7a) and, instead, cuts off the skirt of the king's robe that he may subsequently produce it as a proof of his generosity and goodwill (4b, 5). There is, however, a difficulty which this rearrangement cannot touch. If the interpretation flowing from it is correct, why should David have been filled with remorse when he cut off Saul's skirt, since *ex hypothesi* this was symbolic of his resolve not to harm Saul? The fact that he was filled with remorse makes it clear that the meaning of this symbolic act in v. 5 is not in accord with the interpretation given to it in vv. 8 f., and no rearrangement of verses can dispose of this difficulty. What seems to have happened is that the cutting off of Saul's skirt has been reinterpreted in vv. 8 f. so as to become symbolic of the qualities of restraint and mercy which it is desired to attribute to David. Verses 4-7, however, cannot be fitted into this scheme and should be examined on their own merits without any attempt at rearrangement.

David's men tell him that Yahweh has delivered Saul into his hands and, acting on this assumption, David cuts off the skirt of Saul's robe, but no sooner has he done this than he is filled with remorse. When Samuel announced that Yahweh had rejected Saul from being king, he too cut off the king's skirt (see Commentary on 15.27). This symbolized the taking away of kingship from Saul and the giving of it to David (15.28). It should perhaps be understood there and here not as a mere symbol, but as a symbol having the power to bring about the event which it represents, so that it is as if that event were already fulfilled. David's action must be so understood and this explains why he is subsequently seized with remorse. By cutting off Saul's skirt he is following Samuel in rejecting Saul as Yahweh's anointed, and is accepting the theological justification for the attack on Saul's person which has been formulated by his men (v. 4). But he immediately repents of this step; Saul is still Yahweh's anointed after all, and David is no longer convinced that either Samuel's act or his own can deprive him of his sacral status and open up the way for an attack on his person. Hence he chides his men for having put the idea into his head and refuses to countenance an attack on Saul (vv. 5-7). David's behaviour in v. 8 is in accord with this attitude of reverence to Yahweh's anointed, for there he makes deep obeisance to Saul, and the lack of unity in the chapter is seen in v. 10, where David in the same breath says that Saul is Yahweh's anointed and that Yahweh has delivered him into his hands. The two statements are incompatible. If Yahweh has delivered Saul into David's hands, Saul has ceased to be Yahweh's anointed.

The main concern of the chapter is therefore imperfectly joined to another theme—the inviolability of the person of the anointed. Once a sacral king, always a sacral king; and neither Samuel nor David can deprive Saul of his status. It may be conjectured that this Messianic (in the strict sense) theology was formulated at a period when the sacral status of the Davidic king in the Jerusalem cult had become an important article of faith. In order to uphold it it was thought necessary to draw out its logic so far as to include the non-Davidic Saul. This was an outpost which had to be defended in order to assert that the charismatic endowment of the Davidic king could not be taken away from him, that he could never be lawfully deposed by any human authority and that it was always a sin to do violence to his person.[4]

CHAPTER 25

NABAL REFUSES TO PAY FOR PROTECTION

25.1-13

1. Paran Groll. p. 159. G^B: 'Maon', Groll. p. 156. This is doubtless correct (cp. v. 2).

2. Carmel Located in Judah, not the Carmel of northern Palestine. Groll. p. 146, Carmel (1).

[4] Cp. Bentzen, *Introduction* II, 94 f.

3. churlish and ill-behaved Or: 'hard and malevolent'.

6. And thus you shall salute him It is doubtful whether MT can mean this. The literal translation is: 'And thus you are to say to him that lives.' Or: 'And you are to say thus: "To him that lives!"' i.e., a form of greeting. V: 'to my brethren', hence the emendation, 'And thus you are to say to my brother.'

11. water RSV follows MT. G: 'wine'.

13. RSV follows MT. The words, 'And every man of them girded on his sword; David also girded on his sword', do not appear in G^B.

THE INTERVENTION OF ABIGAIL

25.14-35

17. ill-natured The Hebrew word can hardly mean this. Either 'worthless' or 'confused', that is, 'wrong-headed'. See Commentary on 1.16. (Similarly in v. 25.)

18. five measures According to S. R. Driver[1] a measure is equivalent to $2\frac{2}{3}$ gallons.

22. to David RSV follows G. MT 'the enemies of David' is not apposite. The point of the oath is to bring punishment on David's own head, if he does not fulfil what he swears.

25. Nabal As the RSV translation makes plain there is word-play on Nabal of which 'fool' is not an entirely satisfactory translation. The word refers to a condition of intellectual and moral obtuseness which produces both impiety and unsocial behaviour.

regard i.e., do not take any notice of.

26. bloodguilt Rather 'bloodshed'.

and from taking vengeance with your own hand The sense

[1] S. R. Driver, *Notes, in loc.*

is correct, but the rendering is very free. Rather: 'and that your own hand should save you'; i.e., he should leave it to Yahweh to settle the wrong done to him by Nabal.

be as Nabal Again word-play on the name Nabal. 'Be wrong-headed and confused.'

28. Forgive the trespass This is a little difficult, since Abigail has not transgressed against David in the sense of doing him a wrong. The meaning evidently is that she has taken a liberty in confronting him and addressing him so boldly; i.e., 'forgive the presumption', although the Hebrew does not normally have this sense.

evil shall not be found in you The evil from which Abigail would save David is that of engaging in the indiscriminate slaughter of Nabal's establishment simply because he suffered a personal affront from a churlish individual.

29. If men rise up This presupposes an emended text. MT: 'and a man has arisen.' This could be interpreted as referring specifically to Saul, and Abigail then assures David that, in relation to this particular and acute peril, he is in the safe custody of Yahweh (bound in the bundle of the living with Yahweh).

30. according to all the good that he has spoken concerning you This is the sense required, but it is necessary to emend MT to get it.

prince over Israel The same word is used of Saul in 9.16 and 10.1, and of David in 13.14. See Commentary on 9.16.

31. no cause of grief or pangs of conscience Literally: 'a tottering and stumbling of heart' which might mean 'a false step and error of judgment', but more probably 'a false step and remorse of conscience'.

or for my lord taking vengeance himself More exactly: 'and that my lord should save himself'; cp. Commentary on v. 26. Perhaps 'hand' should be inserted with G, i.e., 'and that the hand of my lord should save himself'. The meaning then is that David will not take a false step or have remorse of conscience through having shed blood and pursued a policy of self-help. David will be wise not to assume the role of an avenger.

DAVID MARRIES ABIGAIL

25.36-44

37. his heart died within him i.e., his will to live drained away. With HE BECAME AS A STONE compare our idiom 'he was petrified'.

39. who has avenged the insult Literally: 'who has contested (and won) the case of my insult.' The terminology is legal; cp. 24.12, 15. See Commentary on 24.15 where the same phrase is used.

43. Jezreel Groll. p. 154, Jezreel (2).

44. Gallim Groll. p. 150, Gallim (1).

Despite the theological filter and the euphemistic language (vv. 7, 15) the nature of the work in which David and his men are engaged is plain enough. It is blackmail with the threat of violence in the background. They are a self-constituted and unwholesome police force pressing their services on such wealthy flockmasters as Nabal and, when Nabal refuses to pay up, their reaction is that of a gang which has been denied its protection money. We can appreciate why it would not be an unmixed blessing for the citizens of Keilah to be 'delivered' from the Philistines by such ruffians, (23.1 f.) and why both they and the Ziphites were prepared to assist Saul in his pursuit of David. Nabal looks on them with extreme distaste. They are runaway slaves and, as the owner of this kind of property, he views with alarm a trend for slaves to become wasting assets (v. 10). Abigail grasps all the implications of Nabal's refusal to supply rations and knows that they are all in deadly danger, since David will not stop short of wholesale murder. It is for this reason that she acts with speed and incisiveness.

Such would appear to be the historical background, but the episode is reorientated in agreement with the author's point of view. What is he trying to say? According to his representation the scene is dominated by Abigail, a woman with good looks and a shrewd head, whose persuasive advocacy turns David aside from a rash and ill-considered punitive expedition. Abigail's case is that it is both inexpedient and immoral that David should slaughter a large number of innocent people, because he has been piqued by Nabal's meanness. He has few enough friends and must, at all costs, avoid multiplying his enemies. He must not allow himself to be carried away by such personal feuds, for he is engaged in a holy warfare; he must keep his sword sharp to fight Yahweh's wars, always remembering that he is born to be king and to establish an enduring dynasty. To this end he is to bend his energies with high seriousness, while the settling of personal scores can be safely left in the hands of Yahweh (vv. 26.31).

Hence, after David has accepted Abigail's advice and the rations which she brings, it is Yahweh in person who fights David's case and avenges his insult (v. 39) by striking Nabal down and causing his death (v. 38). The theme of 24 is thus again influential in this chapter (see Commentary on 25.39). David's role is not to avenge himself on individuals who wrong him, since he must leave this to Yahweh. So he is grateful for the better judgment of Abigail (v. 33) who has reminded him that he has higher tasks than the settling of personal insults. In relation to his conflict with Saul (see Commentary on v. 29) she assures him that he is in the safe keeping of Yahweh and that he need not stain his hands with blood in order to be safe from this or any other adversary (cp. 24.12-15).

CHAPTER 26

THE ZIPHITES LAY INFORMATION AGAINST DAVID

26.1-5

1. This verse closely resembles 23.19, and 23.19-29 and 26.1 f. may be divergent accounts of the same incident. This seems more reasonable than the assumption that the Ziphites informed against David on two separate occasions.

on the east of Jeshimon See Commentary on 23.19. 'On the east of' is dubious. Literally: 'beside the face of', i.e., perhaps, 'in front of'.

4. and learned of a certainty OF A CERTAINTY is the same Hebrew phrase as occurs in 23.23 (see Commentary). 'Ascertained' would be an adequate translation. The difficulty, however, is that the process of ascertaining in v. 4 does not appear to add anything to v. 3b, unless 'seeing' implies less precision that 'ascertaining'. For this reason it has been thought that the name of a place is desiderated in v. 4, and that it was in order to discover more precisely the location of Saul's force that David sent out spies. Cp. v. 5: THEN DAVID ROSE AND CAME TO THE *PLACE* WHERE SAUL HAD ENCAMPED.

DAVID AGAIN SPARES SAUL'S LIFE

26.6-12

8. and I will not strike him twice i.e., there will be no need of a second blow.

10. perish More accurately: 'be swept away'.

11. jar The root means 'to be broad' and the vessel is identified by Honeyman[1] with a 'two-handled lentoid pilgrim

[1] A. M. Honeyman, *PEQ*, 1939, p. 89 and fig. 10.

flask' archæologically attested in the Palestinian deposits of the latest Bronze period and found with increasing frequency throughout Early Iron I.

DAVID TAUNTS ABNER

26.13-16

14. to the king RSV follows MT, although David has in fact called out to Abner. Hence the emendation of BH: 'Who are you that is calling out to me?'

DAVID PROTESTS HIS INNOCENCE TO SAUL

26.17-20

19. may he accept an offering Literally: 'may he smell an offering', i.e., sniff it with pleasure and approbation.

that I should have no share Or: 'so that I have no attachment with the portion of Yahweh', i.e., so that I am cut off from the portion of Yahweh. The 'portion of Yahweh' is the promised land of Canaan and so the presupposition is that to be cut off from Canaan is to be cut off from Yahweh. A man's religion is tied up with his citizenship in a given community and, if this political connection is severed, he cannot continue to practise it. Hence, when Naaman wishes to worship Yahweh at Damascus, he has first to load up two mules with the soil of Canaan and transport it to Damascus, thereby creating an enclave of Yahweh's land in his Aramaean dwelling-place (II Kings 5.17). The belief that a god cannot be worshipped outside his own land does not merely involve holding that there can be no worship of a god where he has no sanctuary, but that the land of a strange god is not a fit place to erect such a sanctuary.[2] Albright[3] has argued that particularism of this kind is characteristic of the Early Iron Age, from the twelfth to the ninth centuries BC, and that this contrasts with the international and universalistic tendencies of the Middle

[2] W. R. Smith, *ROS* p. 93.
[3] Albright, *ARI* p. 118.

and Late Bronze Ages. Thus he contrasts the Song of Deborah, (Judg. 5) where, in his view, the universality of Yahweh's power is stressed, with the attitude represented by this verse. Robertson Smith,[4] on the other hand, holds that this delimitation of the area of influence of any god is bound up with the nature of ancient Semitic religion, where the religion of the community is an aspect of its total political organization and cannot therefore be practised except in the context of citizenship. This seems to me to be nearer the mark than Albright's observations.

20. my life RSV follows G. MT: 'a flea' is less in keeping with the context.

SAUL ADMITS HIS ERROR

26.21-25

22. Here is the spear, O king RSV follows the consonantal Hebrew text. As vocalized by the Masoretes the meaning is: 'Here is the spear of the king.'

25. You will do many things and will succeed in them Or: 'You will act resolutely and prove your ability.'

The interest of this chapter is focused in the further probing and exhibiting of David's dilemma and the sympathy of the reader is solicited for him. On the one hand he believes in the validity of his anointing at the hands of Samuel and is persuaded that he has been called by Yahweh to be king over Israel; on the other he is determined to avoid any suggestion of disloyalty towards Saul and is anxious to establish that there has been no treacherous intention in his behaviour. It is intended that we should appreciate how difficult it is for him to assert his belief in his future tenancy of the throne and, at the same time, to maintain his posture of absolute fidelity to Saul. He tries to do this by resolutely refusing to intervene

[4] W. R. Smith, *ROS* pp. 35 f.

personally so as to accelerate his progress to the throne. Saul has made him into an outlaw, but he has done nothing to deserve the king's enmity; he has always acted towards Saul with 'righteousness' and 'steadfastness' (v. 23), and he expects that Yahweh will reward him for the stainlessness of his ethical posture. 'Righteousness' implies a high regard for the social wholeness of the community; he has not trafficked in intrigue; he has done nothing to weaken or divide Yahweh's community. 'Steadfastness' points to the honourable and utterly reliable character of his behaviour in relation to Saul. Not for a moment has he contemplated turning traitor, and, above all, he will not violate the person of the anointed (v. 23).

This great respect for the anointed is seen clearly in the circumstances of David's adventure with Abishai. Here again (cp. 24.4) he is provided with a theological justification for assassinating Saul—it is Yahweh who has provided him with the opportunity (v. 8)—but he is unwavering in his conviction that it is a sin to do violence to Yahweh's anointed. However he makes effective use of the incident; it gives him the chance of taunting Abner who, although specially entrusted with the safety of the king, is so sleepy-headed that David is able to remove the king's spear and a jar of water from under his nose. Yet this was no ordinary sleep; it was a deep sleep of Yahweh (v. 12) and so a sign that David's faith was justified and that Yahweh was at work accomplishing his purpose for David, without involving him in violent action against Saul. This is David's argument. Yahweh must be left to deal with Saul and he will eventually pass from the scene either through the direct action of Yahweh (cp. 25.38) or through dying a natural death or in the heat of battle (v. 10).

More important than the comic deflation of Abner is the demonstration of David's innocence and magnanimity (vv. 22-24) effected by his production of Saul's spear and the jar of water; and, no doubt, there is a serious side also to his abuse of Abner who has proved incapable of guarding the sacred person of the anointed (vv. 15 f.), for this is a doctrine in which David believes and on which he acts. David protests that Saul's attitude is unintelligible to him and must be the result either of Yahweh's disfavour or of the malice of men (v. 19). Saul, confronted with unimpeachable evidence of David's innocence, confesses his folly and error and professes a change of heart. But David does not return to him (cp. v. 21) and at the end of the chapter the situation is unchanged. DAVID WENT HIS WAY AND SAUL RETURNED TO HIS PLACE (cp. 24.16-19).

CHAPTER 27

DAVID ESCAPES TO ACHISH, KING OF GATH

27.1-7

1. there is nothing better for me than that I should escape . . . This is an attempt to translate MT. G: 'There is no betterment for me except I escape . . .'

2. We have already heard of David's experiences at Gath (21.10-15) and we may suppose either that the present chapter is a variant account of the same episode or that it refers to a different occasion. There are a number of cases where two variant traditions of a historical episode or situation would seem to have been incorporated in our book.[1]

6. Ziklag Groll. p. 165. This verse has an aetiological aspect. The fact that Ziklag was part of Judah at the time of writing was explained by the circumstance that it had once been donated by Achish to David. Smith's[2] supposition that the point of this is that Ziklag would naturally have belonged to the northern kingdom is, in view of the location of Ziklag, difficult to understand.

[1] Bentzen, *Introduction* II, p. 93.
[2] H. P. Smith, *ICC, in loc.*

DAVID DUPES ACHISH

27.8-12

8. the Geshurites, the Girzites and the Amalekites Groll. pp. 150, 151, 142. RSV follows MT. G reads only the Geshurites '.

for these were the inhabitants of the land from of old as far as Shur RSV follows MT. The Hebrew is dubious and 'from of old' is probably the corruption of a place name which indicated the other limit of the area defined. There is some support from G for 'Telem' (cp. 15.4, 7), i.e., 'for these were the inhabitants of the land from Telem as far as Shur, up to the land of Egypt.'

10. Negeb Meaning 'dry country' and, since the south of Judah is dry, acquiring the geographical meaning 'south' and applied particularly to the south of Judah. Here the other districts in the same neighbourhood are named after the clans settled in them.

12. made himself utterly abhorred Or, retaining the Hebrew idiom, 'put himself in bad odour'.

David reaches the conclusion that he cannot survive except he leaves Israelite soil and removes himself from Saul's reach; and, with this in mind, he escapes to Achish, king of Gath, taking his domestic and military establishments with him. After a period of residence in the royal city he asks to be put in charge of a military outpost and Achish gives him the command of Ziklag (v. 6). What exactly was behind this request is a matter of speculation, but, at any rate, David represented to Achish that he had no desire to be a hanger-on at court and preferred for himself and his men a more active existence. We may suppose that it would be difficult to hold together such a band of desperadoes or to maintain morale and discipline, unless they were busily employed in the kind of work for which they had a taste. Moreover it is clear that he wanted freedom of manoeuvre and could play the double game which he had in mind only if he were somewhat removed from the control and surveillance of Achish.[3]

The chapter does not conceal the desperate and ruthless measures of which David was capable, but the apology for this presumably is that such measures were necessary if he were to survive and, at the same time, clear his name of any charge of treacherous behaviour towards his own nation. Thus, having been posted to Ziklag, he at once begins to throw dust into his master's eyes. His raids are not what he represents them to be and they are made against tribes hostile to Israel (vv. 8-10). While Achish imagines that David is fouling his own nest and making himself odious throughout Israel, he is in fact pursuing a policy designed to demonstrate that he is no traitor, that he has become the servant of Achish in order to survive, but that he is still fighting Israel's battles. So that Achish may remain in the dark, no one must be spared to tell the story of these raids (v. 11), and, for this reason, David does not shrink from wholesale slaughter. Achish is content with the booty which is brought to him and he believes that either David's own countrymen or neighbouring tribes friendly to them have been the victims (v. 10). It is a gruesome story and there is no theological reason for the massacre as in ch. 15; it has nothing to do with the operation of the ban. (See Commentary on 15.3.) It is a cold and calculating process of extermination in which David engages, and the point of view of the chapter is that he is driven to this in order to stay alive for the moment and to keep the door open for his return to Israel when the hour strikes.

CHAPTER 28

DAVID APPOINTED BODYGUARD TO ACHISH

28.1-2

2. I will make you my bodyguard for life Achish has no

[3] Cp. Noth, *History*, p. 181.

doubt about David's loyalty and stakes his own life on his judgment. He places him in a position of great trust, where he will be the first to suffer if his judgment is defective, but his confidence is not shared by the other Philistine rulers (29.2 f.).

SAUL CONSULTS A NECROMANCER

28.3-10

3. mourned i.e., wailed, made loud demonstrations of grief after the manner of oriental mourners.

the mediums and the wizards More accurately: 'the ghosts and the familiar spirits'. The reference is to two different types of necromancy, the first making use of any ghost and the second employing the particular ghost which was the familiar of the practitioner. In v. 7, where RSV translates MEDIUM, the literal translation is 'possessor of a ghost', that is, one who can give guidance and penetrate the secrets of the future by utilizing the superior knowledge of the spirits of the dead.[1] Cp. Lev. 20.27; Deut. 18.11.

4. Shunem Groll. p. 162; Plate 188, p. 67.

7. Endor Groll. p. 148; Plate 188, p. 67.

8. bring up for me sc. from the dead.

SAUL COMMUNICATES WITH THE GHOST OF SAMUEL

28.11-20

12. Samuel RSV follows MT. There is some support from G for the reading 'Saul' and this makes the sense clearer, since it is not obvious why the recognition of Samuel should make the woman certain that her client was Saul, unless we are to suppose that she inferred that only Saul would have dealings with Samuel's ghost. If 'Saul' is read instead of

[1] S. R. Driver, *Notes, in loc.*; *Deuteronomy (ICC)*[3], 1902, pp. 225 f.

L

'Samuel', the meaning is that she penetrated Saul's disguise and feared that she had been deceived and taken in the act in view of her knowledge that he had rooted necromancy out of Israel (vv. 3, 9).

13. what do you see? Literally: 'for what do you see?' G: 'Tell what you see.'

15. I am in great distress Or, retaining the Hebrew idiom more faithfully, 'I am hard pressed'.

16. and become your enemy ENEMY is a doubtful rendering, unless the word in MT is regarded as an Aramaism and it is unlikely that this is a correct understanding of it. G and S: 'and has become on the side of your neighbour.' 'Neighbour'=David. The appearance of the Hebrew word for 'neighbour' or 'companion' in v. 17 referring explicitly to David lends some support to the reading of G and S in v. 16; cp. 15.28; 18.12.

17. The Lord has done to you RSV follows G and V and five Hebrew manuscripts. MT: 'has done to him'. If G and S are followed in v. 16, it is possible to defend MT, although the effort is perhaps a little forced. 'Him' of v. 17 will refer back to 'neighbour' of v. 16, i.e., the word of Yahweh, communicated by Samuel to David, has been fulfilled, since Saul has been deposed in favour of David (cp. 16.1 f.). YAHWEH HAS DONE TO YOU AS HE SPOKE BY ME is, however, superior and can be associated directly with Samuel's words to Saul in 13.13-15; 15.28 f.; in 15.28 the identical phrase to that of 28.17, 'to tear the kingdom' occurs.

19. and to-morrow you and your sons will be with me RSV follows MT. G: 'to-morrow you and your sons with you are going to fall (sc. in battle).'

20. Then Saul fell at once RSV follows MT. G: 'Then Saul was terrified and fell . . .' This has some support from v. 21: 'and, when she saw he was terrified . . .'.

THE NECROMANCER PREPARES A MEAL FOR SAUL

28.21-25

21. I have taken my life in my hand See Commentary on 19.5.

S. R. Driver[2] argues that 28.3-25 is out of place and should come into the narrative after 30. He notes that in 29.1 the Philistines are still at Aphek (Groll. p. 142, Aphek [1]) and that they do not reach Jezreel (Groll. p. 154, Jezreel [1]) until 29.11. Since Shunem (28.4) is about three and a half miles north of Jezreel, their arrival at that place should be narrated subsequent to 29.11. Verses 3-25 are assigned by Eissfeldt[3] to E, and 27–28.2 to J.

The chapter is to be understood in relation to the observations which have been made on ch. 23. Saul is without the guidance of either prophet or priest as a consequence of his break with Samuel and his massacre of the Elide priests at Nob. His position in the face of severe Philistine pressure is now desperate and in his straits he seeks counsel from Yahweh but none is forthcoming. He looks for illumination through the medium of dreams and he follows the oracular procedure prescribed for Urim and Thummim, but Yahweh is silent. He has no prophet endowed with visionary gifts or the recipient of a word from Yahweh; and he has no accredited priest to wear the ephod and operate Urim and Thummim (cp. 14.3, 18, 36 f., 41 [G]; 23.9).

In this situation he thinks of Samuel, once his confidant, but now dead, and he resolves to communicate with the dead prophet through engaging the services of a necromancer. But there is no comfort or help for Saul in his communication with the ghost of Samuel, for the voice of the prophet from the world of the dead speaks the same word as had been uttered by him in the land of the living. The ghost of Samuel confirms

[2] S. R. Driver, *Notes, in loc.*
[3] Eissfeldt, *Einleitung,* pp. 307 f.

that Saul has been rejected and that the blessing of Yahweh has passed to David (vv. 16 [G] and 17). He is no longer the anointed and he is vainly trying to hold on to a kingdom which Yahweh has torn from his grasp. Saul's failure in obedience was final and there can be no reversing of the verdict already passed (v. 18, cp. 13.13-15; 15.28 f.). There are in fact signs from Yahweh to be read if Saul will open his eyes and look at them, but they are a confirmation of his rejection and contain no seeds of hope. His present impotence to deal with the Philistine menace is nothing but Samuel's word of rejection endorsed by the incontrovertible logic of events. Saul is alienated from Yahweh and his army will be delivered into the hands of the Philistines (v. 19).

This is the same theology as the framework of the Book of Judges (cp. I Sam. 7.3 f. and 12.6-12) and it is interesting that Saul's resort to necromancy infringes a prohibition of Deut. 18.11 and Lev. 20.27. The words of Lev. 20.6 should also be noted: 'If a person turns to ghosts and familiar spirits and goes whoring after them, I will turn my face against that person and will cut him off from among his people.' The same Hebrew idiom, 'to cut off', occurs here and in I Sam. 28.9. If this account of Saul's behaviour is in fact regulated by Yahweh's words in Lev. 20.6, the intention is to represent that he began his reign as the chosen of Yahweh, implementing his will, but subsequently went whoring after ghosts and so was ripe for 'cutting off'. At any rate the process of deterioration to which Saul was subject is being illustrated. At the beginning of his reign he acted with vigour to extirpate necromancy from Israel and it is because of his past record as an extirpator of necromancers (v. 3) that the woman is terrified when she discovers the identity of her client (see Commentary on v. 12). Now he has gone cap in hand and in heavy disguise to make use of a woman who dabbles in ghosts. A more damning portrayal could hardly have been contrived and this is what the author wants to achieve. This is but an aspect of Saul's general defection from the will of Yahweh; he is near the end of his tether and there will be no relief for Israel from the Philistines until David, Yahweh's anointed, takes the reins of kingship into his grasp.

CHAPTER 29

DAVID SENT BACK FROM THE FRONT

29.1-11

1. by the fountain RSV follows MT. G^A reads 'Endor' of which S. R. Driver[1] says that it is too far off to be probable.

lords of the Philistines The Hebrew word translated LORDS is used only of the leaders of the five Philistine city-states. (See Commentary on 6.4.) It has been connected with the Greek word (thought to be non-Greek in origin) 'tyrant'.[2]

2. by hundreds and by thousands i.e., military formations of differing sizes were passing in review, with David and his men bringing up the rear among the contingent of Achish.

3. for days and years RSV follows MT. G: 'for a year or two years'.

since he deserted to me RSV follows G. TO ME is not present in MT. Achish looks on David as a runaway slave who has exchanged one master for another. It has already been noted that even the highest royal official was regarded as the 'slave' of his master. (See Commentary on 8.14.)

4. he become an adversary S. R. Driver,[3] 'thwarter'. That is, David will be working against the Philistines and not with them; he will be looking for a way to wreck the operation.

Would it not be with the heads of the men here? David has run away from the service of Saul (v. 3), and the suggestion here is that the only way open to him of effecting a reconciliation with his former master is to make a gift to him of the heads of the Philistine soldiers, just as once before he had

[1] S. R. Driver, *Notes, in loc.*
[2] Noth, *History*, p. 164 n. 1.
[3] S. R. Driver, *Notes, in loc.*

won Michal by making a present of two hundred Philistine foreskins (18.27).

5. Is not this David . . . ? The point is that this refrain was sung in celebration of David's slaughter of the Philistines (cp. 18.7; 21.11).

10. with the servants of your lord RSV follows MT. G and V: 'you and the servants of your lord'.

who came with you . . . RSV follows MT. Between 'with you' and 'and start early' G reads: 'and go to the place where I have given you a command and do not set a base word in your heart, for I have a high opinion of you.' David's relationship to Achish was probably a feudal one. He had been granted a piece of land (Ziklag) and was obliged to perform service with his mercenary force.[4]

It might have been expected that this dismissal of David from the front would have been attributed to Yahweh—an intervention by which David was saved from fighting against his own people. In fact the orientation of the narrative is quite otherwise and the suspicions of the Philistine rulers are not viewed as Yahweh's way of extricating David from a difficult situation. On the contrary the presupposition of the narrative is that his dismissal is a disappointment and even a setback to him (v. 8), for he was hoping to operate with his men as an effective fifth column and to sabotage the Philistine operation against Israel. But the other 'tyrants' were not so gullible as Achish and the refrain with which the women had once celebrated his slaughter of the Philistines was too much for them to stomach (v. 5). So they decided that he was an intolerably bad security risk and that he ought not to participate in the campaign. David, however, is still held in high esteem by Achish and enjoys his complete confidence. Hence he lies consummately in protesting his loyalty and reliability and in asserting that he is being badly treated (v. 8), but Achish has

[4] Noth, *History*, p. 164.

been overruled by his hard-headed colleagues and David and his men have to withdraw.

An interesting critical point is the reappearance of the refrain (v. 5) which had already been David's undoing at Gath (21.11). The question has already been asked (see Commentary on 27.2) whether 21.10-15 and 27.1 f. refer to two separate occasions on which David sought asylum at Gath or whether they are widely diverging accounts of a single occasion. The appearance of the refrain in both would seem to lend some support to the latter alternative. Here, at any rate, is a feature common to both accounts, although, according to the first, it was Achish who regarded it as damning testimony, while, according to the second, it was the other Philistine rulers. It is an attractive conjecture that the core of the tradition was that this refrain had once proved to be David's undoing at Gath, and that this was variously embroidered with a view to elaborating the circumstances attending the occasion.

CHAPTER 30

THE AMALEKITES SACK ZIKLAG

30.1-6

2. the women and all who were in it RSV follows G. MT: 'the women who were in it'.

DAVID PURSUES AND OVERTAKES THE AMALEKITES

30.7-20

9. the brook Besor A stream south of Ziklag the exact site of which is unknown (Groll. p. 145).

where those stayed who were left behind Or: 'and those who were surplus stayed (there)'. The natural meaning of this is that he did not require six hundred men for the operation and left behind those who were surplus. Verse 10, however, reveals that the two hundred left behind were too exhausted to cross the wady Besor. The two pieces of information are not necessarily contradictory. David picked for the expedition the four hundred in the best physical condition and left the less fit to look after the baggage (v. 24).

10. were too exhausted The cognate noun means 'corpse'. Hence we get the flavour of the idiom if we translate 'were too dead tired'.

14. Cherethites Probably a sub-tribe of the Philistines and the name may be connected with that of Crete from where the Philistines are stated to have come.[1] (Caphtor=Crete, Amos 9.7.)

16. dancing This is dubious, although it is supported by Köh., who gives the primary meaning of the root as 'to bound', 'to dance', and so 'to walk in procession'. The meaning 'festive procession', 'pilgrimage' is well-established in Hebrew and Arabic for the cognate noun, but the semantic development posited by Köh. is not certain. The meaning here may simply be 'behaving as at a festival', i.e., 'junketing'.[2]

17. until the evening of the next day Literally: 'until the evening of their to-morrow', an expression which does not occur elsewhere in the Old Testament, and which has been called in question for this reason. A conjectural emendation gives the reading: 'until the evening and put them under the ban', i.e., exterminated them, because they were 'holy' and devoted to destruction. (See Commentary on 15.3.) There is, however, no sufficient reason (in the absence of textual evidence) for introducing the theology of the ban into this chapter.

19. sons or daughters, spoil or anything that had been taken RSV follows MT, with a change of punctuation. G: 'Nothing small or great was missing, either of the spoil or of the sons and daughters, or of anything which they had appropriated.'

[1] Cp. S. R. Driver, *Notes, in loc.*
[2] Cp. S. R. Driver, *ibid., in loc.*

20. and the people drove those cattle before him BEFORE HIM has the support of V, but G and V do not express 'David' at the beginning of the verse, and instead of THOSE CATTLE G reads 'the spoil'. MT: 'they drove before those cattle' which makes no sense. The verse has been extensively emended to read: 'And they took all the sheep and the cattle and drove them before him and said: "This is the spoil of David."'

THE DIVISION OF THE SPOIL

30.21-31

21. and, when David drew near to the people, he saluted them MT cannot be so translated. The translation must be: 'And David drew near with the people (i.e., those who had been on the expedition with him) and asked after their welfare' (i.e., the welfare of those who had been watching the baggage). It has been objected that this does not give the meaning which is desiderated, since it is those left behind who should be asking after the welfare of those who have been out after the Amalekites. 'Asked after their welfare' would, in the context, be most naturally understood not just as a conventional greeting, but as a specific enquiry about the success or non-success of the operation against the Amalekites. Hence the conjectural emendation: 'and they (those left behind) drew near to the people (David's expeditionary force) and asked how things had gone.'

22. base Or: 'confused', 'wrong-headed'. See Commentary on 1.16.

23. with what the Lord has given us RSV follows MT. Instead of 'You are not to do thus, my brethren, with what Yahweh has given us' (MT), G^B reads: 'You are not to do thus after what the Lord has given us.'

27. Bethel Groll. p. 145, Bethuel (2).

Ramoth of the Negeb Site unknown, perhaps to be identified with Ramah of the South (Josh. 19.8).

Jattir Groll. p. 153.

28. Aroer Groll. p. 143, Aroer (3) (identical with Ararah).

Eshtemoa Groll. p. 149. The site of Siphmoth is unknown.

29. Racal Probably Carmel should be read with S. See Groll. p. 146, Carmel (1).

30. Hormah Groll. p. 152.

Borashan Groll. p. 143, identical with Ashan and probably the modern Khirbet 'Asan, north west of Beersheba.

Athach Probably identical with Ether (Josh. 19.7). See Groll. p. 149, Ether (2).

31. Hebron Groll. p. 152.

This chapter describes how David recovers from a disaster which threatens to destroy his prestige among his own following. When he and his men return to Ziklag only to find it burned to the ground, there is a strong feeling abroad that David is responsible for this tragedy and the mood of his men is so savage that the word is raised to stone him. He has shown himself to be incompetent and lacking in foresight; he ought to have foreseen that in following Achish to the front he was leaving Ziklag exposed to marauding bands (vv. 1-6).

It is through Yahweh's help and David's awareness that he needs this help that the disaster is not irretrievable. David has Abiathar and the ephod (see Commentary on chs. 23 and 28) and so an authoritative and reassuring answer to a crucial question: Should he pursue the Amalekites? (vv. 7-8). Here he may be asking implicitly whether the Amalekites have already slaughtered the wives and children. At any rate the notice in v. 1 that the Amalekites had killed no one is evidently intended to register a providential circumstance which enabled David to restore a situation which might, in the normal course of events, have been beyond all mending. 'Deliver' or RESCUE in the oracular answer (v. 8) is to be understood as Yahweh's guarantee that David would succeed in recovering the captive wives and children from the Amalekites unharmed.

Thus Yahweh is still presiding over the destiny of his anointed and the discovery of the Egyptian is not fortuitous; he is used of Yahweh to lead David to the place of revenge and recovery. Nor would David's men have had the benefit of his information had they not shown kindness to him when they knew no reasons for giving him food and befriending him except those of humanity (vv. 11-15). So, in the end, what might have been a fatal miscarriage of David's generalship turns out to be no more than a temporary setback from which he effects a complete recovery. David knows that it is Yahweh who has worked this deliverance, so that, when his men say, THIS IS THE SPOIL OF DAVID, he asserts that it has been bestowed by Yahweh and insists that all must share in it, those who kept the baggage no less than those who took part in the operation (vv. 23 f.).

The emendation proposed for v. 17 would introduce the theology of the 'ban' into the chapter, but it does not seem to have a place there. If it did, it would apply to the spoil of the Amalekites no less than to the Amalekites themselves, but the spoil is distributed and not devoted to destruction. (See Commentary on chs. 15 and 27). The point of the chapter is rather to show how sensitive David is to any charge of incompetence or failure in generalship and how he recovers the lost ground with the help of Yahweh. In making this recovery he shows qualities of fairness and foresight which augur well for the future, establishing a precedent for the manner of distributing spoil among his own men (vv. 23-25), and thereby building up morale and *esprit de corps* and enriching his influential supporters throughout Judah whose friendship will serve him well in the future, when he lays claim on their allegiance (vv. 26-31).

CHAPTER 31

THE DEATH OF SAUL

31.1-7

1. Mount Gilboa Groll. p. 150; Plate 188, p. 67.

3. and the archers found him This has been understood to mean 'hit him', but more probably it means simply 'came upon him', although it might mean 'found his range'.

and he was badly wounded RSV follows G. MT: 'was in great anguish from'. G is superior.

4. and make sport of me See Commentary on 6.6. Probably here with the developed sense of 'abuse', 'torture'.

6. and all his men RSV follows MT. These words are not expressed by G. The reference is not to all the army of Saul, but to the men around him (cp. v. 7).

7. on the other side of the valley Referring to the valley or plain of Jezreel (Groll. p. 154; Plate 188, p. 67). THE OTHER SIDE means the north side of the valley and 'the other side of Jordan' the territory east of Jordan. Thus, according to this verse, there was a general and far-spread panic among the Israelite population following Saul's defeat.[1]

SAUL'S BODY RESCUED FROM THE PHILISTINES

31.8-13

9. and sent messengers This presupposes an alteration in the vocalization of MT, which, as it stands, must mean 'and they consigned them', i.e., the head and armour of Saul.

to carry the good news to their idols RSV follows G and also I Chron. 10.9 (I Chron. 10 has been excerpted from I Sam. 31 with small variations and, in this instance, it preserves a better text). MT: 'to announce the good news in the house of their idols.'

[1] Noth, *History*, p. 178.

10. the temple of Ashtaroth The singular 'Ashtoreth' rather than the plural 'Ashtaroth' is desiderated. S. R. Driver[2] has suggested that the incorrect appearance of the plural here may be due to its occurrences elsewhere in the book (7.3 f.; 12.10) and believes that the reference is to the temple of Astarte at Ashkelon. Astarte was goddess of the evening start and must have originally been identical with Ashtar, god of the morning star, who was androgynous, being male in the morning and female in the evening. As evening star Ashtar became the feminine Ishtar in Mesopotamia and Ashtartu (Greek Astarte) in Canaan. Astarte was a goddess of sex and war and no doubt appears here in the character of a martial goddess.[3] In connection with the laying up of arms in sanctuaries see Commentary on 21.9.

and they fastened his body to the wall of Bethshan The parallel passage in I Chron. 10.10 reads: 'and they fastened his skull in the temple of Dagon.' (On Dagon and his temple at Ashdod see ch. 5.) MT has been emended to read: 'and they exposed his body on the wall of Bethshan', although it is doubtful whether the emendation can give this sense. Robertson Smith[4] suggests that the fastening of Saul's body to the wall is connected with the belief that a corpse is taboo and a source of dangerous supernatural infection, so that great care has to be taken in its proper disposal. In this case the funeral custom which neutralizes the danger of the corpse to the living is its exposure between earth and heaven before the deity. On Bethshan see Groll. p. 145.

12. and they came to Jabesh RSV follows MT. G and S: 'and they brought (them) to Jabesh.'

and burned them there These words do not appear in I Chron. 10.12. It was unusual for the Hebrews to burn their dead and we can only speculate on why Saul's body was disposed of in this way. It may have been in order to forestall

[2] S. R. Driver, *Notes, in loc.*
[3] Albright, *ARI* pp. 74 f., 83 f.
[4] W. R. Smith, *ROS* p. 370.

the risk of exhumation by the Philistines or it may have been to destroy the defilement which his body had suffered at the hands of the Philistines, since, after this catharsis, his bones were buried under the sacred tamarisk at Jabesh.[5]

There is no element of surprise in the disaster which breaks in upon Saul, for we have been well prepared for it and an atmosphere of doom has been systematically created around his person. Yet the scale of it is terrible, for it engulfs not only the king and his three sons, but the whole of Israel. It is a moment of national catastrophe. Nevertheless the doomed king commands our sympathy and even our awe and we are encouraged to feel that he is a man of stature who confronts his fate like the hero of a Greek tragedy. He is too big a man to end up as the toy of his enemies and, if his armour-bearer will not despatch him, he will not hesitate to fall on his own sword.

And, however terrible the theological sanctions which have been invoked against him, the memory of his courage and chivalry is not dead in Israel, so that, at a moment when they might have been preoccupied with recriminations, or paralysed by defeat, the men of Jabesh recall that he had once saved them from the Ammonites (11.1-11) and risk their lives to rescue his corpse and those of his sons from the uncircumcised Philistines (v. 4). So they bear Saul back to their own city and accord his bones the honour of burial, for, although rejected by Yahweh, he was nevertheless to the end the anointed of Yahweh and it was right that Israelites should treat him so (cp. 24.6, 10; 26.9-11). No one but Yahweh might judge him, and now that the terror of this judgment had been consummated it was fitting that his bones should rest under the tamarisk tree in Jabesh, the place where he had won his first victory at a time when there was not a whisper of rejection to spoil his reputation or darken his days.

[5] W. R. Smith, *ibid.*, p. 372 n. 3.

II SAMUEL

NEWS OF SAUL'S DEATH BROUGHT TO DAVID

1.1-16

9. for anguish has seized me The reading of G may point to 'dizziness' which would agree with S. Köh., on the basis of a cognate Accadian word, renders 'bodily weakness'. This meets the case better than 'dizziness'. The position is that Saul has fallen on his sword (v. 10), but feels that the onset of death is unbearably slow. ANGUISH of RSV is what is needed, but there is no evidence that the Hebrew word can mean this. The primary meaning of the root is 'interweave'.

and yet my life still lingers Literally: 'for all of my life is still in me', i.e., 'I am fully conscious (and in great agony)'.

10. after he had fallen i.e., after his being impaled on his sword. The Amalekite's assessment of the situation was that Saul was mortally wounded and so he fell in with the king's request and terminated his agony.

armlet The primary meaning of the word is 'pace-chain', a chain fixed from ankle to ankle which restricted or regulated the length of pace. The word is used here with the more general sense of 'bracelet'. This was evidently part of Saul's regalia.

12. for the people of the Lord and for the house of Israel PEOPLE OF THE LORD and HOUSE OF ISRAEL have been thought to be tautologous phrases and the emendation 'people of Judah' has been suggested in agreement with G.

13. I am the son of a sojourner SOJOURNER refers to a special class of alien resident among the Israelite community whose status as a free individual was guaranteed, but who did not enjoy the privileges of full citizenship.[1] Thus SON OF A SOJOURNER presumably means 'son of an Amalekite who

[1] W. R. Smith, *ROS* pp. 75 f.

made his home in Israel' and so he was evidently serving with Saul's army in some capacity or other and he is explaining how it comes about that he, an Amalekite, and so a traditional enemy of Israel, (cp. I 27.8; 30.1 f.) was in the ranks of Saul's army.

DAVID'S LAMENT OVER SAUL AND JONATHAN

1.17-27

17. lamentation Or 'lament' or 'elegy'. This type of composition differs from the normal rhythm of Hebrew poetry, where it is customary for the second member or *stichos* of the line to balance the first. This is a balance both of rhythm and of thought and is called 'parallelism'. The rhythm of the elegy, on the other hand, is sometimes called the *qīnā* rhythm (*qīnā* is the Hebrew word for 'lament' or 'elegy'). In the Hebrew lament the first member of the line preponderates over the second and is marked off from it by a pause. The function of the second member is not to achieve balance, but to produce a tapering-off effect or an echoing of the first. This gives the poetry the character of a plaintive lilt. The most celebrated example of this kind of composition in Old Testament literature is this lament of David for Saul and Jonathan.

18. and he said that it should be taught to the people of Judah RSV follows G. MT: 'And he gave orders to teach to the people of Judah a bow.' It has been supposed that 'bow' is the title of the lament which follows and that this is derived from the mention of the bow of Jonathan in v. 22. This is improbable as is the assumption that the word is an Aramaism meaning 'accurately' or 'veraciously'. i.e., 'And he gave orders that it should be taught veraciously to the people of Judah.' BH emends conjecturally, prefixing 'and he said' to v. 19 (with G[L]), transposing 'to teach the people of Judah' after 'Jashar' and deleting 'bow' with G. Thus: 'Behold it is written in the Book of Jashar in order to teach the people of Judah. And he said . . .' Another conjectural emendation reads: 'Behold it is written in the Book of Jashar: "Discern hard tidings, O Judah." And he said . . .' There is no satisfactory elucidation of this verse.

the Book of Jashar Or: 'The Book of the Upright.' This is the second mention of sources used in the composition of Books of Samuel. Cp. 'The Law of the King' in I 10.25.

19. thy glory Literally: 'the glory' (or, 'adornment'), referring to Saul and Jonathan. Or the Hebrew word could mean 'the gazelle'. This has been understood as a reference to the fleetness of Jonathan, but S. R. Driver[2] objects that the poet's thoughts do not turn particularly to Jonathan until vv. 25b-26 and that it is unlikely that the poem would open with an epithet applicable to only one of the heroes. The word has been explained by Robertson Smith[3] in quite a different way. 'The gazelle is slain upon thy high places' may be an allusion to some ancient sacrifice connected with the fact that deers and antelopes of various kinds were sacred animals in various parts of the Semitic area and particularly in Phoenicia. These were exceptional sacrifices of the type illustrated by the annual stag sacrifice at Laodicea on the Phoenician coast which was regarded as a substitute for the more ancient sacrifice of a maiden, and they are connected with the myth of a virgin who was immolated when the city was founded and was subsequently worshipped as a goddess. The maiden and later the stag are thus theanthropic victims; in them the death of the goddess is re-enacted. Thus the poet is saying that the death of Saul and Jonathan is a sacrifice of mystic and awful significance. It should be noted, however, that in the Ugaritic literature 'bulls' and 'gazelles' are picturesque designations of grandees[4] (similarly 'ram'='duke'); 'gazelle' here may therefore be a reference to Saul.

is slain upon thy high places RSV follows MT. G^B: 'Erect a pillar, O Israel, for these who died on thy high places of

[2] S. R. Driver, *Notes, in loc.*
[3] W. R. Smith, *ROS* pp. 466-68.
[4] Gordon, *UM* p. 270, No. 972; G. R. Driver, *CML* pp. 136, 150.

wounds.' G^A. Erect a pillar, O Israel, on thy high places for the dead.'

21. Ye mountains of Gilboa . . . This illustrates the element of incantation in the poem. The poet's words are words of power; they have a magical effect and as soon as they are spoken they constitute an effective curse against the mountains of Gilboa.

nor upsurging of the deep This rendering is based on a conjectural emendation. MT: 'fields of offerings'. 'Offerings' is used particularly of produce from the land, i.e., first fruits. Hence 'fields of offerings' are fields bearing produce from which first fruits are offered. The translation of the verse is, however, difficult. 'You mountains of Gilboa let no dew nor rain come upon you nor upon you, fields of offerings' represents rather a desperate attempt to make sense out of the verse. Perhaps 'descend' should be read in v. 21a with G, and 21a and 21b rearranged so as to read: 'You mountains of Gilboa let not the dew descend (on you) nor rain on you, fields of offerings' (deleting 'and' before 'fields' with G^L). Other conjectures are 'fields of gloom', 'fields of deceit'.

was defiled S. R. Driver[5]: 'rejected with loathing'; i.e., the point, according to Driver, is not the defilement of Saul's shield, but the fact that it is now derelict and abandoned.

not anointed with oil i.e., no longer kept in a state of good preservation. Shields, whether made of metal or leather, were oiled to keep them in good condition. The rendering NOT ANOINTED WITH OIL presupposes an alteration in the vocalization of MT, but it is doubtless correct.

24. who clothed you daintily in scarlet Rather: 'who clothed you in scarlet together with luxuries'. It is uncertain whether the phrase can be understood adverbially to mean 'pleasurably' or 'luxuriously' or 'daintily'. The emendation 'together with fine linen garments' has been suggested.

[5] S. R. Driver, *Notes, in loc.*

27. the weapons of war Saul and Jonathan are conceived figuratively as weapons of war. (So S. R. Driver.) Perhaps, however, the reference is rather to Jonathan's bow (mentioned in v. 22) and Saul's shield (v. 21) and sword (v. 22), i.e., to the weapons of the heroes of which explicit mention has been made in the poem. For the close association between a warrior's weapons and his person see Commentary on I 18.4.

Eissfeldt[6] holds that vv. 1-16 are a narrative of two strands, L and J, and that the lament (vv. 17-27) is to be considered genuine and, for the most part, the work of David. It was inserted into its present context by J. With regard to the lament attention should be called to the 'How . . . !' which is so characteristic of this type of composition. Normally this 'How . . . !' appears at the beginning of the lament, but here it first occurs with the second member of the first line and is twice repeated thereafter as part of the refrain 'How are the mighty warriors fallen!' (vv. 25, 27). In the context of the lament 'How . . . !' means 'How different!' and points to the character of the funeral song which sharply contrasts the 'now' and the 'then', the joy and splendour of life with the desolation of death. S. R. Driver[7] has called attention to the accents of humanism which predominate in this lament and has remarked on the absence of religious thought of any kind. It is likely, nevertheless, that the funeral song, as a literary type, originally had religious connections and was associated with ancestor worship or the lament for the dead god. In the Old Testament these connections are severed because of their incompatibility with the nature of Yahwism.[8]

The elegy opens with an intimation of the death of the heroes Saul and Jonathan (v. 19), and then it is commanded that the news be not disseminated in the cities of the Philis-

[6] Eissfeldt, *Einleitung*, pp. 311, 316. Albright agrees with Eissfeldt in attributing the dirge to David (*ARI* p. 126); cp. Bentzen, *Introduction* I, pp. 135 f.; II, pp. 94 f. Although I have assumed that David is the author, it may be that the ascription of the lament to him should be explained rather as part of the artistry of the real author.

[7] S. R. Driver, *ibid., in loc.*

[8] Bentzen, *Introduction* I, p. 135.

tines, where it would be a cause for gloating to the enemies of Israel. There follows the curse on the mountains of Gilboa where the two heroes fell and where the weapons which were so much a part of them (see Commentary on v. 27) lie useless and derelict (vv. 21 f.). Of Saul and Jonathan it is said that in life and death they were not divided (v. 23) and, for these sentiments, Bentzen[9] has charged the author with insincerity. The phrase may mean no more than 'they were closely associated in life and died together on the same battlefield.' Even if it means more than this, no one ought to expect the writer of an elegy to introduce criticism of the dead into his work or to parade evidences of discord between Saul and Jonathan (cp. I 20.30 f.; 22.8). This would ruin the aesthetic effect after which he is striving. The lament has its own canons and does not become insincere because it passes over discord and disharmony and looks only for what can be praised and will contribute to tranquil recollection. Thus the poet recalls the association of father and son, a partnership which had worked great things for Israel, and he also recalls the intimacy between himself and Jonathan, but he naturally does not destroy what he has achieved in these two respects by pointing out that the one relationship was destructive of the other, although in fact Jonathan forfeited the friendship of his father, because he preferred David and loved him as his own life (I 18.1-4; 20.17). But this the writer of an elegy must pass over in silence and it is right that he should do so. David is thus warm and generous in his tribute to Saul, obliterating from his memory the evil which had been done to him and remembering only the qualities which had inspired devotion and admiration. And for Jonathan there is a special tenderness in this commemoration, for David had been joined to him in a brotherhood closer than that of blood and had been saved by him at a time when there was but a step between him and death.

Theological attitudes which we have already noticed are struck again in this chapter. No Israelite was willing to be a party to the slaughter of the Elide priests at Nob, for the priest

[9] Bentzen, *ibid.*, p. 136.

is holy to Yahweh and violent action against him can never be justifiable. It was the foreigner, Doeg the Edomite, who carried out Saul's orders (I 22.18 f.). It is in agreement with these theological scruples that the death-blow should have been dealt out to Saul by a non-Israelite, for the king also was a sacred person. It is true that the circumstances are different in this case and that the Amalekite did no more than Saul begged him to do, but this, in the eyes of our author, is not a justification of his conduct, although it must seem to us that, if he did no more than perform a mercy killing at Saul's request, he is not deserving of the inhuman treatment meted out to him. But the dogma which determines the point of view of this chapter is that of the inviolability of the person of the anointed (v. 14, cp. I 24.3 f.; 26.7 f). His death at the hands of the Philistines in battle would have been Yahweh's judgment on him; his falling on his own sword would have meant that he had taken his own life. What was not permissible, since he was Yahweh's anointed, was that another human hand should intervene in order to expedite the judgment of Yahweh. It is this theology which is thought to justify the harsh and inhuman behaviour of David towards a stranger in the midst (v. 13) who had tried to do his best for Saul in his death throes.

DAVID AS KING

II 2-8

CHAPTER 2

DAVID ANOINTED KING AT HEBRON

2.1-4

4. It was the men of Jabesh-gilead who buried Saul It is doubtful whether MT can be so translated. Perhaps MT should be emended to read: 'And they informed David saying: "The men of Jabesh-gilead have buried Saul."' Another emendation gives the reading: 'And they informed David saying that the men of Jabesh-gilead had buried Saul.'

DAVID'S MESSAGE TO JABESH-GILEAD

2.5-7

6. steadfast love and faithfulness i.e., may Yahweh in his dealings with you show the same constancy of affection and unwavering loyalty as you have shown to Saul. Cp. Commentary on I 26.23.

and I will do good to you This presupposes a necessary emendation of MT, which reads 'this good', although no specific good is in view.

7. and be valiant Literally: 'and become sons of valour'. David is probably asking here for military support, since the word 'valour' is closely associated with martial prowess. His message to Jabesh-gilead on this occasion has been interpreted as an astute political move.[1] He identifies himself with the men of Jabesh-gilead in their veneration for Saul and claims that he is the legitimate heir to the loyalty and affection which

[1] Bright, *History*, p. 176.

they lavished upon the dead king. This, however, is not the point of view of our author whose narrative has a religious orientation. David has been represented as one who always acted on the assumption that the person of the anointed was inviolable (I 24.3 ff.; 26.7 ff.; II 1.14), and he discovers, in the men of Jabesh, those who also venerate the person of Saul. Saul is dead and the house of Judah has anointed him king over them, ratifying his earlier anointing at the hands of a prophet of Yahweh (I 16.13). David is a legitimate successor to Saul and it is right that the men of Jabesh should transfer their affection from the person of the dead king to his person.

ISHBOSHETH IS MADE KING BY ABNER

2.8-11

8. Ishbosheth Originally Eshbaal, meaning probably 'Baal exists'[2] (cp. I Chron. 8.33; 9.39). Apparently the name was later interpreted as 'man of Baal' and then the pejorative '*bosheth*' (shame) was substituted for 'Baal'.

Mahanaim Groll. p. 156. Abner established a 'refugee government' out of the reach of the Philistines.[3] The impression given is that Ishbosheth had little choice in the matter. He was the figurehead, but the real power lay with Abner and the army which he commanded.

9. Ashurites RSV follows MT which is probably corrupt. Read either 'Geshur' with S and V or 'Asher'. For the tribal areas mentioned in the verse see Groll., Map 15, p. 66. Ishbosheth was made king over ALL ISRAEL, but THE HOUSE OF JUDAH FOLLOWED DAVID (v. 10). Noth[4] discerns here the beginning of the limited political concept of Israel as distinct from its earlier and comprehensive significance as the name of the twelve-tribe amphictyony.

[2] Albright, *ARI*, pp. 113, 207 n. 62.
[3] Bright, *History*, p. 175; Noth, *History*, p. 183.
[4] Noth, *ibid.*, p. 184.

10. house of Judah This refers not simply to the tribe of Judah, but to a confederation of southern tribes. Noth[5] argues that these tribes had a special association in a six-tribe amphictyony (Judah, Caleb, Othniel, Cain, Jerahmeel and Simeon) which was centred on the celebrated tree sanctuary at Mamre[6] near Hebron, and he thinks that it was probably at this shrine that David was anointed king (v. 4). If this assumption is correct, it means that David's anointing as king was an amphictyonic act performed at the central sanctuary of the six tribes. It also means that these six tribes had acted independently of the other six with whom they were also associated in the larger twelve-tribe amphictyony. In this connection, however, it should be noted that Ishbosheth is made king without the consent of the tribes at the pleasure of Abner. Since no principle of dynastic rule was then established, he lacked the marks of a legitimate king. He had not, unlike David, been nominated and anointed by a prophet, nor was he anointed king at a sanctuary by the Israelite tribes. It is reasonable to assume that the rite of anointing was performed for David by Abiathar, who would also be involved with the ephod in David's enquiry of Yahweh at the beginning of the chapter (v. 1).

THE SKIRMISH AT GIBEON

2.12-17

12. Gibeon Groll. p. 150.

13. and met them at the pool of Gibeon Gibeon was a border town of Benjamin and had strategic importance for both sides. This may explain why the two forces, whether by chance or design, met there. WENT OUT in vv. 12 and 13 means went out on a military assignment (cp. I 18.30). THE POOL OF GIBEON is mentioned again in Jer. 41.12. It was the source of the city's water supply and was connected to it by an under-

[5] Noth, *Das System der zwölf Stämme Israels*, pp. 107-111; *History*, p. 182.
[6] W. R. Smith, *ROS*, pp. 116, 193.

ground tunnel.[7] The use of SERVANTS in connection with both forces may be significant. (See Commentary on I 8.14.) Both groups of combatants were composed of professional soldiers, attached to the establishments of David and Abner respectively (cp. I 14.52; 16.18).

14. and play before us The youths were to participate in some kind of game and so provide amusement for the two forces. What this game was is not clear from what follows, but v. 16 would suggest that a type of wrestling was intended.

15. twelve for Benjamin . . . and twelve of the servants of David It has been suggested that what is portrayed here is not play but representative warfare. The issue between David and Ishbosheth (or Abner) is to be settled by representative combat just as the issue between Israel and the Philistines was decided by the fight between David and Goliath (I 17). It has been conjectured that the intention was to reunite the divided Israel, but that this was frustrated by the death of all the combatants and that the result was an intensification of the opposition of the two groups.[8] All this, however, is risky speculation and there is an insurmountable linguistic objection to this line of interpretation, namely, that the Hebrew verb in v. 14 means 'to play' or 'to sport' and not 'to engage in representative warfare'.[9]

16. and thrust his sword in his opponent's side Literally: 'with his sword in his partner's side', i.e., a circumstantial clause. G: 'And each fastened his hand on the head of his partner and his sword in his partner's side.' BH would insert 'the men of Benjamin'. Thus: 'And each of the men of Benjamin caught his opponent . . .' The meaning then is that there was a conspiracy on the part of the men of Benjamin to act treacherously against the twelve of Judah who were done to death. Without this insertion the verse means that all twenty-four died simultaneously, and, while there is no sufficient

[7] G. A. Barton, *Archaeology and the Bible*[7], 1937, p. 171 and Fig. 63.
[8] R. de Vaux, *RB* 65, 1958, p. 125.
[9] Hertzberg, *ATD* p. 205 n. 2.

reason for emending, no explanation is offered how what should have been a friendly contest erupted into a slaughter. It is this perplexity which has prompted the representative warfare theory noted above.

Helkath-hazzurim i.e., 'field of flints' or 'field of flint-knives' or 'field of sword-edges'. Or (emended) 'field of the ambushers' (so G) or 'field of sides' (referring to the way in which the youths died).

ABNER KILLS ASAHEL

2.18-32

21. his spoil i.e., what is stripped off a dead warrior as loot.

22. How then could I lift up my face . . . ? Cp. our idiom, 'How could I look your brother Joab in the face?' Abner, a seasoned warrior, does not wish to injure Asahel whose experience and skill are less than his enthusiasm.

23. with the butt of his spear Literally: 'with the back of his spear', although the Hebrew is dubious. 'Backwards' has been conjectured instead of 'with the back of the spear'; i.e., he drove the reversed spear backwards into the stomach of Asahel.

24. Giah Its location is unknown and the text may be corrupt. G: 'valley'.

27. As God lives . . . in the morning The force of the verse is not well conveyed by this translation. Literally: 'As God liveth (I say) that, unless you had spoken, that then, only after the morning, would the people have risen up each from after his brother'; i.e., David's men would have continued to pursue their adversaries throughout the night and beyond daybreak, had not Abner called for a halt to the fighting. 'Risen up' has the special military sense of calling off an action.

29. the whole forenoon The meaning of the root is 'to

divide in parts'. Hence THE WHOLE FORENOON which is 'the whole of one part of a day'.[10] Another suggested rendering is 'cleft' or 'gorge'. Thus: 'And they journeyed (over) the entire gorge.'

31. But the servants of David . . . of Abner's men This requires the deletion of 'and' which appears in MT before 'of Abner's men'. G: 'But the servants of David had slain of Benjamin, of Abner's men, three hundred and sixty.' The words 'they were dead', which appear at the end of the verse in MT, are superfluous. Abner's force is described as Benjamite (cp. v. 13), because it is composed of the body of professional soldiers who had been attached to Saul (cp. I 14.52).

32. and the day broke upon them at Hebron i.e., they reached Hebron at daybreak.

David, still a vassal of the Philistines[11] (v. 9a), is anointed king by the house of Judah (see Commentary on v. 10), probably at an ancient shrine near Hebron and he subsequently addresses the men of Jabesh-gilead (who were in Abner's sphere of influence), commending them for their loyalty to Saul and their veneration for his person and representing that he is the one to whom they should transfer their allegiance. Ish-bosheth is no more than a puppet king, without the necessary credentials of Hebrew kingship, whereas he is Yahweh's anointed, the successor of Saul, nominated by Samuel and accepted by the house of Judah (see Commentary on v. 7).

The remainder of the chapter poses some problems to the interpreter, principally those noted in connection with vv. 14-16. The representative warfare theory is attractive, but it conflicts with the plain sense of v. 14. The intention of the author is perhaps rather to represent that the two forces of professional soldiers were involved in a battle which they did not seek by the suicidal behaviour of the youthful hotheads on both sides. It should be kept in mind that David had once been a 'servant' of Saul and that confronting one another

[10] W. R. Arnold, *American Journal of Semitic Languages* 28, 1912, pp. 274 f.

[11] Noth, *History*, p. 183; Bright, *History*, p. 175.

across the pool of Gibeon were those who had once been colleagues at Saul's court.

This restraint and distaste for bloodshed is seen in Abner's attitude to Asahel. He advises him to try conclusions with a warrior of less stature and feels a professional embarrassment in injuring someone who is not in the same class as himself in respect of skill and experience, and who, moreover, is the brother of an old colleague. Certainly Joab declares that his men are thirsty for blood (v. 27), and this may imply that they had a special reason for feeling injury and desiring revenge. This would be the case, if the emendation of BH in v. 16 (see Commentary) were accepted. The twelve young men of Judah had been massacred by the treacherous and concerted action of the twelve from Benjamin and it was this which sparked off the fighting and made the SERVANTS OF DAVID hot for revenge. The words of Abner to Asahel can also be accommodated by this interpretation. Thus SEIZE ONE OF THE YOUNG MEN (v. 21) means 'Seize one of those responsible for the atrocity'. All this, however, resting as it does on a conjectural emendation, is necessarily speculative.

Bentzen[12] has described vv. 10-11 as framework notes similar to those found in the Book of Kings (cp. I Kings 2.11), and S. R. Driver[13] would delete v. 10a which he regards as a late and unauthoritative insertion into the text. Noth,[14] on the other hand, holds that the notice about the duration of Ish-bosheth's reign is trustworthy and that it 'cannot be refuted on textual or material grounds'.

CHAPTER 3

LIST OF DAVID'S WIVES AND SONS

3.1-5

2. at Hebron Since David had at least two wives consider-

[12] Bentzen, *Introduction* II, p. 95.
[13] S. R. Driver, *Notes, in loc.*
[14] Noth, *History*, p. 186.

ably earlier (I 25.42 f.), Noth[1] has suggested that some of his sons may have been born before the period of his residence at Hebron. Such lists are usually regarded as old material incorporated by the compiler of the Books of Samuel[2] (cp. I 14.49-51; II 5.13-16; 8.16-18).

3. Chileab The name is suspect and may be due to dittography. The parallel passage (I Chron. 3.1) reads 'Daniel' and G has a reading which is thought to be a corruption of 'Dodiah'.

Geshur Bright[3] has suggested that David contracted this marriage for political reasons in order to gain an ally in Ishbosheth's rear. Geshur was an Aramaean state north-east of the sea of Galilee. See Groll. p. 150.

5. David's wife But it is not obvious why it should be noted of Ithream that she is David's wife, when the preceding five are also his wives. S. R. Driver[4] has observed that, on the analogy of 3a, the name of Ithream's first husband might have been expected and he thinks that 'David' is due to a *lapsus calami* or to a transcriptional corruption. Hertzberg[5] prefers the assumption that 'wife of David' is used of Ithream, because she is David's favourite wife.

ABNER QUARRELS WITH ISHBOSHETH

3.6-11

6. was making himself strong in the house of Saul i.e., he was the power behind the throne and had attained a position of complete predominance. This interpretation is favoured by S. R. Driver[6] who, nevertheless, notes that this verb is not

[1] Noth, *History*, p. 200.
[2] Bentzen, *Introduction* II, p. 94.
[3] Bright, *History*, p. 176.
[4] S. R. Driver, *Notes, in loc.*
[5] Hertzberg, *ATD in loc.*
[6] S. R. Driver, *Notes, in loc.*

elsewhere used pejoratively. In view of this fact the meaning may rather be 'was firm in his attachment (loyalty) to the house of Saul'. This agrees well with what follows which describes the break in what had up till then been a firm allegiance to Ishbosheth.

7. the daughter of Aiah After these words G^L reads: 'And Abner took her.' Some Hebrew manuscripts, G and V read 'Ishbosheth' before 'said'. To take possession of a deceased king's harem was to stake a claim to the throne,[7] but this idea is perhaps not present here (cp. II 16.22). Abner was king in all but name, but the point may be that the weakling Ishbosheth is trying to assert a regal authority which he does not possess and Abner rates him for the absurdity of his pretensions.

8. a dog's head of Judah 'of Judah' does not appear in G. The pun is on the word 'dog', since this Hebrew word has the same consonants as 'Caleb', the name of a tribe of the house of Judah. The dog in the Old Testament is used metaphorically in such a way as to show that it was an object of contempt.[8] Abner is saying that no one is going to treat him as if he belonged to the Judaean tribe with the name of a dog. He has been the prop of Ishbosheth's regime and, if he were to withdraw his support, it would collapse, but, instead of gratitude, he receives castigation for a trivial and niggling FAULT CONCERNING A WOMAN. (So RSV following G. MT: 'the error of the woman'.)

10. from Dan to Beersheba See Commentary on I 3.20.

ABNER TREATS WITH DAVID

3.12-16

12. at Hebron RSV follows G^L. MT can hardly be trans-

[7] Cp. Bright, *History*, p. 176.
[8] See especially D. W. Thomas, '*Kelebh*, "dog": its origin and some usages of it in the Old Testament' in *Vetus Testamentum* 10, 1960, pp. 410-27.

lated ‘where he was’ and the Hebrew word may be a corruption of ‘Hebron’.

To whom does the land belong? MT: ‘saying: “To whom is a land?”, saying: “Make your covenant ...”’ G seems to show that in the Hebrew text used by the translators ‘make’ followed immediately on the first ‘saying’, i.e., ‘“To whom is a land?”, saying’ was not present.

your covenant The idiom (see Commentary on I 11.1) here seems to mean no more than a private political bargain. Its fuller significance is preserved in v. 21, where it refers to the religious ceremony and contract by which the tribes of Israel accept David's kingship over them.

13. you shall not see my face i.e., I shall not meet you with a view to negotiations.

unless you first bring MT: ‘except before your bringing’ which is grammatically improbable. G: ‘except you bring’.

15. her husband RSV follows G. MT: ‘a man’. Noth[9] argues that the tradition according to which David became Michal's husband in the context of his victory over Goliath (I 18.27; 25.44) is late and historically incorrect and that the reference to this tradition here is shown by the context to be secondary. What he means by this, I suppose, is that the negotiations are between David and Abner and there is no reason why Ishbosheth should intrude into the account. Thus he holds that Abner and not Ishbosheth should be the subject of v. 15, and it may be noted that the reappearance of Abner in v. 16 would tend to support this. It is he who tells Paltiel to go home and who delivers Michal to David. There are, however, no grounds in textual criticism for these alterations.

16. Bahurim Groll. p. 144 and plate 192, p. 69.

[9] Noth, *History*, p. 184 n. 1.

ABNER CONFERS WITH THE ELDERS OF ISRAEL

3.17-19

18. I will save RSV follows some Hebrew manuscripts, and all the Versions. MT: 'he saved'.

19. Abner also spoke to Benjamin The tribe to which the house of Saul belonged and which was particularly attached to it by ties of tribal loyalty and considerations of self-interest (cp. I 22.6 f.).

JOAB REVENGES ASAHEL'S BLOOD

3.20-30

25. your going out and your coming in . . . Joab represents that Abner is not sincere in his negotiations with David and that his intention is to collect as much information as he can concerning David's situation at Hebron.

26. cistern of Sirah S. R. Driver suggests that this should be identified with 'Ain Sara, about a mile north of Hebron on the road to Jerusalem.

27. took him aside into the midst of the gate RSV follows MT. G, 'took him to the side of the gate', is less awkward.

privately Literally: 'in quietness', i.e., he sought a corner away from the public eye.

so that he died for the blood of Asahel his brother The preposition 'for' indicates explicitly the idea of blood revenge, i.e., 'to pay for the blood of Asahel his brother'. This was the most primitive and sacred of kin obligations[10] and the nearest kinsman on whom it fell was called 'the redeemer', because he had to redeem the blood of his dead kinsman by spilling the blood of his killer (cp. Num. 35.12, 19-27; Deut. 19.6, 12).

[10] W. R. Smith, *ROS* pp. 32, 72, 272.

28. before the Lord Literally: 'from with Yahweh'. The acquittal is thought of as proceeding from Yahweh.

29. May it fall upon S. R. Driver,[11] on the basis of Jer. 30.23 where the same verb is used, suggests that the metaphor may be that of a storm breaking. 'May it (the blood of Abner) break (like a storm) on the head of Joab.' Köh. holds that it is the idea of transference which is involved in this usage. 'May it (the blood of Abner) be transferred to the head of Joab . . .', i.e., may the responsibility be his and not mine.

or who holds a spindle The word translated 'spindle' means primarily 'whorl', the disk on a spindle which steadies its motion. It is thus a case of the part standing for the whole. The meaning is, 'May you have men fit only for womanly occupations.' S. R. Driver[12] appositely cites the Greek phrase 'Hercules with the distaff' which is also a metaphor for effeminacy. Thus David's curse invokes on the house of Joab disease, effeminacy, suicide and hunger.

who is slain by the sword The phrase is the same as that used of Saul (I 31.4) and the RSV here does not bring out its meaning. The rendering should be 'falls on the sword' and the reference is to suicide, associated with the kind of massive disaster which would drive a man to self-destruction.

DAVID ORDERS MOURNING FOR ABNER

3.31-39

31. mourn See Commentary on I 28.3.

33. And the king lamented This is the second lament attributed to David. (See Commentary on II 1.17.) By means of this lament David publicly disassociated himself from the death of Abner.[13]

as a fool dies 'fool' embraces a wider range of folly than

[11] S. R. Driver, *Notes, in loc.*
[12] S. R. Driver, *ibid., in loc.*
[13] Cp. Bentzen, *Introduction* I, pp. 135 f.

our English word. It comprises ethical obtuseness, impiety and intellectual incapacity. It is the last of these which is probably in the foreground here.[14] Abner was an experienced soldier and a seasoned negotiator; he was versed in the procedures of statecraft and yet he died in circumstances which made him look like a simpleton. Joab caught him in an uncritical mood when he was unsuspecting and all his defences were down, although he could have defended himself, had he been on his guard (v. 34). It is this which David remarks on with astonishment.

37. and all Israel Not only the house of Judah, but the other tribes who were on the point of accepting David as their king. His emphatic disassociation of himself from Abner's death thus effected what he had hoped it would and the fruits of his negotiations with Abner which might have been wasted through the recklessness of Joab were preserved.

The quarrel over Rizpah was no more than the occasion of Abner's break with Ishbosheth, for it emerges in the course of the chapter that there were more fundamental reasons for this transfer of allegiance. The opening verse notes that the position of Ishbosheth was progressively deteriorating, while David's power was assuming ever more impressive proportions. Clearly Abner's approach to David was not simply the consequence of a fit of pique, but was based on a long-term appraisal of political trends and was a response to what he judged to be the realities of the political situation. It is therefore not surprising that he had little difficulty in persuading the elders of Israel of the wisdom of his move, since they had themselves for some time been on the edge of such a decision (v. 17). Yet the power in the north is seen to be in his hands and he is confident that any policy which he initiates will have the backing of the tribes (vv. 8, 12). The tribe of Benjamin was a special case, but Abner's powers of persuasion prevailed with them also (see Commentary on v. 19). It seems that David believed it to be vital that he should have Michal the

[14] *Pace* S. R. Driver, *Notes, in loc.*

daughter of Saul as his wife (or that she should be restored to him; see Commentary on v. 15). He may have calculated that this would help to end the feud between Judah and Benjamin and make the latter tribe feel that it still had a stake in the royal house. Or it may have seemed to him that with the daughter of Saul as a wife his status would be enhanced and his title to inherit the throne of all Israel strengthened.[15]

There is no good reason for doubting that David's attitude to Abner's assassination was what the chapter represents it to have been, for Joab's act might have caused the Israelite tribes to recoil from their allegiance to David just at the moment when their acceptance of him appeared to be secure. Whether the degree of moral revulsion felt by him was strong or weak, political wisdom demanded that it should be manifest everywhere, among the Judaean tribes and beyond, that he had had no part in it and that it had embarrassed and angered him.[16] Noth's[17] conjecture that Joab's motive for killing Abner was a more complicated one than blood revenge (see Commentary on v. 27) and that he feared lest Abner's accession to David's establishment would endanger his own position finds no support from the text.

This chapter gives the impression of being a reliable and untendentious piece of historical writing and the theological point of view does not obtrude, although it is not entirely lacking. The deepest reason why DAVID GREW STRONGER AND STRONGER, WHILE THE HOUSE OF SAUL BECAME WEAKER AND WEAKER (v. 1) was that Yahweh had sworn to transfer the kingdom from the house of Saul and to set up the throne of David over Israel and Judah from Dan to Beersheba (vv. 9 f.). Again Abner, in his conversation with the elders of Israel, reminds them that Yahweh has made a promise to David saying: BY THE HAND OF MY SERVANT DAVID I WILL SAVE MY PEOPLE ISRAEL FROM THE HAND OF THE PHILISTINES AND FROM THE HAND OF THEIR ENEMIES (v. 18). We may doubt

[15] Cp. Noth, *History*, p. 200.
[16] Cp. Noth, *ibid.*, pp. 185 f.
[17] Noth, *ibid.*, p. 185; cp. Bright, *History*, p. 176.

whether Abner would have used such theological language, but we recognize the point of view which appears elsewhere in the book. David is Yahweh's anointed and cannot be effectively opposed or obstructed in his inexorable progress towards the throne of all Israel.

CHAPTER 4

THE ASSASSINATION OF ISHBOSHETH

4.1-12

1. When Ishbosheth, Saul's son RSV follows G. 'Ishbosheth' is not present in MT.

his courage failed Literally: 'his hands were drooping'.

dismayed Or: 'demoralized'.

2. Now Saul's son had RSV follows MT, with a small emendation. G: 'Now Ishbosheth, son of Saul, had . . . .'

Beeroth i.e., 'wells'. This place is mentioned in association with Gibeon, Chepirah and Kiriath-jearim in Josh. 9:17 as a Canaanite town which for a long time maintained its independence in Israel.[1] It is usually identified with el-Bireh, a village with several springs or wells, nine miles north of Jerusalem[2] (Groll. p. 144).

3. The Beerothites fled to Gittaim . . . The purpose of this notice is to explain why the inhabitants of Beeroth took their revenge on the son of Saul. Saul had evidently come into conflict with them and had driven them from their city, so that they had been forced to flee to Gittaim (meaning 'two wine presses', situation unknown) and became sojourners there. (On the significance of SOJOURNERS see Commentary on II 1.13.) Baanah and Rechab were professional soldiers, 'captains of guerilla bands', attached to the establishment of Ish-

[1] Cp. Noth, *History*, pp. 145 f.
[2] S. R. Driver, *Notes, in loc.*

bosheth. Bright[3] regards Saul's action against Beeroth as an aspect of the harsh measures which he took against the Gibeonite confederacy (see Commentary on v. 2 and II 21.1 f.) and suggests that the reason for this may have been that they had collaborated or were suspected of having collaborated with the Philistines. The Gibeonites and the inhabitants of the dependent towns were not Israelites but Amorites, but, according to Josh. 9, they had been in a treaty relationship with Israel since the conquest (cp. II 21.2).

4. as she fled in her haste Or: 'as she hurried away in alarm to escape'. The meaning of the verb is that of starting up in fright and this is not very well conveyed by RSV.

Mephibosheth A distorted form, the original being either Meribbaal (I Chron. 8.34; 9.40a) or Meribaal (I Chron. 9.40b). On the substitution of 'bosheth' for 'baal' see Commentary on II 2.8. This notice about Mephibosheth may be regarded as a preliminary intimation that he is to enter the narrative at a later place (II 9).

6. And behold the doorkeeper of the house . . . RSV follows G. MT: 'And thither they came into the interior of the house, takers of wheat, and they wounded him in the stomach and Rechab and Baanah, his brother, escaped (or, 'slipped in'). The sense of MT is defective; 'takers of wheat' cannot be translated 'as though fetching wheat'; 'they wounded him in the stomach' is premature and wrongly anticipates v. 7.

slipped in RSV follows G, but the verb in MT normally means 'escape'. S. R. Driver,[4] however, holds that 'slipped in' is in accord with the primary sense of the root and cites I 20.29, 'let me slip away'.

10. which was the reward I gave him for his news This presupposes an emendation of MT which as it stands is grammatically difficult and obscure. It has been translated; 'that

[3] Bright, *History*, pp. 168 f.
[4] S. R. Driver, *Notes, in loc.*

I might give him a reward for his good tidings', in which case the words are to be understood as macabre irony. Or: 'to whom I ought to have given a reward for his good tidings'; i.e., it would have been generally regarded as normal and reasonable had I rewarded the Amalekite in view of the fact that Saul had persistently sought my life. Both these 'translations' read a good deal into MT which is very cryptic. T: 'who expected that I would give him a reward for his good tidings.' Köh. suggests that it is the messenger's fee which is alluded to.

David's attitude to Ishbosheth's assassination is intelligible as political shrewdness, based on the same reasoning as moved him to disassociate himself from the death of Abner. He was not in such a hurry to become king of all Israel as to require the services of professional assassins. He was already acceptable to the tribes of Israel and Ishbosheth was not a formidable obstacle in his path. Moreover the assassination was an embarrassment to him, because it might impair the loyalty he had almost won and reawaken suspicions and misgivings.

David's behaviour is, however, represented as having a theological motivation and one which has already been noticed (I 24, 25). Yahweh is at work on David's behalf bringing him to the office for which he has been anointed and David will not do anything to try and increase the tempo of this divine process. More particularly he is confident that Yahweh will deliver him from all danger and adversity and will bring to judgment those who have wronged him (I 24.12-15; 25.25-31; II 4.9), and so he refuses to take revenge on his own behalf. Baanah and Rechab claim the support of Yahweh for their murder of Ishbosheth (v. 8), just as David's associates had tried to convince him that he had a theological justification for killing Saul, since Yahweh had delivered him into his hand (I 24.4; 26.8). David sees the case of Ishbosheth as quite different from that of Saul. Baanah and Rechab argue that, since Saul was his enemy, Ishbosheth must also be counted as his enemy, and this is in agreement with the old belief in the solidarity and indivisibility of the family (see Commentary on I 22.1). David argues in agreement with Ezek. 3.16-21; 18. His reasons for his attitude to Ishbosheth are thus different from those which were influential in the case of Saul. Saul had wronged him and shown a bitter and unremitting hostility towards him and David had restrained himself from retaliation because of his belief that Yahweh would vindicate him, but also for the special reason that Saul was Yahweh's anointed and that no violence should be done to his person.

Ishbosheth, on the other hand, is not Yahweh's anointed and so these special considerations do not apply. His is a much simpler case. He has not wronged David in any way and he is a 'righteous' man in this sense, so that David will not associate himself with what he regards as a cruel and sordid affair (v. 11). He feels that Baanah and Rechab are more culpable than was the Amalekite and he orders that they be put to death and their hands and feet exposed to public view at Hebron. Moreover he gives to Ishbosheth the same honours of burial as he had accorded to Abner, just as he had applauded the action of the men of Jabesh who rescued the corpses of Saul and his sons from the uncircumcised Philistines (II 2.4b-7).

CHAPTER 5

5.1-5

THE ELDERS OF ISRAEL MAKE DAVID KING AT HEBRON

2. it was you that led out and brought in Israel i.e., Even when Saul was king it was to you that the nation looked as the leader and directing genius of its affairs.

and the Lord said . . . In choosing David as king the elders are guided by their knowledge that he has been designated by Yahweh as king over all Israel. Yahweh has commanded him to exercise such oversight and control over Israel as a shepherd exercises over his flock. Cp. 3.9 f., 18 where Abner refers to David in the same terms.

and you shall be prince over Israel On PRINCE see Commentary on I 9.16, where the term is applied to Saul. It is used of David here and in I 13.14; 25.30 and elsewhere.

3. and King David made a covenant with them . . . On the idiom 'cut a covenant' see Commentary on I 11.1. David was first anointed by the prophet Samuel as king-designate (I 16.13) and his acceptance by the house of Judah (II 2.4) and the tribes of Israel at Hebron may be regarded as the human or democratic ratification of his election by Yahweh as attested by a prophet. His acceptance by Judah and Israel took place at Hebron, probably at its ancient sanctuary (see Commentary on II 2.10), and the religious character of the transaction in both cases is emphasized by a further act of anointing, but no reference is made to any covenant between David and the house of Judah. A similar pattern is perhaps to be discerned in the case of Saul, although the passages dealing with his acceptance by Israel are obscure and perhaps suspect. (See Commentary on I 10.20 f.; 11.14 f.) At any rate he was anointed by Samuel and then acclaimed by the people[1] (I 10.24), but there is no mention of any further act of anointing. (Cp. I 11.14 f.)

DAVID MAKES JERUSALEM HIS CAPITAL

5.6-12

6. the blind and the lame will ward you off This presupposes a small emendation of MT. The meaning is that the fortress is so impregnable that the blind and the lame are an adequate defence against David. This confidence is expressed by the closing words of the verse, DAVID CANNOT COME IN HERE.

7. the stronghold of Zion, that is, the city of David This refers to the south-east hill of Jerusalem on the northern and highest part of which stood the temple and on the south,

[1] Cp. Noth, *History*, p. 226.

contiguous with the temple, the royal palace of Solomon.[2]

8. let him get up the water-shaft The Hebrew verb cannot be translated 'get up' or 'ascend'; such a rendering requires an emended text. The word translated 'water-shaft' by RSV is a celebrated crux on which there has been much discussion.[3] We may leave it untranslated for the moment and render MT thus: 'Whoever strikes down the Jebusite, let him touch (or, 'arrive at') the *ṣinnōr*.' Even if *ṣinnōr* means 'water-shaft', Simons'[4] rendering, 'Whoever strikes down the Jebusite and arrives at the water-shaft,' is grammatically dubious. According to Simons it is not a question of climbing up the shaft, but simply of obtaining control of the foot of it, since this would effectively cut off the fortress from its water supply and make surrender inevitable. The belief that it is an ascent of the water-shaft to the city which is referred to has prompted the unjustifiable translation, 'Let him reach (sc. the city) through the water-shaft.' This water-shaft is identified with the tunnel known as 'Warren's shaft'.[5] Again *ṣinnōr* has been thought to refer to a part of the body; *membrum virile* and 'throat' have been suggested and Albright[6] has tried to deal with the philological obscurity in which the word is wrapped and has argued that its primary meaning is 'joint'. He translates: 'Let him strike a joint', i.e., all the Jebusites are to be lamed. The Jebusites located the lame and the blind on their walls in order to vaunt the strength of their fortress and to mock at the puny resources of David, and the revenge prescribed by David is that all the defenders of the fortress are to be made cripples. The parallel passage in I Chron. 11 is widely divergent. The verb used there to describe Joab's initiative, 'ascended', might be thought to lend support to the 'water-shaft' interpretation of this verse. If *ṣinnōr* does in fact mean 'water-shaft' and we emend to read, 'Let him

[2] S. R. Driver, *Notes, in loc.*; J. Simons, *Jerusalem in the Old Testament*, 1952, pp. 60-68.
[3] See G. Bressan, *Biblica* 25, 1944, pp. 346-81.
[4] J. Simons, *op. cit.*, p. 172.
[5] J. Simons, *ibid.*, Fig. 22, p. 166.
[6] W. F. Albright, *JPOS* 2, 1922, pp. 285-90.

ascend the water-shaft', the remainder of the verse only makes sense if a verb is inserted into the text. Thus S. R. Driver[7] suggests 'and smite the lame and the blind'. Cp. RSV, TO ATTACK THE LAME AND THE BLIND. 'To attack' is not present in MT.

who are hated by David's soul RSV follows the Masoretic vocalization. The consonantal text would read: 'they hate the soul (or, 'life') of David.' If we ignore the Masoretic punctuation, we might read: 'and with the lame and the blind they (i.e., those who have been made cripples, following Albright) hate David's life.' This verse, however, is full of unsolved difficulties.

The blind and the lame . . . This is given as a proverbial saying and its origin is accounted for in the same way as the 'proverbs' in I 10.12 and 19.24. S. R. Driver[8] argues that HOUSE means 'temple' (so G: 'house of the Lord') and that the meaning of the saying is: 'Beggars (i.e., the blind and the lame) shall not come into the temple.' He holds that this 'proverb' is a late gloss deriving from an erroneous exegesis of v. 6b, namely, 'except you remove the blind and the lame (sc. from the Israelite army) who say: "David will not enter here."' Cp. T: 'except you remove the sinners and the guilty', and similarly in v. 8 T substitutes 'sinners and guilty' for 'blind and lame'. It is impossible to decide what this 'proverb' means, since the explanation offered of its origin is so enigmatic. It could conceivably have the same kind of general application as 'Is Saul also among the prophets?', and mean: 'There are some things which are not done because they conflict with accepted patterns of behaviour.' Thus instead of saying (as we should say) 'It isn't done', a man would say: 'The blind and the lame (i.e., beggars) do not come into the house.' But the connection of this with the episode in which it is supposed to be grounded cannot be traced.

9. and David built the city THE CITY is not present in MT,

[7] S. R. Driver, *Notes, in loc.*
[8] S. R. Driver, *Notes, in loc.*

but is found in the parallel passage in I Chron. 11.8. 'Millo' means 'filling' and probably refers to a mound or rampart of earth or to a solid tower. Elsewhere the name is always associated with the building operations of Solomon and it has been suggested that the reference to it here may be anachronistic; i.e., the writer referred to the Millo in order to define the outward limit of David's building operations, although the Millo did not exist in David's time.[9]

10. the God of Hosts See Commentary on I 17.45.

11. Verse 12 would follow naturally after v. 10 and so Noth[10] has suggested that v. 11 was originally part of the context of II 8.1-14, and that it was transferred to its present position because it refers to Jerusalem. It is an important notice of the cultural and trading links between David and Phoenicia, since it marks a tendency which greatly increased in Solomon's time. David has now attained to a sufficient royal dignity to require a palace as one of its material manifestations.

LIST OF CHILDREN BORN TO DAVID IN JERUSALEM

5.13-16

13. from Jerusalem The parallel passage (I Chron. 14.3) reads 'in Jerusalem'.

16. Eliada Originally 'Beeliada'. Cp. I Chron. 14.7 and G^B and G^L. On the substitution of El for Baal compare Commentary on II 4.4.

DAVID DEFEATS THE PHILISTINES

5.17-25

17. the stronghold S. R. Driver[11] argues that this cannot refer to Zion, because the verb 'go down' is inappropriate in

[9] J. Simons, *Jerusalem in the Old Testament*, pp. 131 f.
[10] Noth, *History*, p. 197 n. 2.
[11] S. R. Driver, *Notes, in loc.*

relation to it. He holds that the stronghold intended is Adullam (see Commentary on I 22.4). Noth[12] points out, however, that the same Hebrew word is used of Zion in v. 9 and believes that STRONGHOLD here must be a deliberate allusion to v. 9, although it is a secondary feature and not original to the text of v. 17. Cp. I Chron. 14.8, 'he went out against them.' Verse 17 is the direct continuation of v. 3, the narrative being interrupted by vv. 4-16 which may have been a later insertion, and the appearance of 'stronghold' in v. 17 may be connected with this process. Noth's assumption that there may be a literary reason for the extant order is attractive. The writer first mentions the climax of the campaign, the capture of Jerusalem, and then goes on to recount the details of the war against the Philistines.

18. the valley of Rephaim Groll. p. 160. Driver[13] and Noth[14] identify it with the modern el-Baq'a, immediately west of Jerusalem.

20. Baal-perazim Groll. p. 144. Meaning 'Baal of the eruptions', a name presumably derived originally from a fountain bursting out from the hill side which the local Baal was thought to inhabit.[15] It is plain, however, that in this verse Baal is a title of Yahweh, since the name is explained from the circumstance that Yahweh has burst through the enemies of David like an erupting flood, and so is 'Lord of Eruptions'. According to this aetiology Baal-perazim commemorates the victory wrought by Yahweh for David over the Philistines.

like a bursting flood Or, perhaps, with S. R. Driver,[16] 'like the breaking of waters through (a dam)'.

21. left their idols there RSV follows MT. G and I Chron. 14.12: 'gods'. The Philistines brought their gods to battle to fight for them just as the Israelites brought the ark (I 4.1 ff.).

[12] Noth, *History*, pp. 187 f. n. 1; p. 188 n. 1.
[13] S. R. Driver, *Notes, in loc.*
[14] Noth, *History*, p. 188.
[15] Cp. W. R. Smith, *ROS* pp. 95-108.
[16] S. R. Driver, *Notes, in loc.*

23. You shall not go up RSV follows MT. G has the additional words 'to meet them'.

go around to their rear This presupposes a dittography in MT. Without this emendation the translation 'Lead (your men) round to their rear' is possible.

24. the sound of marching The noise in the trees is to be a sign to David (cp. I 10.1 ff. and I 14.8 ff.) and, when he hears it, he will know that Yahweh has gone out in front to strike down the army of the Philistines (cp. I 7.10 f.).

bestir yourself Or, keeping the Hebrew idiom, 'look sharp'.[17]

25. Geba In G and I Chron. 14.16, 'Gibeon'.

Gezer Groll. p. 150.

The critical problems associated with this chapter have been touched on in the Commentary on v. 17. The main narrative consists of vv. 1-3, 17-25, 6-10, 12. A possible reason why 6-10, 12 precede 17-25 has been mentioned above. In relation to the main narrative vv. 4 f., 11, 13-16 are secondary material. Bentzen[18] has described vv. 4 f. as framework notes after the manner of those in the Book of Kings (e.g., I Kings 2.11) and vv. 13-16 as 'old material'. On v. 11 see the Commentary.

The historical value of the material in this chapter can only be briefly noticed. In anointing David as king at Hebron the house of Judah was committing itself politically without prior consultation with the 'tribes of Israel'. (See Commentary on II 2.10.) Now the 'tribes of Israel' follow suit, but they too are acting only on their own behalf and the fact that both Judah and Israel have accepted David as king does not mean that the old concert of the amphictyony has been restored. The two parts have been united for the time, because David has sufficient personal stature to hold them together, but the reasons for their separatist tendencies have not been removed

[17] S. R. Driver, *Notes, in loc.*
[18] Bentzen, *Introduction* II, pp. 94 f.

and will reassert themselves after the death of Solomon.[19]

The other significant political fact with which this chapter deals is David's choice of Jerusalem as his capital. This was clearly related to the kind of kingdom over which he envisaged that he was to preside. He was to build a society of a different character and with different social presuppositions from what Israel had up till then known. In Jerusalem there was available to him the ready-made organization of a well-established city-state and, moreover, it was not part of the sphere of influence of any of the tribes. Thus it was 'David's city' where his civil and military establishments had their headquarters and from which he could effectively implement his centralizing policies.[20]

In accepting David as their king the elders of Israel realize that they are doing no more than confirming Yahweh's choice, and that, even when Saul was king, David was the *de facto* if not the *de jure* leader of Israel (v. 2). The chapter takes up again a point of view which has earlier been prominent, namely that Yahweh was with David and that this was both the guarantee of his success and the ultimate reason for it (vv. 10, 12, 25; cp. II 3.1). Just as in his contest with Goliath David looked to Yahweh and put little reliance in the orthodox accoutrements of war (I 17.37, 45-47), so here it is Yahweh who goes out in front of the Israelite army to strike down the Philistines (v. 24; cp. I 7.10 f.).

The other important theological element which reappears here is David's dependence on the ephod (and so on Abiathar) for ascertaining the will of Yahweh. We are not told explicitly in this chapter what was the manner of David's enquiring of Yahweh (vv. 19, 23), but, since his first access to Yahweh for guidance follows immediately upon the attachment of Abiathar to his establishment, it is a reasonable assumption that this was the oracular procedure which he followed here. His use of it is explicitly attested in two places (I 23.9 f.; 30.7).

[19] Cp. Noth, *History*, p. 187.
[20] Cp. Bright, *History*, p. 179.

CHAPTER 6

DAVID BRINGS THE ARK TO JERUSALEM

6.1-15

2. to Baale-Judah This does not translate MT, which reads 'from Baale-Judah.' Moreover in MT Baale-Judah is apparently not a place-name, but means 'the citizens of Judah'. Thus the translation of MT would be: 'And David arose and went with all the people who were with him of the citizens of Judah to bring up from there. . . .' The words 'from there' are an indication that 'Baale-Judah' is a corruption of a place-name which originally stood in the text. This is confirmed by the parallel passage in I Chron. 13.6, where it is explained that Baalah is an alternative name for Kiriath-jearim. Cp. Josh. 15.9 f. The original text here was probably 'Baalah of Judah', Judah being added to distinguish this Baalah from other places of the same name; cp. Josh. 19.8, 44.

3. upon a new cart In view of the potent holiness of the ark, already illustrated by the stories in I 4-6, only a cart which had not previously been in profane use was a suitable and safe receptacle for it. The same notion may be present in v. 14. Had David kept on his ordinary clothes for his religious duties, they would have become taboo, i.e., infected with the holiness of the ark.[1]

3-4. And Uzzah and Ahio, the sons of Abinadab, were driving the new cart with the ark of God. RSV is based on G^B. MT: 'And Uzzah and Ahio, the sons of Abinadab, were driving the new cart and they brought it from the house of Abinadab which is on the hill with the ark of God.' S. R. Driver[2] holds that 'and they brought it from the house of Abinadab which is on the hill' has been accidentally repeated from v. 3a. He would insert 'And Uzzah was proceeding' before 'with the ark'. (So also BH.) This would mean that

[1] W. R. Smith, *ROS* p. 451.
[2] S. R. Driver, *Notes, in loc.*

Uzzah was walking at the side of the ark and Ahio in front of it. In the words 'the house of Abinadab which is on the hill' Porter sees a mythological allusion and cites as a parallel the imprisonment of the god in a mountain at the beginning of the Babylonian New Year Festival and at Ugarit.[3]

5. with all their might, with songs RSV is based on the parallel passage, I Chron. 13.8. MT: 'with everything, juniper trees and lyres . . .'

6. the threshing-floor of Nacon RSV follows MT. It is unlikely that 'Nacon' can be a proper name. The meaning of the phrase must be 'a fixed threshing-floor', but this is not satisfactory and a proper name is desiderated. The parallel passage, I Chron. 13.9, reads, 'the threshing-floor of Chidon'.

for the oxen stumbled The normal usage of this Hebrew verb is transitive and not intransitive. Thus: 'for the oxen let (it) fall.' Köh. explains this as 'left the cart to itself', i.e., nearly upset it. G: 'wheeled it round'.

7. because he put forth his hand to the ark RSV follows I Chron. 13.10, of which S. R. Driver[4] thinks the MT of this verse is a mutilated fragment. It has, however, been translated as 'and he struck him down there on the ground of irreverence' (Köh.).

beside the ark of God RSV follows MT. G: 'before God' which is the reading of both MT and G of I Chron. 13.10.

10. Obed-edom, the Gittite i.e., 'a devotee of Edom'. 'Edom' is almost certainly the name of a deity. Thus he was not a worshipper of Yahweh, but his experience of the ark is represented as having been more equable and profitable than that of those who came into contact with it during its previous sojourn in Philistine territory, when it was also in Gath (I 5.9).

13. had gone six paces David was uncertain how he ought to handle the ark. In view of Obed-edom's experience he regarded

[3] J. R. Porter, *JTS* 5, 1954, pp. 169 f.
[4] S. R. Driver, *Notes, in loc.*

it as a desirable acquisition, but its removal to Jerusalem was fraught with hazards and the consequence of a false step had been shown on an earlier occasion (vv. 6 f.). As soon as the initial process of disturbing the ark had been effected without calamity, a sacrifice was offered to Yahweh, partly as a thanksgiving that his previous anger had been appeased and partly as an inauguration of the ceremony which was to follow (vv. 14-19). The meaning is not that a sacrifice was offered every six paces.

15. with shouting and with the sound of the horn 'Shouting' may refer to a particular ritual cry. The same word occurs in I 4.5, where the army of Israel greet the ark as it is brought into the camp, and this suggests that, among its other meanings, the word was used of the ritual response with which it was appropriate to greet the ark. This 'shouting' in association with the sound of the trumpet or, more accurately, ram's horn, is found also in Ps. 47.5 in a cultic and ceremonial context. S. R. Driver[5] holds that the psalm, in this particular, is dependent on our verse, but the reverse may be true, and this description of the bringing up of the ark to Jerusalem by David may have been filled in by details borrowed from the ceremonial of the ark in procession in the Jerusalem cult. This is an aspect of Porter's[6] approach which is valuable, but it would seem to me to be more reasonable to suppose that this was an attempt to connect the new central sanctuary with old amphictyonic procedures rather than to interpret the episode in terms of the myth and ritual categories of the Ancient Near East. The 'dancing' would also fit into a cultic context[7] (vv. 5, 14-20).

MICHAL DESPISES DAVID

6.16-23

17. peace-offerings See Commentary on I 10.8.

[5] S. R. Driver, *Notes, in loc.*
[6] J. R. Porter, *JTS* 5, pp. 165 f.; cp. Bentzen, *Introduction* II, p. 94.
[7] Cp. Porter, *ibid.*, p. 166.

19. a portion of meat This interpretation goes back to Kimchi, but there is no basis for it in MT. Köh., on the basis of an Arabic cognate, suggests 'food of the traveller', i.e., date-cake. Here again Porter discovers a coronation rite—the date-cake has associations with the New Year Festival.

21. It was before the Lord RSV follows MT. G has the additional words: 'I dance, blessed be the Lord.' 'I dance' is necessary to the sense.

as prince over Israel See Commentary on II 5.2.

22. more contemptible than this i.e., I shall in the future demean myself even more than you suppose me to have done to-day.

23. had no child It is not easy to decide what is the significance of this piece of information. Is it no more than a factual notice or does it contain the suggestion that this was Michal's punishment for her behaviour on this occasion? Porter argues that this chapter describes a coronation rite connected with David's assumption of kingship in Jerusalem and that a central feature of this rite is the celebration of a sacred marriage in which the king and his consort represent the god and the goddess. The purpose of this sacred marriage is to safeguard the succession and so give continuance to the dynasty. Because of Michal's scorn David refused to consummate the marriage with her and so she remained childless for the rest of her life.[8] Noth[9] observes that in taking Michal to wife David would have in mind that a son born to her would be an exceptionally well-qualified candidate for the throne of all Israel and might be expected to command the support of the tribe of Benjamin.

The ark was important to David, because it had been the most hallowed cult object of the Israelite tribes and in it the power of Yahweh was thought to be particularly concentrated. Moreover in bringing it to Jerusalem he was seeking to trans-

[8] J. R. Porter, *JTS* 5, pp. 165 f.; cp. Bright, *History*, p. 186.
[9] Noth, *History*, p. 200.

fer there the prestige and traditions which had belonged to former central sanctuaries, where the ark had previously resided. Jerusalem, possessing the ark, was to become the new amphictyonic centre, and David hoped to capture thereby the allegiance and devotion which the central sanctuary had in the past claimed and won from the Israelite tribes. By representing that there was this continuity between the old and the new regime and by enlisting old and tenacious religious loyalties he expected to enhance the stability of his kingdom.[10]

An interesting aspect of this portrayal is that David himself is represented as being unsure of how to proceed in relation to the ark. The ark is still the dangerous and explosive force which it was seen to be in I 4-6 and David's first attempt to transport it from Kiriath-jearim to Jerusalem ends with the death of Uzzah, who had the misfortune to come into contact with its lethal holiness, when he was trying to right the cart. David was apparently sufficiently discouraged by this to postpone his intention of bringing it to Jerusalem and he conveyed it instead to the house of Obed-Edom, an inhabitant of Gath. The impression which is gained from the narrative is that he was experimenting with a force about which he was desirous of learning more and whose transport presented a problem to him. When the effects of the ark on Obed-Edom are good, he is reassured and resumes the operation of bringing it to Jerusalem. But, even at this stage, he proceeds tentatively and gingerly (see Commentary on v. 13).

Michal's attitude is that of a king's daughter towards a king who does not behave in accordance with his station. She finds no pleasure in seeing her husband in the role of a naked ecstatic, enacting the excesses of a whirling dervish. Whether or not David's behaviour on this occasion was calculated or spontaneous is difficult to decide. It was in his own interests to be in the centre of the picture and to emphasize by his personal participation that he venerated the ark. It is ironical that Michal disapproved of his ecstatic dancing, for her father had once behaved in a similar way and he too was then thought to

[10] Noth, *History*, p. 191; Bright, *History*, p. 179.

have acted out of character and station. (See Commentary on I 10.12.)

There is one critical point which deserves mention. It is clear that II 6 is a continuation of I 6. There the narrative breaks off with the ark in the house of Abinadab at Kiriath-jearim, and here it takes up with David's attempt to remove it from there to Jerusalem.

CHAPTER 7

NATHAN DISSUADES DAVID FROM BUILDING A TEMPLE

7.1-7

2. but the ark of God dwells in a tent David feels that the ark of God which he has brought up to Jerusalem should be as adequately housed as he himself is and he proposes that a HOUSE (i.e., temple) should be built for it, comparable in craftsmanship and magnificence to the residence which Phoenician craftsmen had built for him.

5. Would you build me a house to dwell in? The question implies (cp. v. 7) that David ought not to build a temple for the ark, and the ark, as in the earlier chapters, is thought of as embodying the presence of Yahweh (cp. I 4-6; II 6). Nathan, having agreed to David's proposal and given it Yahweh's blessing (v. 3), now conveys to him an express word from Yahweh forbidding the building of a temple.

6. but I have been moving about in a tent for my dwelling More accurately: 'but I have been moving about in a tent and in a dwelling.' The significance of the words 'a dwelling' is probably to be seen as a contrast with the opening words of the verse, 'I have not *resided* in a temple . . .' The translation of RSV does not show that 'dwelt' and 'dwelling' are from different roots; 'dwelling' is used in the sense of temporary lodging, whereas 'residence' is indicative of a permanent resting-place. It should not be assumed that the writer is ignorant of the fact that the ark had, since the settlement in Canaan, been housed at Shiloh and elsewhere in conditions of relative permanence. From his point of view these locations were no more than 'dwellings', because, throughout the period, Israel was still on the move and Yahweh's place was at the head of his people.

7. judges RSV follows the parallel passage, I Chron. 17.6. MT: 'tribes', concerning which S. R. Driver[1] observes that there is no evidence that any tribe was ever commissioned to govern Israel.

to shepherd my people Israel This metaphor again points to the mobility of Israel. In order to discharge their duties the 'judges' had to be on the move fending for Israel as a shepherd does for his flock. These are the conditions which have been typical from the historical moment when Yahweh gave her a sense of nationhood ('SINCE THE DAY I BROUGHT UP THE PEOPLE OF ISRAEL FROM EGYPT TO THIS DAY'), and at no time did Yahweh indicate to the 'judges' that the moment had come for the nation finally to settle down to a static existence and so for the ark, as the symbol of Yahweh's presence, to receive a permanent home.

NATHAN ASSURES DAVID OF THE PERMANENCE OF HIS DYNASTY
7.8-17

9. And I have been with you . . . and I will make for you Yahweh has been with David and it is because of this that he survived terrible dangers and emerged from an apparently hopeless position to become king of Israel. The promise for the future is thus linked to what Yahweh has already accomplished for David, and so it is related to the main theological tendency of the earlier story of David's chequered career. The final purpose of Yahweh's choice of him is that he should be the founder of an enduring dynasty.

[1] S. R. Driver, *Notes, in loc.*

10-11. As formerly from the time that I appointed judges over my people Israel RSV follows G. MT: 'as formerly and from the time . . . FORMERLY may then be taken to refer to the period preceding the settlement in Canaan, i.e., the sufferings in Egypt. The main exegetical difficulty of the verse, however, is connected with the words FROM THE TIME THAT I APPOINTED JUDGES OVER MY PEOPLE ISRAEL. S. R. Driver[2] holds that the blessings secured by the settled government of David are being contrasted with the era of insecurity through which Israel passed in the period of the Judges. This is probably a correct understanding of the words, but a difficulty is constituted by the fact that, according to the Book of Judges, the appointing of 'judges' were the occasions on which the tribes were rescued from servitude and apostasy and restored to Yahweh. It is therefore possible (following MT) that Israel is being promised a period of rest and security under the rule of David comparable with what was achieved in former times (i.e., during the deliverance from Egypt and the journey to the Promised Land) and through the rule of the 'judges'.

11. Moreover the Lord declares to you . . . The transition from first to third person is abrupt and awkward. Here Nathan is reporting Yahweh's word; elsewhere he reproduces the words of Yahweh. Although the form of this verse differs from that of the rest of the oracle, this may be a mark of earliness rather than lateness.[3] Cp. the oracle in Ps. 110.2 ff., which is also in reported speech.

will make you a house The use here of the same Hebrew word as appears in the first section of the chapter would seem to represent a deliberate attempt to link the proceedings recorded in vv. 1-7 with what follows. David is not to build a 'house', that is a temple to Yahweh, but Yahweh will establish a 'house' (i.e., a dynasty) for David.

[2] S. R. Driver, *ibid.*, *in loc.*

[3] So L. Rost, *Beiträge zur Wissenschaft vom Alten und Neuen Testament* 42, 1926, pp. 58 f.

12. I will raise up your son after you Literally: 'I will raise up your seed.' This verse does not refer specifically to Solomon; it is rather a guarantee that the Davidic dynasty will be perpetuated. The same is true of vv. 14 and 15 which do not refer to Yahweh's dealings with Solomon, but with his relationship to the Davidic king; cp. I Kings 2.4; Pss. 89.30-37; 132.12, where Nathan's prophecy is applied to David's sons, i.e., his posterity. Verse 13, which is a particular reference to Solomon, does not fit easily into the general context of the chapter. Here 'house' is used again in the sense of temple as it was in vv. 1-7 and no indication is given why what was forbidden to David should be permitted to a successor. The theological objections raised in vv. 1-7 would apply equally to Solomon and, in the face of them, the explanation of I Chron. 22.8, that David was precluded from building because he was a man of blood, would carry no weight. Verse 13 would therefore seem to be a later interpolation. According to Eissfeldt[4] it is Deuteronomic.

14. I will be his father and he will be my son This may reflect a belief, held elsewhere in the ancient Near East and particularly in Egypt, in the divinity of the king. That the Davidic king was believed to stand in a peculiarly intimate relationship to Yahweh is clear from the language of certain of the Psalms (Pss. 2.7-9; 89.19-37), and this has been thought to reflect the mediatorial role occupied by the king in the Jerusalem cult.[5] The allusion to 'chastening' or 'correction' recalls the language of Prov. 1-9, where it is associated with the process of acquiring wisdom through the exercise of parental discipline. The son becomes wise through availing himself of that wisdom which is the fruit of experience and by submitting to the correction and discipline of his father. A similar father-son relationship is said to exist between Yahweh and

[4] Eissfeldt, *Einleitung*, p. 316. Also A. Weiser, *Introduction to the Old Testament*, p. 168.

[5] See especially A. R. Johnson, 'The Role of the King in the Jerusalem Cultus', in *The Labyrinth*, edited by S. H. Hooke, 1935; also *Sacral Kingship in Ancient Israel*, pp. 93 f.

the Davidic king; the king will be subject to correction, but he will not be cast off as Saul was (vv. 15 f.).

DAVID'S PRAYER TO YAHWEH
7.18-29

19. for a great while to come Literally: 'from afar'; i.e., Yahweh has permitted David to look into the future and discern the enduring structure of his dynasty, so that he now sees that Yahweh's purposes stretch beyond his personal dealings with himself. His bringing of David to the throne of Israel, marvellous though it was, is now viewed as a small thing compared with the establishment of an enduring Davidic dynasty.

and hast shown me future generations RSV rests on a conjectural emendation. MT: 'and this is the law for men.' It is difficult to make sense of this. It has been taken to mean: 'To show me such kindness is to deal with me as if you were a man and not God.' This is forced.

21. Because of thy promise RSV follows MT. I Chron. 17.19 reads: 'for thy servant's sake'. A rearrangement of the words of the verse has been proposed. Thus: 'For thy servant's sake and according to thy heart hast thou done to make thy servant know all this greatness.'

23. what other nation on earth . . . ? MT: 'And what single nation is there on the earth like thy people Israel with whom God went to redeem (them) to himself as a people and to appoint for himself a name and to perform for thee great and terrible things with respect to thy land from before thy people whom thou hast redeemed to thyself from Egypt, nations and its God (or, emended, 'gods')?' The verse thus presents a scene of hopeless confusion and it may be that some of this stems from alterations of the original form of the verse which were dictated by theological scruples. An attempt to restore the original text, guided by G and I Chron. 17.21, reads: 'What other (G) nation is there on the earth like thy people Israel with whom God went to redeem (them) as his people and to appoint for himself a name and to perform for them great and terrible things so as to drive out (Chron.) from before his people a nation and its gods? ' It is assumed that the original form of the verse considered the case of a nation other than Israel in its relationship to its god (or gods) and that this was later felt to be theologically objectionable. The confusion now present in the verse (the change from third to second person) is the consequence of efforts to erase the objectionable matter.[6] It should be noted, however, that the conjectural emendation is susceptible of a different exegesis; ' with whom God went ' may be taken with ' thy people Israel ' and not with ' What other nation is there on the earth? '; cp. RSV.

26. and thy name will be magnified for ever Israel is a historical manifestation of the nature and purposes of Yahweh and through Israel Yahweh operates effectively in the affairs of men. A similar thought is present in v. 23. Yahweh has entered into a partnership with Israel in order ' to appoint for himself a name ', i.e., in order to make his presence felt in the sphere of historical existence; in order to acquire a reputation by expressing himself historically through a nation and its institutions. In this way he becomes a force to be reckoned with in the world. He is incarnate in Israel.

The main problems of interpretation are associated with vv. 1-17. Verses 8-16 have been described as a prose rendering of Nathan's oracle to David, examples of such prophetic oracles in metrical form being found in Pss. 2, 110.[7] Nathan's oracle, although it bears the marks of later revision, is held to date, in its original form, from the time of David[8] or prior to the death of Solomon[9] and it has been supposed that the cultic situation to which such a royal oracle belongs is the king's accession to the throne at the New Year Festival.

The chapter has been welded into a unity, but this unity

[6] Cp. S. R. Driver, *Notes, in loc.*
[7] Bentzen, *Introduction* I, pp. 160 f.
[8] Bentzen, *ibid.*, p. 161.
[9] Noth, *History*, p. 224.

does not go very deep and vv. 1-7 presuppose a theological emphasis which is not easily reconciled with that of vv. 8-29. The connection between the two sections has been made by a play on the Hebrew word for 'house'. In vv. 1-7 it means 'temple' and in vv. 8-16 'dynasty'. David proposed to build a 'house' for Yahweh and Yahweh, having vetoed the proposal, intimated his resolve to establish a 'house' for David. This literary device does not go any way towards establishing an intrinsic connection between the two sections. The link between v. 7 and v. 8—the 'judges' were shepherds of Israel and David was taken from shepherding his flock to be a prince over Israel—is equally superficial.

The two sections, vv. 1-7 and vv. 8-29, are theologically far apart. What we have is not one oracle of Nathan but two, the first in vv. 1-7 and the second in vv. 8-16. The first states that Nathan forbade David to build a temple to Yahweh. This oracle sets a high value on Israel's nomadic heritage and is acutely conscious of the dangers associated with the stage of cultural development at which a permanent residence is built for a deity. The phrase 'house of cedar' (vv. 2, 7) has a special significance in this connection. We read in an Ugaritic text: 'As for the temple ('house', the same word as occurs in this chapter) let them finish it off with cedars.'[10] The fear expressed in vv. 1-7 is that, with the political reorganization effected by David, Israel is being conformed to the pattern of the states which surround her and that, with the erection of a temple for the ark, she is in danger of losing sight of the unique part of her religious heritage. She will forget the route along which she has been led by Yahweh in her earlier history and, worse still, she will believe that she has reached her destination. The writer insists that Israel must not look for such a resting-place nor must she seek to immobilize Yahweh in a temple. She is a pilgrim nation and, although she has reached the Promised Land, this does not mean that she is to settle down and acquire the institutions of her neighbours. The ark is not to be laid up in a temple, because Yahweh

[10] *Baal*, II. v. 10. The translation is that of G. R. Driver, *CML*, p. 97.

whose presence it symbolizes is still on the move and he calls to his people to follow him in faith and obedience in the way of their mission and destiny.

The second oracle, on the other hand, supplies a theology of kingship. The reign of Saul was brief, because Yahweh rejected him, but David is the man of his choice and the throne bestowed on David is to be perpetuated by his posterity. In David's time Israel will have rest from her enemies (cp. 7.1; this is another indication that vv. 1-7 and 8-16 are not intrinsically connected and do not make a real unity) and, after his death, Yahweh's covenant love will remain constant towards an unending line of Davidic kings. Yahweh will correct the Davidic king as a father would discipline his son, but the relationship of peculiar intimacy established between the two by covenant will never be abrogated. This theology reflects the unique mediatorial role occupied by the king in the Jerusalem cult and so presupposes the existence of just such a temple as is rejected in vv. 1-7.

CHAPTER 8

MILITARY SUCCESSES OF DAVID[1]

8.1-14

1. Methegh-Ammah Perhaps meaning 'the bridle of the mother-city'; i.e., David assumed control of the mother-city or capital.

2. And he defeated Moab . . . Why he dealt so savagely with Moab is not indicated, although some explanation is called for in view of the fact that he had once relied on the hospitality of Moab for the safety of his father and mother. It has been inferred from this that he had kin associations with Moab and this would agree with the genealogy which traces his descent from Boaz and Ruth, the Moabitess (Ruth 4.17 ff.). His treatment of Moab may have been a punitive procedure

[1] See Groll. p. 66, Map 16.

adopted by a military victor whereby two out of every three males of the defeated army were put to death. It is passed over in silence in the parallel passage (I Chron. 18.2).

3. Zobah A small Aramaean kingdom near Damascus.[2]

Hadadezer Meaning 'Hadad is help'. Hadad was the ancient Semitic storm god who became the Lord *par excellence* of the Canaanite pantheon and so was equated with Baal.

to restore his power It is doubtful whether the Hebrew can yield this meaning. I Chron. 18.3 reads: 'to establish his dominion' (cp. RSV: 'to set up his monument'). The subject is Hadadezer.

4. And David hamstrung all the chariot horses This points to the fact that David's army was still, for the most part, infantry, since otherwise he would have made more constructive use of this valuable war material.

8. Betah Tebah should probably be read. This is supported by G^L and I Chron. 18.8 (Tibhath). For Tebah (Tibhath) see Groll. p. 164 and for Berothai, p. 145. Both places were located in an area where copper was mined and this is the significance of the statement that David 'took very much bronze'.

9. Hamath Groll. p. 151.

12. Edom RSV follows I Chron. 18.11, G and S. MT: 'Aram', i.e., Syria (Damascus). There is no sufficient reason for changing MT, especially since the conquest of Edom is not recorded until v. 13.

13. And David won a name for himself. When he returned, he slew eighteen thousand Edomites in the Valley of Salt. RSV follows G. MT: 'And David won a name for himself when he returned from his routing of eighteen thousand Syrians in the Valley of Salt.' 'Edom' is certainly to be preferred here to 'Aram', since we know from another passage (II Kings 14.7)

[2] On the location of Zobah and the extent of David's empire see Albright, *ARI* pp. 130 f.; Noth, *History*, pp. 195 f.

that the Valley of Salt was located there. Even with this emendation MT is still difficult, because v. 14 presupposes a statement that David won a victory over Edom and not a statement that his reputation was enhanced when he returned from his successful campaign in Edom. This difficulty is met by the text of G, which has been adopted by RSV. Alternatively it has been supposed that three words may have fallen out of the text as a consequence of the near identity of 'Aram' and 'Edom' in the Hebrew consonantal script.[3] Thus: 'And David won a name for himself. When he returned from his rout of Syria, he struck down Edom in the Valley of Salt.' According to I Chron. 18.12 it was Abishai who won this victory over Edom and, according to the title of Ps. 60, Joab.

DAVID'S OFFICIALS
8.15-18

15. and David administered justice and equity to all his people i.e., David was jealous of the rights of his people and was concerned with the right ordering and welfare of the community. These words are an important part of the ethical vocabulary of the prophets, but here their reference is probably more specialized and they allude to David's judicial activities. The meaning is that he was accessible to his people and was prepared to act personally in the capacity of judge in order to hear their claims and, if necessary, redress their wrongs. Thus, in canvassing the loyalty of the people, Absalom represented that David was no longer in touch with his people; that he had ceased to frequent the 'gate' (the recognized forum where he would be easily accessible to all) and that it was no longer possible to count on his personal interest in upholding the rights of individuals and ensuring that justice was done (II 15.4).

16. Jehoshaphat, son of Ahilud, was recorder Begrich[4]

[3] S. R. Driver, *Notes, in loc.*
[4] J. Begrich, 'Sōfēr und Mazkīr', in *ZAW* 58, 1940-1, pp. 1 f.

argues that both this office and that of SECRETARY or 'scribe' were borrowed by Israel from Egypt and that the more complex character of David's kingdom in comparison with that of Saul made necessary the creation of such offices. At any rate it is clear that both Jehoshaphat and Seraiah were principal secretaries of state, since they occur in this list of the inner circle of government. The 'scribe' as a higher civil servant is an international figure in the ancient Near East and occupies a prominent place in a genre of Egyptian literature.[5] This tendency to govern by means of a cadre of officials was a new departure in Israel and Absalom's remarks (see above) are perhaps connected with it. Under Solomon this bureaucracy grew to such dimensions as to create serious social and economic problems in Israel. It also signified the adoption of a political structure which came into conflict with the older Israelite values of corporate life.

17. And Zadok, the son of Ahitub . . . RSV follows MT. In I 22.20 Abiathar is described as 'one of the sons of Ahimelech, son of Ahitub' and it is likely that this verse should be emended to read: 'And Zadok, and Abiathar, son of Ahimelech, son of Ahitub, were priests.' The name of Zadok appears here for the first time in association with that of Abiathar and it has been conjectured that he was priest of the Jebusite shrine and that he was elevated to the position of joint high priest with Abiathar as an act of political sagacity and an attempt to assist the growing together of the conquerors and the conquered.[6] It is probable that the designation 'son of Ahitub' is an attempt to confer on Zadok a priestly pedigree acceptable to later Israelite priestly scruples. Cp. I Chron. 6.8, where Zadok appears in a genealogy of the sons of Levi.

18. The Cherethites and the Pelethites These were foreign mercenaries who were at the king's special disposal and constituted his bodyguard. The Cherethites have been associated

[5] J. B. Pritchard, *Ancient Near Eastern Texts Relating to the Old Testament*, 1950, pp. 412 f.

[6] See especially H. H. Rowley, 'Zadok and Nehushtan', *JBL* 58, 1939, pp. 113-31.

with Crete and the Pelethites (not very convincingly) with the Philistines.

The contents of this chapter are derived from old material —royal annals (vv. 1-14)[7] and official lists (vv. 15-18).[8] The victory over the Philistines may be that already recorded in II 5.17-25, in which case it is mentioned here so that the victory over Israel's most formidable enemy may be included among the impressive succession of victories which followed Nathan's oracle (8.1, 'after this') But it is Yahweh who gives victory to David (vv. 6, 14) and his awareness of his role is expressed by the dedicating (sanctifying) of his spoil to Yahweh (v. 11).

If the theology of the chapter is drawn out it seems to say that David was an empire builder of great renown (v. 13), but that he was more than this. He was Yahweh's servant who knew that he was not building for himself nor for a day, but that the dynasty of which he was the founder would be as sure and steadfast as Yahweh's covenant love had made it. The Davidic king had transcended the vicissitudes of history, because Yahweh had incorporated him in his scheme of things for Israel and the world.

[7] Noth, *History*, p. 220.
[8] Bentzen, *Introduction* II, p. 94.

THE NARRATIVE OF SUCCESSION

II 9-20

CHAPTER 9

DAVID SHOWS KINDNESS TO JONATHAN'S SON

9.1-13

4. Lo-Debar Its site is unknown, but it was in Transjordan, near Mahanaim (Groll. p. 156).

6. Mephibosheth See Commentary on II 4.4.

7. your father In the looser sense of 'grandfather'; cp. vv. 9, 10, YOUR MASTER'S SON.

8. a dead dog See Commentary on II 3.8; cp. I 17.43; 24.14.

10. That your master's son may have bread to eat; but Mephibosheth your master's son shall always eat at my table RSV follows MT. The difficulty is that, if Mephibosheth is to enjoy David's hospitality, he does not appear to stand in need of the produce of his estate in the way presupposed by the preceding half of the verse. Hence the emendation of BH (partially supported by G^L); 'that your master's household may have bread to eat'. H. P. Smith,[1] however, suggests that Mephibosheth would require an income to maintain himself at court and that Ziba is told to cultivate the former royal estate of Saul so that Mephibosheth may have the proceeds.

11. at David's table RSV follows G. MT: 'at my table' which makes no sense.

David's behaviour towards Mephibosheth flows from the covenant which he had once concluded with Jonathan. (See Commentary on I 20.14-17.) On that occasion David was put

[1] H. P. Smith, *ICC, in loc.*

on oath not to cut off his covenant love from Jonathan and his family, when he became king. It is this covenant love which David now fulfils towards Mephibosheth. The same Hebrew word (*ḥeseḏ*) occurs in I 20.14 f. and II 9.1, 3, 7. With 'the covenant love of God' (II 9.3) compare 'the covenant love of Yahweh' (I 20.14).

It is natural to enquire whether the place occupied by this incident, at the beginning of a section dealing with David's difficulties in establishing his own position and in securing the continuance of his dynasty, has any significance. We are perhaps meant to feel a deep concern for the stability of David's rule and for the security of the Davidic house. These are matters of the greatest moment which transcend David's personal ambitions for himself and his family, since Yahweh has declared through Nathan (II 7.12-16) that the perpetuation of the Davidic dynasty enters into his purposes for Israel. David is therefore bound, in obedience to Yahweh, to take every precaution to safeguard his position, since he holds so much in trust for the future of Israel. It would then have appeared to the thinking of his day an act of common political sagacity to dispose of the surviving members of Saul's family. But David has already made his attitude clear in this respect by his treatment of the assassin of Ishbosheth. (See Commentary on II 4.) Here David was confronted with two conflicting demands in both of which obedience to Yahweh was involved. He was bound, in obedience to Yahweh, to safeguard his throne, but he was equally bound to honour his covenant with Jonathan to which Yahweh had been a witness (I 20.14). David resolved this conflict of obligations by assigning priority to the alternative which involved his personal integrity and his love for a dead friend, although he knew that in so doing he might be hazarding a public trust. And, in fact, he had to pay the price for his constancy to Jonathan, for, at a time when the revolt of Absalom had put his throne in jeopardy, Mephibosheth entertained the idea of re-establishing the dynasty of Saul (II 16.3). David is therefore represented as a man of great qualities; one who carries a heavy responsibility on behalf of Yahweh and Israel, but who disdains to make these responsibilities an occasion for any defection from the covenant which he swore with Jonathan.

CHAPTER 10

THE AMMONITE INCIDENT AND THE SUBSEQUENT WAR

10.1-19

4. shaved off half the beard of each The Hebrew word for 'elder' has the same consonants as that for 'beard'. Hence the beard was a symbol of seniority, dignity and rank in the community and to mutilate it was deliberately to deflate, denigrate and humiliate.

6. Beth-Rehob, Zobah, Maacah, Tob See Groll. Map 16, p. 66. For Zobah see also Commentary on II 8.3.

7. And all the host of the mighty men RSV follows G^L and T. MT: 'All the host, the mighty men,' i.e., 'mighty men' in apposition to 'host' (army) and defining it more exactly. The meaning of MT then is that it was a specialist force which was sent to Rabbah under Joab, made up of David's professional solders who were distinguished both for their skill and their valour. Support for MT is perhaps to be seen in the reference to picked troops in v. 9, since these would seem to have comprised the whole and not part of the force. (See Commentary on v. 9.)

9. When Joab saw . . . i.e., he realized that he would have to fight on two fronts and he disposed his forces accordingly.

some of the picked men of Israel More accurately: 'from the total of the picked men of Israel', i.e., the force was entirely one of picked men.

16. Helam Groll. Map 16, p. 66.

This supplements the account of David's military actions in ch. 8[1] and it now appears that the immediate cause of the hostilities with Ammon was the deadly affront which was offered to his ambassadors. On the occasion of a change of king in Ammon David had sent envoys on a courtesy visit in order to convey his condolences to Hanun on the death of his father and to assure him of his continuing cordiality. The Ammonite interpretation of this gesture has a striking nuance of modernity. Hanun was advised by his leading statesmen that this embassy was not what it seemed to be and that it was in the nature of a subversive spy ring. He accepted this advice and humiliated the ambassadors by mutilating their beards and reducing their flowing robes to an indecent brevity.

David felt great concern at this insult, and in ordering the men to remain at Jericho until their beards were grown, he was thinking not only of the damage to their esteem which would be done if they returned to Jerusalem with mutilated beards, but also of the necessity of giving the minimum of publicity to the incident for the sake of his own prestige. Ammon's pretensions, it would seem, far outran her resources of war and so, having engineered a conflict with David, she drew several Aramaean states into it in the role of mercenaries (v. 6). When the alliance was defeated by Joab and Abishai, only Hadadezer felt so dissatisfied with the outcome as to seek to reverse it by engaging in another trial of strength with David. In this he was joined by the Aramaeans of Damascus (8.5), but this new alliance was decisively defeated by David at Helam. There is one point where it is difficult to harmonize the two accounts. According to 8.3 Hadadezer was defeated by David when he went to re-establish his power at the Euphrates; according to 10.16 he included in his force Aramaeans from beyond the Euphrates (his writ apparently ran as far east as this), but the decisive battle was fought at Helam in Trans-Jordan.

[1] In making this assumption I am following Noth, *History*, p. 194. Cp. Bright, *History*, p. 181. Bright supposes that the events recorded in 8.3-8 were subsequent to the Ammonite war recorded in chs. 10-12 (p. 181 n. 38).

CHAPTER 11

DAVID SEDUCES BATHSHEBA

11.1-13

1. In the spring of the year So this phrase has been commonly understood. It has been argued that the period for large-scale military operations was the end of the winter rains.[1] Snaith,[2] however, contends that 'at the return of the year' refers to the new year which coincided with the end of the vine harvest. (See Commentary on v. 11.) The notice refers to a campaign against Ammon subsequent to that of ch. 10.

2. he saw from the roof . . . The beginning of David's sin was in his assuming the part of a peeping-Tom. It has been suggested that it was Bathsheba's intention to be seen while she bathed, but there is no reason to suppose that this was so. Rather David's eye alighted on her from his vantage point and then he decided to watch. This proved to be a fatal step, for, when his desire was inflamed, he used his power as king to satisfy it. We may suppose that he was missing the company of his soldiers who were campaigning against Ammon and that he felt at a loose end in Jerusalem. He was in the dangerous condition of searching for something with which to divert himself and then one sin led to another.

4. Now she was purifying herself . . . i.e., she had just finished menstruating and her bath probably marked the end of her state of ritual impurity.

8. and wash your feet It has been suggested that 'feet' is a euphemism for 'private parts', but this is unlikely. On the other hand 'wash your feet' means more than just 'refresh yourself after your journey' (H. P. Smith[3]). How

[1] So Noth, *History*, p. 177.
[2] N. H. Snaith, *The Jewish New Year Festival; its Origin and Development*, 1947, pp. 32-34.
[3] H. P. Smith, *ICC, in loc.*

Uriah himself interpreted it is seen in v. 11: SHALL I THEN GO TO MY HOUSE TO EAT AND DRINK AND LIE WITH MY WIFE?. It would seem that Uriah, as a soldier engaged in a campaign, was bound by a vow of sexual abstinence[4] and that this vow was so stringent as to debar him even from entering his house or lying in his bed. David, in ordering him to wash his feet, was perhaps alluding to the ritual ablution associated with release from the vow.

11. The ark and Israel and Judah dwell in booths This is usually taken as a reference to the army campaigning against Ammon and to the ark in their midst. This interpretation may be questioned for the following reasons: (*a*) Although there is evidence that the ark accompanied the army of Israel in the earlier period (I 4.5), this would be the only reference to the practice in the time of David. (*b*) Although ALL ISRAEL refers to the tribal militia[5] in v. 1, it is doubtful whether ISRAEL AND JUDAH in v. 11 is to be similarly understood. (*c*) The second half of this verse is certainly a reference to the army and it states that the professional soldiers of David were camping in the open. If the specialist troops were camping in the open, would the tribal militia be living in huts made of branches? It may therefore be the case that Uriah is speaking of two different things in the two halves of the verse. If 'the return of the year' in v. 1 means 'the spring', and if we allow an interval of about six months for events to mature, we may assume that Uriah's recall to Jerusalem coincided with the autumnal (New Year) Feast of Tabernacles. He may therefore be adducing two reasons why he should not go home and have sexual intercourse with his wife. The civilians are living in a state of sanctity in booths observing the Feast of Tabernacles; the soldiers too are in a state of holiness for the prosecution of the war. How then could he agree to enter his house and lie in bed with his wife? There are reasons for supposing that, when the Israelites lived in booths during

[4] W. R. Smith, *ROS* p. 455.
[5] Noth, *History*, p. 198 n. 1.

the Feast of Tabernacles, they were interdicted from entering their houses.[6] As for the sojourn of the ark in a booth this would be a symbol of the theology expounded in II 7.4-7 (see Commentary). The way in which the writer compresses the various events of this chapter should be noted. There is no indication that any time elapses between the various episodes. No sooner, it seems, has David had intercourse with Bathsheba than she knows herself to be pregnant. Uriah is recalled, refuses to be putty in David's hands, is sent back to the front and murdered. This compactness contributes to the sense of high drama which is communicated by the chapter.

12. and to-morrow I will let you depart In fact Uriah was not permitted to depart on the morrow. Instead David plied him with food and drink in the hope of undermining his scruples, but the ruse was unsuccessful. HE DID NOT GO DOWN TO HIS HOUSE (v. 13). AND THE NEXT should probably be detached from v. 12 and attached to v. 13, thus: 'And on the morrow David invited him . . .' (So G^L and S.)

DAVID CONTRIVES THE MURDER OF URIAH

11.14-27

16-17. he assigned Uriah . . . Joab does not carry out David's instructions to the letter. He is ordered to locate Uriah where the fighting is hardest and then to withdraw all support from him. (DRAW BACK FROM HIM in v. 15 presumably means not only 'draw back from him in person' but also 'order the soldiers who are supporting him to withdraw'.) It would seem that Joab was not prepared to carry out David's orders in precisely this way. If he had, it would have been obvious to all who were present that Uriah had been deliberately left to die and the effect on the morale of David's crack mercenary force would have been disastrous. There were other foreigners besides Uriah among them and they too were selling their skill to David. Hence an incident such as this would have created a sense of intolerable insecurity in their ranks. It must

[6] W. R. Smith, *ROS* p. 484.

be made to appear that Uriah had died a soldier's death and that no suspicious circumstances attached to it, and, in order that this might be so, he must not die alone. So Joab initiated a tactical move which he knew to be unwise and which would hazard the lives of the participants, in order that Uriah might die in company.

20. Why did you go so near the city to fight? Joab is aware that his tactics were bad and so he can anticipate David's question and also his mood. He has contravened an elementary military maxim and he knows that David will point this out immediately. He is confident, however, that there is one piece of information which will cause David to see the action in another light—the intimation that Uriah was one of those who fell.

22. At the end of this verse a speech from David, corresponding to that anticipated by Joab in vv. 20 f., is desiderated and appears in G. Thus, after ALL THAT JOAB HAD SENT HIM TO TELL, G reads: 'all the war news. And David was angry with Joab and said to the messenger: "Why did you go so near to the city to fight? Did you not know that you would be struck down from the wall? Who struck down Abimelech, son of Jerubbaal? Did not a woman throw an upper millstone on him from the wall and so he died at Thebez? Why did you go close to the wall?"' The messenger then answers: 'Because the men gained an advantage over us . . .' (v. 23). RSV follows MT in v. 22, but does not translate 'because' in v. 23.

25. Do not let this matter trouble you . . . David is dismayed when he first hears of the casualties among his men and he does not connect the news with the letter which he sent to Joab by the hand of Uriah. This is a further indication that Joab has carried out the order in terms different from those stipulated by David. Whether or not he entirely approves of the manner in which Joab has contrived Uriah's death, he is no longer disposed to censure him once he hears that Uriah is among the dead.

This chapter is not concerned with assessing the degree of Bathsheba's guilt or with the enquiry whether she was a willing paramour or whether she was coerced. The statement that she mourned for Uriah (v. 26) may mean that she had a real affection for him, but it may mean no more than that she performed the formalities of mourning. In any case it is David's behaviour which is the burning topic and no conclusion drawn concerning Bathsheba can serve as a mitigating factor. The concluding verse, 'But the thing that David did was evil in the eyes of Yahweh,' leads on to the reproof of Nathan in ch. 12, but it also explains the orientation of the narrative in ch. 11. It is not only or principally that David, as an individual, should be seen as frail and base, but that David, as the 'anointed', and the man singled out by Yahweh as the founder of an enduring dynasty, should be reduced to the thraldom of lust and become the architect of the murder of a loyal officer.

Consider the picture. David plays the part of a peeping-Tom and decides to devour the woman on whom he has spied. He uses his power as king to achieve his end and, when it becomes necessary to cover up the consequences of his act, he recalls Uriah from the front and bids him go and lie in bed with his wife. He bestows a gift on him—a sinister present. It was the kind of gift which is given to tie the hands of the man who receives it and to make it difficult for him not to do the giver's bidding. The technique of reducing a man's freedom of action by embarrassing him with bounty has been well-tried and often used. It may be that Uriah sensed some part of the truth and knew that David's eagerness to have him in bed with his wife was not disinterested. But he would not be bribed nor was his sense of what was right destroyed by the drink with which David plied him. Hence Bathsheba's pregnancy had not been covered up and so David had to take another step and engineer Uriah's death.

The painting of such a picture as this is as clear an indication as could be desired that whatever the nature of the special covenant relationship between Yahweh and the Davidic king (see Commentary on II 7), the king is still a man, subject to human passions and temptations. The question which the writer expects us to ask is: How will Yahweh react to David's behaviour? Is David, the man of Yahweh's choice, and the one on whom the future of Israel hinges, above the law of Yahweh? The way in which this question is to be answered can already be seen in v. 27: 'But the thing that David did was evil in the eyes of Yahweh.' The Davidic king has been portrayed as possessed of human infirmities and as a great sinner. Any image of him as a god-like figure has been destroyed; and it will be seen in what follows that, in respect of the moral demands of Yahweh, he is one among his brethren.

CHAPTER 12

NATHAN DENOUNCES DAVID

12.1-14

1. And the Lord sent Nathan David did not have a monopoly of charismatic endowment in Yahweh's community. Nathan too was chosen of Yahweh and authorized to confront even the king with a word of condemnation and judgment.

3. and he brought it up More accurately: 'and he kept it alive'; i.e., it was a motherless lamb which he reared artificially.

5. deserves to die Literally: 'is a son of death'. David is acting in his capacity of supreme judge in the community (see Commentary on II 8.15), whose responsibility it is to redress wrongs and guarantee justice to the poor, and is passing sentence of death.

6. fourfold RSV follows MT. G: 'sevenfold'. S. R. Driver[1] suggests that the proverbial sevenfold (Prov. 6.31) may be original and that 'fourfold' may represent an alteration in the interests of legal precision (cp. Ex. 22.1).

[1] S. R. Driver, *Notes, in loc.*

10. the sword shall never depart from your house This is usually referred to the violent deaths of David's sons, Amnon, Absalom and Adonijah, and also to the later purge of Athaliah (II Kings 11.1). The threat that his wives would commit adultery in public is connected with the subsequent behaviour of Absalom towards his harem (II 16.20-22). Note that the principle of *lex talionis* operates (Ex. 21.24; Lev. 24.20; Deut. 19.21), so that the punishment fits the crime.

14. you have utterly scorned the Lord MT: 'the enemies of the Lord'. The meaning would then be: 'you have brought Yahweh into contempt with his enemies', but this is to force the Hebrew and 'enemies of' should probably be deleted.

THE DEATH OF BATHSHEBA'S CHILD

12.15-23

16. and David fasted and went in and lay all night upon the ground MT should perhaps rather be translated: 'And David fasted without respite and would go to spend the night lying on the ground.' i.e., he did this night after night during the child's illness.

21. You fasted . . . David had reversed the conventional procedure and his officials ask him to explain his behaviour. He had behaved like a mourner before his child was dead and now, with the child dead, he is disregarding the rites of mourning. David justifies himself by saying that he did what he could to influence Yahweh to spare the child's life while there was hope, but now there is nothing more he can do. I SHALL GO TO HIM, BUT HE WILL NOT RETURN TO ME (v. 23) would seem to be a reference to Sheol and the translation, 'I am journeying to him, but he will not return to me' brings out David's meaning. The child cannot be brought back from the shadowy world of the dead, but, in fulfilling the law of his mortality, David is travelling towards that world.

THE BIRTH OF SOLOMON

12.24-25

Solomon Perhaps 'Recompense', that is, for the child who died. Or 'Peace', the sign of the restoration of 'wholeness' in respect of David's relationship to Yahweh. The alternative name communicated by Nathan, 'Beloved of Yahweh', assured David of Yahweh's changed attitude towards Bathsheba's second child.

DAVID FINALLY SUBDUES AMMON

12.26-31

26. and took the royal city In view of v. 27 ROYAL CITY should perhaps be emended to 'city of waters' or 'water-city'. The water-city was a large cistern, roofed over so as to be concealed, and connected with the city proper by an underground passage. Through it citizens could go in time of siege to obtain water from the cistern[2] (cp. the Siloam tunnel in Jerusalem). On the other hand it may be that Joab is speaking loosely in v. 26 and defines ROYAL CITY more precisely as 'water-city' in v. 27.

28. and it be called by my name This reflects the usage of calling a city by the name of its conqueror, as Jerusalem was called the city of David. Joab does not wish to arrogate to himself a right which belongs to David as king and commander-in-chief of the army.

30. their king RSV follows MT. G: 'Milcom'—the deity of the Ammonites whose name the king of Ammon would bear (cp. I Kings 11.5).

and in it was a precious stone Following I Chron. 20.2, S and T. MT: 'and a precious stone'.

31. and set them to labour . . . This is a difficult verse. It

[2] G. A. Barton, *Archaeology and the Bible*[7], pp. 171, 260.

says either that David tortured the defeated Ammonites or that he put them to forced labour. RSV understands it to mean the latter and this is the view which is now generally held, although the balance of probability is hard to determine. I Chron. 20.3 reads: 'And he sawed them with saws' and this supports the 'torture' interpretation. It has been suggested that the barbarity of the Ammonites in war (Amos 1.13) may have been a reason for David's savagery (cp. his treatment of Moab, II 8.2). The 'forced labour' interpretation would certainly be superior were it not that it requires the emendation of MT at a crucial place. Thus MADE THEM TOIL AT THE BRICK KILNS (or, 'made them toil at the brick moulds',[3] i.e., at brick making) presupposes the alteration of one consonant of MT. The meaning of the verb without this alteration is 'made them pass over (or, through)'.

Nathan, who in Yahweh's name spoke to David a word of promise, (II 7) reappears to uphold the authority of Yahweh in his community. He does this firmly and so as not to brook contradiction and yet he does it with finesse. He does not go out of his way to be unnecessarily blunt or offensive and yet he is relentless in his exposure of David's sin and fearless in the word of denunciation which he speaks. He builds up a hypothetical case to which he asks David, as supreme judge, to listen and then he invites his judgment on it.

The case concerned a poor man who adopted a motherless lamb as a domestic pet. He had no interest in its commercial value; it was one of his family and as domesticated as a dog. Neither this man nor his children would ever have entertained the idea that it might be killed for food, for their relationship to the lamb was on another and different plane. It is this which makes the conduct of the big commercial breeder all the more despicable and inhuman. He was rearing animals for the market on a large scale, but, instead of taking one of his own to meet the claims of a traveller on his hospitality, he seized the pet lamb of the poor man and had it slaughtered. He did not

[3] S. R. Driver, *Notes, in loc.*

want to lose face by acting in defiance of tradition and refusing hospitality to the traveller, but his hospitality was to cost him nothing and yet to cost another family what could not be measured in money.

When David heard the case, he could not contain his anger and sentenced the breeder to death on the spot. The irony of the situation was that he was sentencing himself and did not know it. So Nathan went on to disclose that David himself was the subject of the sentence which had just been passed. It was therefore an ingenious way of making his point and wringing an admission of guilt from David. The reason for Nathan's interview with the king was now clear and the two men were no longer at cross purposes. Nathan too was Yahweh's servant speaking with authority to another of Yahweh's servants—the king. David learned that he was no absolute monarch and that he might not make his subjects into his toys. There was a moral balance in Yahweh's community which the prophet would not fail to maintain and which the king might not disturb with impunity.

David's confession of sin means much to Nathan, because he now knows that David understands how dismally he has betrayed his trust towards Yahweh and Israel. David apprehends the enormity of his failure. I HAVE SINNED AGAINST YAHWEH. It is the onset of this chastened mood—this return to truth and duty—which paves the way for Nathan's assurance of forgiveness. But forgiveness does not mean that Yahweh's judgment is abrogated, for the consequences of David's sin cannot be cancelled and the punishment must fit the crime. More immediately Yahweh's judgment will fall on the child who was the fruit of his sin—Bathsheba's child will die. It is by this that David is most moved and the singleness of his concern for the child reveals in a better light the man who has sunk so low. It is the child's fate, and not the more far-reaching consequences of his sin for himself and his posterity, which fills his mind. So he fasts and prays without respite for the sick child, consumed with concern for the innocent victim of his sin.

The episode closes on a note of reconciliation. Uriah is dead and Bathsheba is David's wife. David has sinned and cannot undo the evil which he has wrought nor turn back Yahweh's judgment, but Yahweh can bring good out of evil. David cared for the child who died and his love for it was a good thing; and from his union with Bathsheba a second child is born who is doubly named. Solomon means 'Recompense' or 'Peace' and this is not a child doomed to die because of the sin of his parents, but one 'Beloved of Yahweh'.

CHAPTER 13

AMNON RAPES TAMAR AND ABANDONS HER

13.1-19

2. was so tormented that he made himself ill i.e., he was ill through frustration and unsatisfied desire.

3. a very crafty man The Hebrew word translated CRAFTY is the ordinary one for 'wise' and this passage shows that it need not have any ethical tendency. It means here that Jonadab's plan was shrewd in its conception and would enable Amnon to satisfy his desire. In this respect it was the work of a 'wise' man. The fact that he used his ability to achieve an immoral end is not thought to impair his wisdom, since, in this context, 'wise' does not contain any element of ethical evaluation.

5. Let my sister Tamar come and give me bread to eat Amnon was to pretend that his appetite was poor and that he needed some special inducement to eat, and to suggest that Tamar should come and coax him with a diet agreeable to his digestion.

12. do not force me Basically, 'humiliate me', meaning here, 'rape me'. Amnon is seen here and in the following verses in a very poor light. It is the premeditated character of his outrage of Tamar which is so damnable. It is not that he acts impulsively when an unexpected opportunity is offered him of satisfying his lust; rather it is a carefully laid plan which we can see unfolding stage by stage until the point is reached where all the servants are dismissed and he has Tamar at his mercy in his bedroom (vv. 10-14).

13. speak to the king, for he will not withhold me from you This disclosure deepens Amnon's guilt, because it reveals that he could have married Tamar if he had so desired. We have no reason to doubt that Tamar is speaking the truth or that we are being offered an important clue for the understanding of Amnon's behaviour. Tamar was his half-sister and there was no bar to his marrying her. What he wanted, however, was not to marry her but to seduce her. This fact may explain the odd statement in v. 2, FOR SHE WAS A VIRGIN AND IT SEEMED difficult (RSV IMPOSSIBLE) TO AMNON TO DO ANYTHING TO HER. It may also explain why his love turned so quickly to hatred, although this may be related to the circumstance that she had refused to give herself to him and that he had had to resort to rape. At any rate, having done her a deadly wrong, he goes on to behave towards her like a monster of cruelty. Tamar assumes that, for better or for worse, she now belongs to him and counts his abandonment of her a greater wrong than his first act of brutality (vv. 15 f.). Hence she adopts the rites of a mourner as a widow who has lost her husband might have done and she lives like a widow (v. 20, A DESOLATE WOMAN) in her brother's house.

16. No, my brother . . . RSV follows G^L. MT does not make good sense.

17. out of my presence The Hebrew is indicative of contemptuous dismissal and, at this point, the cruelty of Amnon's behaviour to Tamar is extreme. He speaks to his servant in such a way as to give the impression that she has been making a nuisance of herself and forcing her unwelcome attentions on him. He adds deceit to brutality and tortures her outraged feelings beyond all healing.

18. a long robe with sleeves The same Hebrew phrase as is used of Joseph's robe (Gen. 37.3). The meaning is in doubt, but it probably means 'an ankle-length robe' rather than 'a multi-coloured robe'.

ABSALOM BIDES HIS TIME

13.20-22

21. he was very angry RSV follows MT. G^L and V have the additional words: 'But he did not vex the spirit of Amnon, his son, for he loved him, because he was his first-born.' Whether or not these words belong to the original text they are an apt comment on David's attitude. He was angry, but his anger was weak and ineffective, because he was a too indulgent father and his anger was smothered by sentimentality. The words 'because he was his first-born' may indicate that David looked on Amnon as the next king and that this was a further reason why he took no action against him. The phrase, however, may imply no more than that David's first-born had a special place in his affections.

22. neither good nor bad Probably an idiom for 'not a single word'. It would seem that Absalom did not want immediately to make an issue of the outrage, and he played it down in a way which could not have given much comfort to his sister (v. 20). It is hard to decide what his motives were. He may have thought it unwise that members of the royal house should wash their dirty linen in public; he may have been anxious not to embarrass David nor publicize a scandal which would have impaired the authority of the king and his house. At any rate he was determined to kill Amnon and was prepared to await a favourable opportunity. In the interval he would give him no indication of his thoughts or feelings. Absalom may have been motivated, as has been suggested,[1] by the desire to get rid of one who stood between him and the throne, but, if this is so, it is not entertained by the narrator of this chapter.

[1] Noth, *History*, pp. 200 f.

ABSALOM KILLS AMNON

13.23-29

23. Baal-Hazor Groll. p. 144. Ephraim here is to be equated with Ophrah (Ophrah [1], Groll. p. 158).

27. all the king's sons go with him RSV follows MT. After these words G, L and V add: 'and he made a feast like a royal feast'. For sheep-shearing as a time of feasting see I 25.4.

ABSALOM A FUGITIVE

13.30-39

32. Let not my lord suppose . . . The 'wisdom' (see Commentary on v. 3) of Jonadab is again evident in his advice to the king to discount rumour. He surmises correctly that Absalom is concerned only with killing Amnon.

34. the Horonaim road RSV follows G. MT: 'the road behind him', which is unsatisfactory. The Horonaim road is understood as the road leading from Jerusalem to Upper and Lower Beth-Horon (Groll. p. 145). G has a longer text than MT; thus: 'many people were coming from the Horonaim road on the descent and he told the king saying, "I see men coming down from the Horonaim road on the side of the hill."' RSV keeps the shorter text of MT. Hertzberg,[2] following Alt and Eissfeldt, emends 'Horonaim' to 'Bahurim' on the ground that the Horonaim road would not be visible from the south-east hill of Jerusalem where David's city was. Bahurim is a village north-east of the Mount of Olives through which David passed in his flight from Absalom (II 16.5, Groll. p. 144).

36. wept very bitterly This should perhaps be followed by v. 37b, 'and he MOURNED FOR HIS SON DAY AFTER DAY'. The order would then be 37a, 38b and 39. 38a is a doublet of 37a.

[2] Hertzberg, *ATD*, *in loc.*

38. Geshur An Aramaean kingdom east of the upper course of the Jordan (Groll. p. 150). Absalom's mother was the daughter of its king (II 3.3).

39. And the spirit of the king longed to go forth to Absalom RSV follows G^L. MT is untranslatable. The second half of the verse and the following chapter require that v. 39a should make some reference to the softening of David's attitude towards Absalom. Other conjectures are: 'The spirit of the king ceased to struggle against Absalom' (BH); 'The horror felt by David towards Absalom (gradually) died out' (Hertzberg[3]).

A first step to the understanding of this chapter is the realization that it is part of the 'History of Succession' and that its contents are relevant to this central concern. The narrative does not spare Amnon and certainly canvasses no sympathy for him. He is a brute and a deceiver and Absalom could plead great provocation in mitigation of his murder of him. Yet Amnon is a key figure, because he is David's first-born son and was, in all probability, regarded by David and by himself as the next king, while his behaviour towards Tamar shows that he is totally unworthy of such an honour and responsibility. This situation is further complicated by the circumstance that David is blinded to Amnon's viciousness, his judgment being destroyed by an uncritical paternal indulgence. In the eyes of the narrator perhaps the most important single factor in the total situation is the failure of David to exact punishment on Amnon. If he had acted decisively against Amnon, the rot might have been stopped and Absalom would have been deprived of a reason for taking the law into his own hand.

Absalom himself may have had designs on the throne and may have been moved by ambition and not simply by a determination to vindicate his sister's honour, but this suggestion is not present in the narrative. But, in any case, he did become a candidate for the throne by virtue of Amnon's death, whether this was his design or not, so that his estrangement

[3] Hertzberg, *ATD*, *in loc.*

and exile are highly significant facts in relation to the problem of succession. Moreover the relaxing of David's anger has to be viewed not only as a private reconciliation between father and son, but also as the return to favour of one who may be the next king, and so an event of political significance.

But in fact Absalom did not become king and it may be significant that prior to embarking on his account of violence and intrigue in relation to the succession, our writer recorded how David received a message from Nathan to the effect that Solomon was 'Beloved of Yahweh' (II 12.25). Nathan's appearances are moments of decisive authority (cp. II 7), and this is perhaps another such moment. The strongest candidates for the throne and those whose candidature is most canvassed will not in fact occupy it, because Yahweh's choice has alighted on Solomon. This is a choice which will confound the forecasters, for the beginnings of David's relationship to Bathsheba were covered in shame and the first child was the object of Yahweh's judgment. But Yahweh will not be tied by accepted notions of what constitutes a strong candidature; Bathsheba's first child died for the sins of its parents, but her second child is to be king of Israel.

CHAPTER 14

DAVID AND THE WOMAN OF TEKOA

14.1-20

2. Tekoa Groll. p. 163.

4. When the woman of Tekoa came RSV follows the Versions. MT: 'said'. She appeals to the king as the supreme dispenser of justice in the community. (See Commentary on II 8.15.)

7. And now the whole family has risen FAMILY refers to the larger family or clan. The determination of the clan to fulfil the duty of blood revenge (cp. Gen. 9.6) conflicts with the concern of the woman to perpetuate the name of her deceased husband. She pleads that the ancient law of blood revenge should not apply in this particular case, since, as she is a widow, the future of the household depends on the survival of her one remaining son.

8. and I will give orders concerning you 'I will make an order', in a legal sense. i.e., I will set in motion the machinery which will give effect to my decision in respect of your case.

9. On me be the guilt, my lord, the king . . . This is obscure but it appears that the woman is pressing her case further. RSV translates the second half of the verse as a jussive ('let the king and his throne be guiltless') but this is unlikely. The translation should rather be: 'The guilt is on me, my lord, the king, and on my father's house, but the king and his throne are innocent.' Hertzberg[1] paraphrases this: 'The guilt will be laid on me and my father's house and the king and his throne will be declared innocent,' and he argues that the woman is asking the king to identify himself more emphatically with the decision to stay the execution of blood revenge against her son, so that the clan will see beyond all doubt that it is the king's decision and will not blame her for obstructing them in the execution of their duty. But the verse may be no more than a simple statement of fact. The woman is saying that the consequences of a verdict in her favour are not the same for David as they are for her, because the *locus* of the conflict is in her family. If David prevents the clan from taking revenge, this does not involve him in guilt, since he acts from outside the family. If, however, the woman thwarts the family from fulfilling their sacred duty, she cannot escape guilt, for she is repudiating the solidarity of the family. In other words the woman is pointing out to David that she is involved in a painful conflict of obligations by which he is unaffected. David responds to her plea by guaranteeing her protection, presumably from the family (v. 10) and by swearing the oath which she requests (v. 11).

[1] Hertzberg, *ATD, in loc.*

11. the avenger of blood The nearest kinsman on whom the duty of blood revenge falls (Num. 35.19-27; Deut. 19.6-12). The woman believes that her son's safety will be more adequately secured if David swears by Yahweh that the avenging kinsman will not be permitted to do his duty, and the king allows her plea.

12. Pray let your handmaid speak a word The woman is not yet satisfied. The king has guaranteed the life of her son, but has said nothing about his status. Is he to remain permanently a fugitive? This was an important question for her, for, if the surviving son were effectively to perpetuate the name of his father, he must be reinstated to his proper place in society and allowed to work and live at home. The disguise here, however, is very thin and it is, more or less, dropped in v. 13, where it is clear that Absalom is the subject of her remarks, to be put on again, not very convincingly, in the following verses.

13. Why then have you planned such a thing against the people of God? This can only refer to David's banishment of Absalom and it makes no sense in relation to the woman's son. We are not told at what point in the proceedings David became aware of the real nature of the woman's representations, but he could not have failed to catch her meaning here. The following words must also refer to Absalom: FOR IN GIVING THIS DECISION THE KING CONVICTS HIMSELF, INASMUCH AS THE KING DOES NOT BRING HIS BANISHED ONE HOME AGAIN. The woman is saying that, in banishing Absalom, David is guilty of a sin against the nation (PEOPLE OF GOD). It is against the best interests of Israel for Absalom to be in exile.

14. We must all die . . . These words are more equivocal and might be related to her fictitious son, although HIS BANISHED ONE again points to Absalom. She is saying that life is short and that there is no time to be lost in bringing the exile home.

God will not take away the life of him who devises means

RSV here rests on a conjectural emendation. MT: 'God does not take away life, but takes thought . . .' i.e., God's conduct is more merciful than is yours.

16. the man The avenger of blood mentioned in v. 11.

who would destroy MT can hardly be so translated as it stands and the insertion of 'who seeks' from G gives a smoother reading, i.e., 'who seeks to destroy'.

17. to discern Literally: 'to hear' and again (cp. v. 8) in a judicial context. The woman expresses her confidence that David will 'hear' the case and sift the evidence so as to arrive at a sound judgment.

19. One cannot turn to the right hand or the left i.e., there is no way of evading the impact of the truth of David's words.

ABSALOM RETURNS TO JERUSALEM

14.21-33

24. Let him dwell apart This is a correct paraphrase, but a more accurate translation would be: 'Let him go round to his house' (cp. II 13.20).

26. at the end of every year The Hebrew means no more than 'from time to time'.

by the king's weight Gordon[2] points to the fact that in the ancient Near East there existed variant measures with the same name and he compares such modern examples as the 'short ton' (2,000 lbs.) and the 'long ton' (2,240 lbs.). The specification of the weight as the royal shekel thus removes all ambiguity and ensures precision. Cp. 'the shekel of the sanctuary' (Ex. 30.13, 24). This hints at another aspect of the king's judicial responsibilities. He held the standard by which all other weights were judged and so he was the guardian of the balances (cp. Hos. 12.7; Amos 8.5; Micah 6.11).

[2] Gordon, *UM* p. 38 n. 1.

33. and bowed himself on his face to the ground RSV follows MT. G has the additional words, 'and fell'. Thus: 'And he did obeisance and fell on his face to the ground . . .'

There is an obvious similarity between the technique of the woman of Tekoa and that of Nathan (II 12). Both of them construct a hypothetical case, while they pretend that they are describing a real situation and make an urgent claim on David in his capacity as supreme judge of the community. And in both instances the intention is to win from him a verdict which amounts to self-condemnation and which will compel him to change his attitude. Nathan wants him to see the enormity of his sin against Yahweh and the woman is concerned to make the point that the exile of Absalom is a sin against the people of God. The woman's case is not so immaculately constructed as that of Nathan, nor does it relate so appositely to David's dealings with Absalom as does Nathan's story to the Bathsheba incident. It would seem that we are to equate David with the clan or, more particularly, with the avenger of blood who would kill the widow's surviving son. The woman is alleging that David is so obsessed with taking revenge on Absalom for Amnon's death that he has not appreciated that more is involved here than a feud within the royal family. This is a matter of national importance and in it the nation should have a say. Here the woman's hypothetical case is not entirely apt, for the conflict was between the obligations of the larger family and the survival of the smaller family, and, in this conflict of obligations, priority was claimed for the smaller social entity. But, in the application, the conflict is between what David conceives to be his duty as head of the royal family and what the woman considers to be best for the nation, and it is for the nation that priority is claimed.

Joab's case, presented by the woman, would seem to be that, on political grounds, a reconciliation between David and Absalom was of paramount importance, because only through such a reconciliation could the question of succession be settled. David must put this family squabble behind him and bring back Absalom to court in order that he might be groomed for the throne. David followed this advice only partially by bringing Absalom back to Jerusalem and then denying him the *entrée* to the court for two years, thereby making it clear that he had not forgiven him for Amnon's death nor decided the question of succession in his favour. It appears that, at this juncture, Absalom was, in Joab's judgment, the best candidate for the throne. It was Joab who procured his recall, who went to Geshur to bring him back and who was summoned by Absalom when he had grown tired of kicking his heels. Joab evidently was more patient than his *protégé* and would have preferred to wait for a softening of David's attitude rather than to go and urge him that he should complete his reconciliation with Absalom. Absalom, for his part, was determined to demonstrate to Joab that he was not the kind of man who could be kept waiting too long and he set Joab's field on fire to show that he meant business. This may have marked the beginning of Joab's disillusionment and change of mind with respect to the fitness of Absalom for the throne (cp. Commentary on II 18). In the short term, however, everything worked out well and the chapter ends with the reconciliation of David and Absalom.

CHAPTER 15

ABSALOM COURTS POPULARITY

15.1-6

1. After this Absalom got himself a chariot and horses These were a prestige symbol associated with royal rank (cp. I 8.11; I Kings 1.5). Absalom had therefore settled the question of succession in his own favour and was showing himself to the populace as the next king. The same form of advertisement was adopted by Adonijah.

2. and stand beside the way of the gate Absalom went to the gate where all manner of public business was transacted and where those seeking redress of injustices from the king would be assembled. It is clear that this right of access to the king was highly prized by the community and that he was expected to make himself available to individual subjects so as to ensure that justice was done to them. In preceding chapters allusion is made to David's exercise of such judicial functions on three occasions (II 8.15; 12.1-6; 14.4 ff.). Absalom calculates that an effective way of winning popularity will be to play on David's neglect of his judicial responsibilities and so he goes out of his way to show great personal interest in the individuals who have come to Jerusalem to lay their cases before David. He asks them about their tribe and the city of their origin and tries to create an impression of sympathy and benevolence. He tells them that they have justice on their side and that it is shameful that the king has made no arrangements for the hearing of their suits. It should be noted that Absalom does not go so far as to say: 'O that I were king in the land!' Rather he says that David might have deputed these judicial tasks to him. Thus: SEE, YOUR CLAIMS ARE GOOD AND RIGHT, BUT THERE IS NO MAN DEPUTED BY THE KING TO HEAR YOU. Absalom asserts that, if David delegated these powers to him, he would make himself available at all times to the individual who was labouring under a sense of injustice. These tactics suggest that David's increasing remoteness from the people was a major source of dissatisfaction and, in particular, that individuals who came from a distance to Jerusalem in order to get justice from the king, and who then found that his interest in the rights of the individual was being crushed by an increasingly complex and impersonal administration, could readily be made into missionaries of rebellion. Thus Absalom STOLE THE HEARTS OF THE MEN OF ISRAEL (v. 6).

6. the men of Israel It is difficult to ascertain the meaning of ISRAEL here and elsewhere in the chapter (vv. 2, 10, 13). Noth[1] holds that ISRAEL means the whole nation, since Ab-

[1] Noth, *History*, p. 201; similarly J. Bright, *History*, p. 188.

salom had his main following in Judah, but had also won support among the northern tribes. This interpretation agrees well with the fact that the standard of revolt was raised in the south at Hebron, but it raises certain difficulties in connection with vv. 2 and 6, where ISRAEL might more naturally be understood as referring to the northern tribes. Hence Hertzberg[2] thinks that ISRAEL refers to the northern tribes and that Absalom deliberately chose Hebron in order that the revolt would paralyse Judah and bring about its submission. Cp. II 19.8b f., where 'Israel' can only mean the northern tribes, although it is clear from v. 11 that Judah was also implicated in the revolt. The point of v. 6 is that those on whose sense of grievance Absalom plays have made a journey in order to get to Jerusalem (v. 2) and so the narrative can be understood as alluding particularly to the experience of individuals from the northern tribes who have come to Jerusalem to press their claims for justice. See also Commentary on v. 11.

ABSALOM'S COUP D'ÉTAT

15.7-12

8. It has been customary to follow the Versions in order to get the sense conveyed by RSV, but more recently it has been held that the same sense can be had from MT without emendation.[3]

10. Absalom is king at Hebron This is the recognized formula of proclamation and it means: 'Absalom has begun to reign at Hebron.' On Hebron see Commentary on II 2.10.

11. two hundred men It has been suggested that they were hostages,[4] but they are described as invited guests who accompanied Absalom without having any real awareness of the

[2] Hertzberg, *ATD* on II 15.2, 13.
[3] Gordon, *UM* p. 67.
[4] H. P. Smith, *ICC*, *in loc.*

purpose of his visit to Hebron. They believed that they were going to participate in the ceremony which was the ostensible reason of Absalom's journey. The significance of this notice is that it suggests that Absalom had no following inside Jerusalem. The only fellow-conspirator at court who is mentioned is Ahithophel, and Joab was not implicated (cp. Commentary on II 14).

simplicity i.e., integrity, they were not party to the plot.

12. He sent for Ahithophel . . . The plain meaning of MT is that Absalom sent Ahithophel from Giloh (Groll. p. 150) and the insertion of 'and summoned' with G^L would seem to be necessary in order to give the required sense. Thus: 'He sent and summoned Ahithophel . . .' Giloh is located between Jerusalem and Hebron.

DAVID EVACUATES JERUSALEM

15.13-37

14. servants This refers to David's officials and v. 18 shows that not only his civil servants remained loyal, but also the mercenary force which constituted his bodyguard. David gives two reasons for evacuating Jerusalem. He fears that, if he waits there any longer, his escape route may be cut off and, further, he desires to spare the city the destruction which would result from a clash between his forces and those of Absalom.

17. and they halted BH conjectures, 'and he halted'. The description in v. 18 is then that of David reviewing his followers as they file past him. S. R. Driver[5] with some support from G would read 'his servants' in v. 17a and 'the people' in v. 18a, retaining 'they halted' in v. 17b. 'The servants of the king' are the most influential of David's officials who were in immediate attendance on him and halted with him while the remainder of his following marched past.

[5] S. R. Driver, *Notes, in loc.*

19. Ittai, the Gittite The leader of a mercenary band who had sold his services to David just as the latter had once sold his to the Philistines (I 21.10; 27).

20. and may the Lord show steadfast love and faithfulness to you RSV follows G. MT: 'Take your brethren with you in mercy and faithfulness.'

23. toward the wilderness This is described by S. R. Driver[6] as 'an unparalleled and untranslatable expression'. G^L: 'and all the people passed on before him by the way of Olives which is in the desert.' H. P. Smith[7] holds that the reference is to the road on the south slope of the Mount of Olives. S. R. Driver conjectures 'stood' for 'crossed', i.e., David halted in the valley of Kidron, while his following marched past (cp. v. 17). David's stationary position is presupposed in vv. 25-28, since Zadok and Abiathar set down the ark while they spoke to him.

24. And Abiathar came up and lo, Zadok came also The RSV translation cannot be justified. It is possible that the text is disturbed and that 'Abiathar' has been excised as a consequence of late theological interference in the interests of the Zadokite priesthood and replaced by 'with all the Levites'. The original would then have been: 'Moreover Zadok and Abiathar, the bearers of the ark of the covenant of God, came up . . .' Another possibility is that the verse should be translated as it stands in MT, thus: 'Moreover Zadok came up with all the Levites, the bearers of the ark of the Covenant of God, and they set down the ark of God, and Abiathar presented (an offering).' Cp. II 6.17, where the same Hebrew verb is used in connection with the offering of burnt sacrifices; also I Kings 3.15. In both these passages the ark is associated with the offering of burnt sacrifices.

27. Look RSV follows G. MT: 'Do you see?' i.e., 'Do you see how matters stand?' It is possible that the present

[6] S. R. Driver, *Notes, in loc.*
[7] H. P. Smith, *ICC, in loc.*

text is a corruption of 'Zadok, the chief priest', and that 'the chief priest' is an insertion of the same type as that discussed in the Commentary on v. 24.[8]

you and Abiathar 'Abiathar' is conjecturally restored by RSV and there are three considerations which support this. The Hebrew, literally translated, reads: 'Go back to the city in peace, you (and Abiathar) and Ahimaaz, thy son, and Jonathan, the son of Abiathar, the two of your (plural) sons with you (plural).' Hence (*a*) Since Abiathar's son is mentioned, Abiathar himself must have been previously mentioned. (*b*) The plurals at the end of the verse indicate that both Zadok and Abiathar are being addressed. (*c*) Abiathar is mentioned in conjunction with Zadok in v. 29.

31. and it was told David RSV follows G. MT, which requires emendation, reads: 'And David declared, saying'.

32. Where God was worshipped The reference is to some spot at the top of the Mount of Olives which was frequented as a sanctuary.

Hushai, the Archite G has the addition, 'the companion of David'; cp. v. 37.

The main theological interest in this chapter centres in the attitude of David to Absalom's *coup d'état*. Here the representation has a double-sided character; it is compounded of piety and worldly self-help (cp. Commentary on I 21). One side appears in David's assertion that he is content to leave the issue of Absalom's revolt in Yahweh's hands, for it is he who in the long run will decide the course of events (vv. 25 f.). David's leaving of his concubines in Jerusalem TO KEEP THE HOUSE is perhaps to be interpreted as a gesture of confidence in his ultimate return to the capital, and his insistence that the ark should go back is another such gesture, since to evacuate the ark would be an expression of despair for the future of Yahweh's community. David does not know what the future

[8] Cp. S. R. Driver, *Notes, in loc.*

holds for him personally (perhaps his uncertainty is related to his knowledge that he has sinned against Yahweh and is exposed to judgment, cp. II 12.13 f.), but he has faith in the power of Yahweh to fulfil his purposes for his people. David has been forced to run away before Absalom, but he will not make it seem as if Yahweh also is on the run. Absalom has attempted to wrest the sceptre from Yahweh and to decide prematurely and by force the question of succession, but he will find out that the control of Yahweh's community cannot be won by such smash and grab tactics.

Yet, in the return of the ark to Jerusalem, the other side of David's reaction is manifested, for Abiathar and Zadok with their respective sons return not simply as guardians of the ark, but also as part of David's spy-ring of which Hushai is to be the key member (v. 34). David judges that he must employ every resource of statecraft and espionage in order to counteract the sagacity of Ahithophel. He is clearly of the opinion that the presence of Ahithophel at Absalom's side greatly increases the gravity of his position, for Ahithophel is a seasoned statesman and will give Absalom the very best advice. Hence David is anxious to nullify the counsel of Ahithophel and he proposes to do this by planting Hushai inside Absalom's council of war (v. 34). Hence, while David asserts that it is Yahweh who will decide the issue, he is not precluded from using every device of statecraft in order to frustrate Absalom's designs and ensure the victory of his cause. The assertion that Yahweh is in control does not make the policies and ambitions of Absalom unreal, nor does it excuse David from using all his powers of shrewdness and political calculation in initiating policies which will thwart the aims of the usurper.

CHAPTER 16

ZIBA PROVISIONS DAVID

16.1-4

1. Ziba See II 9.

3. he remains in Jerusalem David is poorly repaid for his kindness to Mephibosheth. See Commentary on II 9.

DAVID STONED BY SHIMEI

16.5-14

5. a man of the family of the house of Saul This is the second affront which David receives from Saul's descendants. Shimei is a near enough relative to Saul to be described as one of his clan (FAMILY means the larger family or clan).

6. And he threw stones at David . . . Note the reference to the three classes of David's retinue. (*a*) The royal officials who kept company with him and who consequently were also a target for the stones. (*b*) The general body of his followers, named THE PEOPLE. (*c*) The professional soldiers. Cp. Commentary on II 15.17.

7. worthless fellow See Commentary on I 1.16.

8. The Lord has avenged upon you Literally: 'The Lord has brought back upon you,' i.e., he has brought upon your head (in our idiom).

9. this dead dog Cp. I 17.43; 24.14; II 9.8. See Commentary on II 3.8.

10. What have I to do with you . . . ? i.e., What is there in common between my attitude and yours in this matter? The RSV translation of the remainder of the verse is not strictly accurate. It should be translated: 'If he curses and if Yahweh bids him, "Curse David", who then shall say, "Why have you done so? "' Note that the saying is directed against Joab as well as Abishai.

12. iniquity So the consonants of MT. The meaning must then be 'the iniquity done to me'. According to the Masoretic vocalization we should read 'my eyes' which has been interpreted as 'my tears'. The Versions read 'my affliction' which best suits the context (so RSV).

14. at the Jordan RSV follows G[L]. The name of a place is desiderated, but is absent from MT.

HUSHAI OFFERS HIS SERVICES TO ABSALOM

16.15-19

15. all the people, the men of Israel RSV follows MT. G: 'all the men of Israel'. On ISRAEL see Commentary on II 15.6.

18. his will I be There are two points to be noted in Hushai's reply to Absalom's question. (*a*) Absalom has been chosen king by Yahweh and by the people and so it is right that he should serve him. (*b*) Nothing could be more natural than that he should want to serve Absalom now that he is king, since he served his father, when he was king. Hushai's advocacy, however, is not very persuasive and he hardly succeeds in his efforts to make a virtue out of what seems to Absalom to be his desertion of David.

AHITHOPHEL ADVISES ABSALOM

16.20-23

20. Give your counsel YOUR is plural and so Absalom's request is presumably addressed to a circle of advisers, but the only advice that counts is that of Ahithophel. He is a prince among counsellors, unerring in his grasp of a situation, precise in his timing and impeccable in his sagacity. David held him in the highest esteem (II 15.31 f.) and Absalom followed his advice.

21. Go in to your father's concubines . . . Ahithophel regards this as an irrevocable step and this is why he wants Absalom to take it. It will make his name stink with his father. No doubt this refers to the personal humiliation of having his concubines appropriated by his son—a humiliation which is outrageous in view of the public exhibition which is made of the act (cp. II 12.11). This, Ahithophel calculated, would destroy any affection which David still had for Absalom and would make it necessary for Absalom to go on with the revolt to the bitter end. The seizing of David's concubines had further significance in that it would naturally be understood as constituting a claim to the throne. (See Commentary on II 3.7.) Ahithophel feared a late reconciliation between Absalom and David which would expose to great danger those who had thrown in their lot with the former. Once it could be seen clearly by his followers that Absalom was irrevocably committed to the revolt this sense of insecurity would disappear and morale would rise.

23. as if one consulted the oracle of God. This is an interesting description of Ahithophel's pre-eminent sagacity. It presupposes two sources of authoritative guidance. On the one hand there is the divine word which is given in response to the request for guidance and is imparted through the oracle; on the other hand there is a guidance which is a human and secular product and which is the fruit of the right use of reason. It depends on the ability to size up all the factors in a given situation and to prescribe the best course of action. These two systems of guidance are conceived as entirely separate—as two universes of truth—and the tribute paid to Ahithophel is that his shrewdness and sagacity are such that his guidance has the same quality of inerrancy as that communicated through the oracle. (Cp. Commentary on II 15, where a corresponding dichotomy in David's attitude to the locus of 'power' is noted.)

David's attitude to Shimei is theologically grounded. Abishai acts in character—a man who believes that force is the final answer to every problem. This, it appears, is a family characteristic shared by Joab (hence YOU SONS OF ZERUIAH in v. 10) and illustrated by their unrelenting determination to kill Abner so as to avenge the death of Asahel (II 2.18 f.). On another occasion Abishai would have killed Saul and finally disposed of David's arch-enemy, had he not been restrained by his master. At that time David had adduced a theological reason for his pacific attitude towards Saul (see Commentary on I 26) and his reaction to Shimei's abuse and violence is similarly regulated. Shimei may be the instrument of Yahweh in his cursing of David and, in this case, it will be part of the judgment ordained by Yahweh for David (v. 10). Although Shimei is actuated by partisan spite and hostility (he was a Benjaminite), David looks to the possibility that this experience may have a constructive significance for himself in his relations with Yahweh. LET HIM ALONE AND LET HIM CURSE, FOR THE LORD HAS BIDDEN HIM (v. 11). The way back to Jerusalem and kingship will not be easy and he must learn first to accept patiently Yahweh's judgment on his sin. He speaks as if he regards his present adversity as the working-out of the judgment prophesied by Nathan and this is an impression strengthened by the circumstance that Absalom's appropriation of his concubines appears to be a fulfilment of Nathan's threat (II 12.11 f.).

CHAPTER 17

AHITHOPHEL'S ADVICE

17.1-4

2. and discouraged Literally: 'and his hands are limp'; cp. II 4.1.

3. as a bride comes home to her husband. You seek the life of only one man. RSV follows G. MT: 'as the return of the whole is the man whom you seek'; i.e., if only David is taken, resistance to Absalom will collapse. This interpretation, however, is forced and G probably preserves the original form of the text. MT has been explained as a copyist's error.

4. and all the elders of Israel Hertzberg[1] holds that ISRAEL means the northern tribes and there is much in favour of this interpretation. It illustrates the difference between the officialdom of Jerusalem and the traditional forms of rule which were still vigorous in the north. Thus Ahithophel is one of a circle of professional advisers in the service of the court and Absalom turns to him for advice. But the northern tribes who have rallied to his cause must also have a say in important decisions and they are represented not by professional civil servants but by those who, in virtue of their seniority and eminence in the tribal structure of society, have the traditional right to deliberate and take decisions.[2] This would be another indication that the main weight of support for Absalom was in the north (cp. vv. 24, 26; see Commentary on II 15.6), although Judah was also involved (II 19.11).

HUSHAI'S ADVICE PREFERRED TO THAT OF AHITHOPHEL

17.5-14

9. And when some of the people fall at the first attack So RSV with very slight support from G. MT is preferable and should be translated as follows: 'When the attacker (i.e., David) opens an attack on them (i.e., Absalom's men), the sound of it will be heard and it will be said (by Absalom's army), "There has been slaughter among the people who follow Absalom."' This translation, however, conceals the form of the Hebrew which is such that it is the reaction of one soldier of Absalom's army which is being described. This individual is selected as representative, i.e., these same

[1] Hertzberg, *ATD in loc.*
[2] Noth, *History*, pp. 108 f.

thoughts will be occupying the mind of every individual soldier.

11. and that you go to battle in person RSV follows MT. G, S and V: 'and that you go in their midst'; i.e., Absalom should lead his army in person and not entrust the operation to Ahithophel (cp. v. 1).

12. and of him and all the men with him not one will be left Literally: 'and of him and all the men who are with him we shall not leave a single person.'

13. and we shall drag it into the valley RSV follows the Versions. IT refers to the city. MT: 'and we shall drag him (David) into the valley.' The remainder of the verse is obscure, but the meaning may be that the pebbles of the wady are to be forced beneath the surface of the ground, when the city is dragged over them. The meaning of the word translated 'pebble' is uncertain.

INTELLIGENCE BROUGHT TO DAVID

17.15-22

16. fords of the wilderness That this is the correct reading is confirmed by the suceeding verses of the chapter which show that David was advised to cross the Jordan (vv. 22, 24). The manuscripts of the Hebrew, however, support, for the most part, the reading, 'plains of the wilderness' (see BH *in loc.*; cp. II 15.28).

17. En-Rogel Groll. p. 149. Meaning 'the Fuller's spring' and situated a little south of Jerusalem.

18. But a lad saw them i.e., on this particular occasion. The tenses are correctly rendered as frequentatives by RSV and they describe the customary procedure of Jonathan and Ahimaaz. The success of David's intelligence organization depended on the ability of these two to keep under cover. Absalom would assume that they had gone with David and so would be unaware that there was a line of communication from Jerusalem to David's camp. David's plans nearly came unstuck at a vital moment.

19. and scattered grain upon it The meaning of the word rendered GRAIN is dubious. Hertzberg[3] agrees with RSV, while Smith[4] follows G^L and T and reads 'fruit'. He suggests that the woman made it appear that she was drying fruit. Köh. suggests the emendation 'grains of sand' i.e., the woman spread sand over the 'mat' or 'cover' and so the entrance to the well was camouflaged.

20. the brook of water The meaning of the word translated BROOK is not known. BH emends, 'They have crossed over from here to the water.'

21. Arise and go quickly over the water They were envisaging the possibility that Ahithophel's advice might still be taken (despite Absalom's words in v. 14).

22. RSV is inaccurate. MT should be translated, with a change in the punctuation, as follows: 'And David arose and all the people who were with him and they were crossing the Jordan up to daybreak, until everyone without exception had crossed the Jordan.

AHITHOPHEL COMMITS SUICIDE

17.23

And he set his house in order There is a subtle stroke in this portrayal. Ahithophel's mind is as clear as a bell; he knows that his advice was sound and that Absalom has preferred folly to sagacity. The unerring logic of his mind now drives him to despair, for he knows that Absalom is heading for disaster and that he is inextricably involved in his ruin. But he is a precise and impeccable thinker to the end and, before he hangs himself, he sets his affairs in order.

[3] Hertzberg, *ATD in loc.*
[4] H. P. Smith, *ICC in loc.*

DAVID IN TRANSJORDAN

17.24-29

25. had set Amasa over the army instead of Joab Cp. Commentary on II 14 and 15.11.

Ithra, the Ishmaelite RSV follows G^{A} and I Chron 2.17. MT: 'the Israelite'.

Abigal, the daughter of Nahash For 'Nahash' G^{L} reads 'Jesse' which agrees with I Chron. 2.16 f. Hertzberg[5] suggests that Nahash may have been the husband of David's mother by a previous marriage, in which case Zeruiah and Abigal were half-sisters. His alternative suggestion that 'Nahash' has strayed into this verse from v. 27 and that 'Jesse' is the correct reading is more probable. Joab and Amasa were cousins and both were nephews of David.

27. Rabbah Groll. p. 160. For Lo-Debar see Groll. p. 155 and for Rogelim, p. 161. Rabbah is the most southerly and Rogelim the most northerly of the three, with Lo-Debar lying between the two. Shobi, a member of the Ammonite royal family, was apparently the local deputy through whom David exercised his rule (cp. II 10.1 f.).

If Yahweh is not on Absalom's side (v. 14), and, if Ahithophel (whose counsel is as if one consulted the oracle of God) is, a stalemate exists. An interesting problem is posed here. Given these two separate and equally valid systems of reliable guidance (see Commentary on 16.23) in what way can Yahweh intervene so as to invalidate the advice of Ahithophel and direct events according to his will?

The answer is not found in a miraculous intervention but in the lack of discretion and judgment in those who decide between the competing policies of Ahithophel and Hushai. Ahithophel's advice shows psychological astuteness and a brilliant simplicity; Hushai's is involved and his observations are a blend of hyperbole (v. 13), banality (v. 9a), and flattery

[5] Hertzberg, *ATD in loc.*

(v. 11). His intention is to give bad advice and so in his own way he is something of an artist and succeeds in what he sets out to do. The real fools are Absalom and the elders of Israel who declare that Hushai's advice is better than Ahithophel's (v. 14) and who are completely incapable of discriminating between a bold and serious plan and the pretentious and bogus strategy of Hushai.

Ahithophel feels the anguish and impotence of the clear thinker whose plan is dropped for a nonsensical alternative. The mental confusion of Absalom and the elders of Israel makes him sick with despair, but he is powerless. His is the impotence of the wise man, when the power to make big decisions is in the hands of fools. He cannot communicate his sagacity and acumen to them and so he goes off in despair, leaving them with their preference for folly.

The irony of Absalom's situation is that he rested his cause on the sagacity of professional political advisers and that he had one adviser whose judgment was impeccable, but that neither he nor the elders of Israel had the critical acuteness to discriminate between wisdom and folly. It was by making use of this circumstance that Yahweh defeated the good counsel of Ahithophel (v. 14).

CHAPTER 18

DAVID'S BATTLE ORDERS

18.1-5

3. But you are worth ten thousand of us RSV follows G and V. MT 'For now there are ten thousand such as we' is not what the context requires. It is David who is the target of the rebels (cp. Ahithophel's proposal to Absalom in II 17.2 f.), and he ought not to expose himself unnecessarily to danger. Hence he is prevailed upon to remain with the tactical reserve. (Literally: 'You should be to us from the city to help,' following the Masoretic vocalization.)

THE DEATH OF ABSALOM

18.6-18

6. the forest of Ephraim Groll. p. 149, Ephraim (3).

7. And the men of Israel were defeated there by the servants of David Cp. ISRAEL in v. 6, and on the difficulty of ascertaining its precise meaning see the Commentary on II 15.6 and 17.4. The form of this verse would certainly lead one to suppose that the rebellion led by Absalom was a popular one and so reinforces the evidence for this conclusion already noted in II 17.4. Here the antithesis is between THE MEN OF ISRAEL and THE SERVANTS OF DAVID; i.e., David's professional soldiers, some of whom were foreigners, were drawn up against a native citizen army (cp. v. 17 and also II 19.8). Absalom had on his side the populace who were attached to the traditional forms of Israelite corporate life and who disliked David's centralized administration.

8. the forest devoured more people that day than the sword This statement is illustrated by the manner of Absalom's death and it means that the special hazards of forest warfare added considerably to the toll of casualties.

9. And Absalom chanced to meet the servants of David i.e., as he was making his way through the forest he suddenly and without warning encountered them.

and he was left hanging RSV follows G and S. MT: 'and he was set'. His fine head of hair which was the crown of his physical beauty and the symbol of his pride and arrogance was his undoing (cp. II 14.25-27, 30 f.).

11. I would have been glad This is inaccurate. Rather: 'I would have been bound', i.e., it would have been incumbent on me.

girdle A type of waistband which not only held the skirt in place but also provided a means whereby various articles such as a sword or a dagger could be carried. 'The better examples are very valuable works of the weaver's art and were probably made of wool in variegated colours.'[1] It was probably such a ceremonial girdle that Joab had in mind.

12. For my sake protect the young man RSV with G and the Versions. MT can perhaps be translated, 'Have a care, whoever you are, of the young man.'

14. I will not waste time like this with you RSV follows MT. G^L and T: 'Therefore I shall begin in your presence,' i.e., begin the process of killing Absalom.

and he took three darts . . . RSV follows G. MT: 'and he took three sticks.' The problem is to determine whether Joab killed Absalom and so refuted the allegation of the previous verse that he wanted another to do the deed, and that he was anxious not to have any part in Absalom's death in view of the angry reaction which might be expected from David; or whether this was no more than a symbolic intimation that the person of the king's son was not inviolate and so a command to his armour-bearers to do Absalom to death. In view of the sacral status of the Davidic king (cp. v. 12, I WOULD NOT PUT FORTH MY HAND AGAINST THE KING'S SON; see Commentary on II 7) it is understandable that the person of his son should have been regarded as inviolate and his killing by ten men should perhaps be regarded as an attempt to establish corporate responsibility for the act. In that case 'sticks' of MT can perhaps be retained and the words 'and thrust them into the heart of Absalom' mean no more than 'and thrust them into the midriff of Absalom', i.e., they do not indicate a mortal blow. That the Hebrew word often translated 'heart' can mean something like 'middle' is seen in the last clause of this verse, WHILE HE WAS STILL ALIVE IN THE *MIDST* OF THE OAK.[2]

18. the pillar which is in the king's valley The King's

[1] G. E. Wright, *Biblical Archaeology*, 1957, pp. 188 f.
[2] Hertzberg, ATD *in loc.*

valley is identified by Groll. (p. 162) with the Valley of Shaveh on the basis of Gen. 14.17. According to Josephus the valley lay within four hundred and forty yards of the old city of Jerusalem. The statement that Absalom had no son conflicts with II 14.27. The identification of this monument with the tomb in the Kidron valley dates, according to Hertzberg,[3] from the sixteenth century of our era. (See Groll. p. 130, plates 375-7.) Albright[4] suggests that, since the erection of a funeral stele was not normal practice in Israel, it should be traced to the influence of Absalom's Aramaean connections on his mother's side.

NEWS BROUGHT TO DAVID
18.19-33

19. The Lord has delivered him Literally: 'has judged him', i.e., has given him the verdict.

20. because the king's son is dead Joab appreciates the implications of Absalom's death and knows that David will have thoughts for nothing but the loss of his son. The word translated TIDINGS in vv. 19, 20, 22, 25, 26 means properly 'good tidings' and is so translated by RSV in v. 31. (See, however, Commentary on I 4.17 and II 18.25.) Ahimaaz, who has been the king's runner since David's evacuation of Jerusalem, wants to deliver what he regards as a final, triumphant *communiqué*, 'the good news' that the rebellion has been crushed. Joab knows that, in view of Absalom's death, his reception by David will be other than what he envisages and he may have had in mind the treatment meted out by David to two previous messengers who imagined that they were bearers of good news (II 1.1 ff.; 4.5 ff.; especially 10). To deliver such a message will not advance Ahimaaz in favour with the king, and Joab does not wish that the wrath of

[3] Hertzberg, *ATD in loc.*
[4] Albright, *ARI* p. 106.

David should descend on the young man's head. It is for this reason that he assigns the task to a negro slave.

22. seeing that you will have no reward for the tidings According to Köh. this refers to the messenger's fee. Literally: 'and to you there is no good news which will find' which S. R. Driver[5] takes to mean, 'there is no news which will bring you a reward.'

24. between the two gates i.e., in the space between the inner and outer gate.

25. If he is alone, there are tidings in his mouth Why is David so sure that a solitary messenger must be a bearer of good news (see above on v. 20)? Hertzberg[6] replies that, if many had been seen running towards the city, this would have been an indication that David's army had been defeated and was in retreat. This is not an entirely satisfactory answer, since the solitary messenger might have been bringing news that David and the reserve in the city were needed at the front (see Commentary on v. 3). It would be possible to argue that the Hebrew word means simply 'news' here and in v. 26 and that the translation 'good news' is proper only in v. 27, where the attributive adjective 'good' appears with the noun. All that David is then saying in vv. 25 and 26 is that it is safe to conclude that the solitary runner will be a messenger. But why should the identification of the runner with Ahimaaz (v. 27) make David so certain that the news was good? Smith[7] replies that he judged the character of the message from the character of the messenger, but this is not convincing.

26. called to the gate RSV follows the Versions. The meaning is that the look-out called to David who was stationed between the two gates (see Commentary on v. 24). MT: 'the gate-keeper'. This is inferior, since the look-out appears to be addressing David directly.

[5] S. R. Driver, *Notes, in loc.*
[6] Hertzberg, *ATD in loc.*
[7] H. P. Smith, *ICC in loc.*

28. Then Ahimaaz cried out to the king RSV follows MT. G^L: 'and Ahimaaz drew near to the king and said' which fits the representation of v. 27 better, since Ahimaaz has still some distance to cover before reaching David. This would require the emendation of one word in MT.

29. When Joab sent your servant, I saw a great tumult MT: 'I saw the great commotion at Joab's sending the servant of the king and your servant.' This does not make good sense, and S. R. Driver[8] suggests that 'the servant of the king' may be a gloss intended to correct the less courtly 'your servant'. The best of the suggested emendations is that of BH: 'I saw the great commotion when Joab, the servant of the king, sent your servant.' It is impossible to believe that Ahimaaz was unable to answer David's question and so it must be concluded that he sensed the atmosphere of the interview and grasped the significance of Joab's dissuasive. Hence his deliberately evasive answer that he was unaware of the circumstances of Absalom's death.

The fascination of this chapter lies in the contrasting attitudes of David and Joab towards Absalom. Both behave in character. David allows his feelings as a father to swamp all other considerations and fails to confront political realities. He acts in the same way as he had done in refusing to punish Amnon for the rape of Tamar (see Commentary on II 13.21). Joab puts the safety of the state first as he had done in his advice to David to recall Absalom. It is true that he has changed his mind about Absalom, but, in making this change, he is guided by the same criteria as had influenced him to procure Absalom's return from exile. Then he had thought that, in the interests of political stability, the question of succession must be settled and he had believed that Absalom was the most promising candidate for the throne. Now he knew that he had been wrong, but it is to his credit that he had seen his mistake and had not been implicated in Absalom's sedition. It may be suspected that from the moment

[8] S. R. Driver, *Notes, in loc.*

that Absalom petulantly set his field on fire, Joab had doubts about his fitness as a future king. Now it was clear that he had been in too much of a hurry to grasp power—unwilling to let his father die as king.

Joab's posture is therefore open-eyed and realistic. Absalom has endangered the very existence of the state by a wild-cat rebellion and is far too bad a political risk to be allowed to live. It is unlikely that there was any element of personal revenge or vendetta in the killing, although it is true that, as a leading member of David's officialdom, he had personal reasons for disliking the leader of a popular rebellion (see Commentary on v. 7). His job was at stake. Nevertheless his consistency is impressive and he is in no mood to apologize to David for his decision. In his dealings with his children David loses all sense of proportion and Joab has deliberately ignored his instructions (v. 5). Nor is he slow in justifying his decision, for he has no time for a king who allows his private feelings to destroy his political judgment.

CHAPTER 19

JOAB REPROACHES DAVID

19.1-8a

3. and the people This refers to those who had fought the battle on David's behalf and so principally to the professional soldiers. The verse points to an incongruous state of affairs arising from David's preoccupation with his private sorrow. The victorious soldiers slink into Mahanaim like thieves as if they had been disgraced on the field of battle and, instead of being welcomed and acclaimed by David as the saviours of the state, are ignored by him.

5. who have this day saved your life . . . Joab no doubt means this quite literally in relation to David and the royal family. He is convinced that Absalom would have instituted a general purge in order to increase the security of his own position by disposing of all rival claimants to the throne. David's harem, on the other hand, would no doubt have been appropriated by Absalom. (See Commentary on II 3.7; 16.21.)

6. that commanders and servants are nothing to you Joab is speaking here of David's cadre of royal officials. COMMANDERS could mean the high officers of his mercenary army or his leading political advisers. In the context it probably means the former and SERVANTS refers to the general body of mercenary soldiers. It was this army that stood between David and the treachery and ruthlessness of Absalom, but now David is so unbalanced by his private grief that he cannot distinguish between his friends and enemies. Joab warns him that his professional soldiers are not the kind of men who will endure his fickleness and advises him that he has come near to committing political suicide (v. 7). He cannot do without his professional army, as the Absalom revolt had conclusively demonstrated, for there is no fund of popular goodwill on which he can draw for the continuance of his regime. Hence he had better arouse himself from his mourning for Absalom and show himself to his soldiers so as to indicate his appreciation of their distinguished services to his throne (v. 8).

ISRAEL'S ALLEGIANCE RETURNS TO DAVID

19.8b-10

9. the tribes of Israel This must refer to the northern tribes (cp. JUDAH in v. 11; see Commentary on II 15.6; 17.4; 18.7).

The king delivered us . . . This is the voice of the people and the YOU of v. 10 must refer to the elders of Israel. This is therefore a popular criticism among the northern tribes of the handling of the situation by their elders. The elders are not criticized for having anointed Absalom as king; on the contrary, the people accept their share of responsibility for this decision. Thus: BUT ABSALOM WHOM *WE* ANOINTED OVER

US . . . (v. 10). They are, however, criticized for their delay in restoring the allegiance of the north to David. In the wake of the failure of Absalom's revolt the people of the north were sufficiently sobered to recall to themselves the virtues of David as a king (v. 9).

DAVID ASKS FOR THE ALLEGIANCE OF JUDAH
19.11-15

11. Say to the elders of Judah It is clear that David was alienated from his own tribe also and that Judah had followed Absalom. That David had depended entirely on his professional soldiers for the crushing of the revolt is confirmed by v. 14, where Judah says to David: RETURN BOTH YOU AND ALL YOUR SERVANTS. For SERVANTS see Commentary on v. 6. This is a further indication of the hiatus between David's centralized administration and the traditional institutions of Israelite corporate life. In addressing the elders of Judah David seeks a reconciliation with those in whom authority was vested according to the old order, so that he may recover a popular basis for his rule. Hence he appeals to the old tribal bond—the cement of kinship. RSV follows MT except that the former deletes TO HIS HOUSE after COME TO THE KING. Perhaps WHEN THE WORD OF ALL ISRAEL HAS COME TO THE KING should be transposed to the end of v. 10 with G (this would furnish the antithesis of 'silence' [saying nothing] and 'word'). In this case we should have to suppose that TO HIS HOUSE at the end of v. 11 is repeated in error from the middle of the verse.[1] Alternatively BH suggests the transposition of TO HIS HOUSE, WHEN THE WORD OF ALL ISRAEL HAS COME TO THE KING to the end of v. 10.

13. And say to Amasa . . . David's decision to depose Joab from the command of the army and to appoint Amasa is astonishing and indefensible. The reason which he appears to give is no reason at all, for Joab was as much his kinsman

[1] So. S. R. Driver, *Notes, in loc.*

as Amasa. (See Commentary on II 17.25.) The army which Joab commanded was probably the tribal militia[2] and it is clear from II 17.25 that this force had followed Absalom. The significance of the statement in II 17.25 that Absalom had set Amasa over the army instead of Joab (cp. II 8.16) is that Joab had remained loyal to David and that the ARMY was consequently leaderless. The fact that Joab had resisted the pull of the force which he commanded and had refused to be an acomplice in the rebellion must enhance our estimate of his devotion to David's regime—an estimate which does not depreciate because there were elements of self-interest in his stand. (See Commentary on II 18.7.) It might therefore be concluded that David acts in a fit of pique against Joab who has crossed him and hurt his pride by uttering a few home truths. If the decision had any political significance at all, it must be interpreted as an attempt to conciliate the rebellious militia by permitting them to keep the commander who had led them in the revolt.[3] Even so it would be hard to find any wisdom in such a decision. A king who punishes a commander for his loyalty and rewards another for his sedition is not one who will inspire confidence in his subordinates.

DAVID SPARES SHIMEI

19.16-23

18. and they crossed the ford . . . RSV follows G. S. R. Driver[4] is inclined to follow G, but suggests as a possible rendering of MT: 'And the ferry boat kept passing over.'

19. let not the king bear it in mind Or: 'that the king should take it into account.' Cp. Commentary on II 16.5 ff.

20. the house of Joseph Referring strictly to the tribes of Ephraim and Manasseh,[5] but used here more loosely of all

[2] Noth, *History*, p. 198.
[3] Cp. J. Bright, *History*, pp. 188 f.
[4] S. R. Driver, *Notes, in loc.*
[5] Noth, *History*, pp. 58 f.

the northern tribes, i.e., of the ten tribes mentioned in v. 43.

21. Shall not Shimei be put to death? Abishai is still of the same mind as he was when the incident involving Shimei took place. (See Commentary on II 16.) It is interesting that he adduces a theological reason as he did also in urging David to kill Saul. (See Commentary on I 26.8.) On that occasion David had countered him with another theological consideration—the sanctity of Yahweh's anointed. It is this which is here pressed into service by Abishai as a reason for killing Shimei.

22. What have I to do with you, you sons of Zeruiah? Cp. Commentary on II 16.10. David felt that he had nothing in common with the ruthless streak which he saw in both Abishai and Joab. Abishai's unyielding hardness towards Shimei is coupled by David with Joab's refusal of mercy to Absalom. They are manifestations of the same hardness which in his present mood he cannot bear.

MEPHIBOSHETH EXPLAINS

19.24-30

25. And when he came from Jerusalem MT: 'When Jerusalem came', i.e., when the inhabitants of Jerusalem came. G: 'When he entered Jerusalem'. Neither reading is satisfactory and what the context requires is the reading of RSV which rests on a conjectural emendation.

27. slandered Cp. II 16.1 ff. There is no means of ascertaining whether the truth was with Ziba or Mephibosheth and this seems to be the conclusion which is reflected in David's decision to divide the land between the two of them.

like the angel of God A tribute to David's wisdom and to his ability to sift the evidence so as to arrive at the truth. Cp. II 14.17, 20 and Commentary on II 16.23 (oracle of God).

DAVID AND BARZILLAI

19.31-40

35. Can I discern what is pleasant and what is not? Barzillai is a wealthy man and was able to help David in his extremity (II 17.27), but it is an uncomplicated patriarchal grandeur which he has enjoyed and he has no desire to exchange this in his old age for the sophisticated life at court. Hence he graciously declines David's offer to make him into a courtier.

38. and all that you desire of me More accurately: 'and all that you choose (and lay) upon me'.

40. brought the king on his way RSV follows MT. G: 'were crossing with the king.'

ISRAEL COMPLAINS

19.41-43

42. Because the king is near of kin to us An answer which would increase rather than allay the suspicions of the northern tribes, since it was essential that they should be reassured that David's special kin relationship to the tribe of Judah would not be reflected in his rule over an inter-tribal society (cp. Commentary on I 22.6). The responsibility for this lack of wisdom must rest ultimately on David, since he had invoked the bond of kinship in asking for the return of Judah's allegiance.[6]

43. ten shares The other tribe excluded with Judah can hardly be Benjamin and may be Simeon[7] about which little is known, but which evidently was settled in the far south.

and in David also we have more than you RSV follows MT. G: 'and also I am first-born (and more senior) than you.'

[6] Cp. Noth, *History*, p. 202.
[7] Cp. Noth, *ibid.*, p. 58.

A noteworthy feature of the History of Succession is the impression of objectivity which it gives. It is not tendentious, nor does it strive to enlist the sympathy of the reader for one side or the other, and the factual character of the narrative in the present instance enables us to grasp the nature of the conflict betwen David and Joab. David, a heart-broken father, is in no mood to be lectured to on what is politically expedient or to be reminded of the first principles of statesmanship. All his achievements as a soldier and politician seem hollow and unreal in this moment of bitter personal sorrow. His strong love as a father swamps every other consideration and he discovers that the life of Absalom meant more to him than the survival of the state which he has built. He assigns priority to the narrow circle of the family and to the unique relationship between a father and a son and he will not accept Joab's doctrine that it was expedient for Absalom to die in order to save the state.

Yet he does not abdicate from political responsibility and he is deeply in the debt of Joab and his professional soldiers. If he had accepted all the conclusions of his discovery that his son meant more to him than his throne, he would have won even more of our sympathy. But he clings to power, only he exercises it while under the influence of tumultuous emotions. To his enemies he is the soul of magnanimity and clemency; he will show mercy to the friends of Absalom where Joab refused to show mercy to Absalom. But his clemency is warped, for, while he overflows with forgiveness to the seditious, he shows a barbed hostility to his friends and ignores the army which shielded him from Absalom's treachery. He resents the straight speaking of Joab and deposes him for a rebel. This, although the political wisdom of his words are above question and although he has served the king with unswerving loyalty. It is not Joab's fault that a state does not exercise mercy to one who has acted treasonably against it. All that he does is to observe the rules laid down by states for their security and he ignores David's order, as he did on a previous occasion (see Commentary on II 11.16

f.), because he believed that it was improper and that David was allowing his feelings as a father to corrupt his political responsibility as a king.

The intention of the narrative is not to apportion blame, but to reveal—and this it does with great psychological insight—the conflict between private feelings and public responsibility in which a statesman may be involved. If Absalom had been another man's son, David would have had no scruples about exacting the penalty for his treason, for then there would have been no inner conflict and he would have made his decision *qua* statesman. But Absalom was David's son and so he was involved both *qua* father and *qua* statesman, and was unable to take a detached view of his crime against the state. He was unable to disassociate himself from a father's love for Absalom in judging what the leader of a crushed rebellion deserved, and this was the root of his conflict with Joab.

CHAPTER 20

SHEBA INCITES ISRAEL TO REVOLT

20.1-2

1. worthless See Commentary on I 1.16.

JOAB ASSASSINATES AMASA

20.3-10a

3. and put them in a house under guard . . . These are the concubines with whom Absalom had had sexual intercourse and it is in consequence of this that David will have no further relations with them. Not only, however, are they now taboo to David but also to every other man. SHUT UP may indicate not only physical isolation but also the consequence of this, namely, denial of all sexual intercourse.[1] LIVING AS

[1] Köh., *in loc.*

IF IN WIDOWHOOD is an attempt to render MT, which is literally 'widowhood of livingness'—an obscure phrase. G: 'living widows'. T: 'widows of a living man'. Hertzberg[2], 'in widowhood for the lifetime (of a man)', claims the support of G for his rendering, although it seems to be nearer to T. If Hertzberg's rendering is accepted, the meaning is that David intended to shut up the concubines for the remainder of his life. Hertzberg cites Tamar as a parallel, but her case is different, since she has to live like a widow in her brother's house because Amnon has abandoned her (see Commentary on II 13.13). It is not clear whether the isolation of the concubines is to be understood primarily in relation to David or whether their connection is rather with the death of Absalom. Hertzberg is of the opinion that the first alternative is correct and so he interprets the segregation as a widowhood for the duration of David's life. But perhaps it is the death of Absalom which explains David's action; Absalom had appropriated these concubines and now that he is dead they are taboo to every other man, including David himself.

5. which had been appointed him Literally: 'which he (David) had fixed for him.'

6. And David said to Abishai S has 'Joab' for 'Abishai' and this is preferred by S. R. Driver[3] on the ground that the mention of Joab in person and not simply the men of Joab (v. 7) is desiderated prior to v. 8. However MT makes good sense here and it should not be set aside. Joab has been deposed from commanding the militia and is in deep disfavour with David and it may be for this reason that Abishai is in charge of this force of professional soldiers. It is true that he was no favourite of David (see Commentary on II 16.10; 19.22), but he may have been less objectionable than Joab at that moment.

take your lord's servants and pursue him On SERVANTS

[2] Hertzberg, *ATD in loc.*
[3] S. R. Driver, *Notes, in loc.*

see Commentary on II 15.14; 18.7. David's plan had been to crush the Sheba revolt not with his professional soldiers but with the militia of Judah and so he sent Amasa, the newly appointed commander, to mobilize this force. Amasa was not able to acomplish this as expeditiously as David required and there was the danger that the situation might get out of hand, if it were not dealt with swiftly and decisively. In order to crush the revolt and to disperse the rebels before they became entrenched David called on his professional soldiers. The second decision was taken because of the need for swift military action, while the first was influenced by political considerations.

and cause us trouble MT: 'and deliver our eye'. G: 'and shade our eyes'. S: 'and pluck out our eyes'. AV margin, 'deliver himself from our eyes', is not a legitimate paraphrase; nor is RV, 'escape out of our sight'. (This is what Köh. suggests on the basis of an emended text.) It may be legitimate to render MT, 'and tear away our eye', that is, damage us irretrievably (which agrees with S). RSV is based on T.

7. Joab RSV is based on G. MT, 'men of Joab', should be retained; cp. v. 11. This was a composite professional force and it included Joab's own troop. It also included Cherethites and Pelethites (see Commentary on II 8.18) of whom Benaiah was the commander[4] (II 8.18; 20.23).

and all the mighty men MIGHTY MEN are professional soldiers who are technically excellent and who have the martial virtues of courage and valour (cp. Commentary on I 9.1).

8. the great stone which is in Gibeon Probably an altar, as Robertson Smith[5] suggests; cp. Commentary on I 6.18. On Gibeon see Groll. p. 150.

Now Joab was wearing . . . MT is obscure but it is better

[4] Noth, *History*, p. 198 n. 4.
[5] W. R. Smith, *ROS* p. 203.

to retain it, for the most part, than to emend conjecturally. G, 'it (the sword) came out and fell' should perhaps be preferred, since MT (followed by RSV) is grammatically doubtful.[6] The girdle is a sword-belt (see Commentary on II 18.11). The general sense is not in doubt—Joab tricked Amasa into believing that he was disarmed.

PURSUIT AND DEATH OF SHEBA

20.10b-22

11. Whoever favours Joab and whoever is for David . . . Joab, following his assassination of Amasa, is now the leader of the expedition against Sheba. (Note the order in v. 10b, JOAB AND ABISHAI.) One of Joab's men (see Commentary on v. 7), standing over the bleeding Amasa, urges THE PEOPLE (v. 12) to follow Joab. But who are THE PEOPLE? It is unlikely that he is addressing any of the force of professionals who had come out from Jerusalem with Abishai and Joab, since this exhortation would be superfluous for them. It is more probable that THE PEOPLE are the militia of Judah who would be acompanying Amasa (see Commentary on II 19.13) when he joined up with the other force at Gibeon. This is therefore the next step by Joab after his assassination of Amasa; it is his attempt to reassume the command from which he has been deposed and he is at pains to make it clear that he is not taking over the militia as an act of disloyalty to David (as Amasa had done when he was appointed by Absalom). A confirmation of this interpretation is found in v. 22 from which it appears that the militia as well as the professional soldiers were engaged in the siege of Abel. Thus: AND THEY DISPERSED . . . EVERY MAN TO HIS HOME (literally, 'tent', cp. Commentary on 18.7). AND JOAB RETURNED TO JERUSALEM TO THE KING. The form of this exhortation (WHOEVER FAVOURS JOAB . . .) may, however, have been the result of hurried improvisation and it is perhaps unwise to read it as a carefully worded formula. Its main purpose, as v. 12 seems to

[6] So. S. R. Driver, *Notes, in loc.*

suggest, was to distract the attention of the militiamen from the bleeding Amasa and, since it did not do this effectively, he was subsequently carried out of view.

14. to Abel of Beth Maacah MT is corrupt and the emendation presupposed by RSV is necessary. The city is in the far north of Palestine (Groll. p. 140).

and all the Bichrites assembled i.e., the men of Sheba's clan (v. 1). MT: 'to Abel and Beth Maacah and they despised him (or, 'and they were assembled') and they entered after him.' This makes no sense and there is no alternative but to make a conjecture at the original. RSV represents the best that can be done.

15. and all the men who were with Joab came This gives the correct sense, but it is exegesis rather than translation. MT: 'And they came and besieged him . . .' Verse 14 (emended) refers to the entry of Sheba and his supporters into Abel and v. 15 reverts to the pursuers.

and it stood against the rampart IT is the mound. The word translated RAMPART has been taken to mean 'outer wall' (Hertzberg)[7], and S. R. Driver[8] suggests that it may refer to the space between the outer and inner walls occupied by the moat (cp. Köh.).

and they were battering the wall to throw it down Or: they were doing demolition work to bring it down.' G: 'they were laying plans to bring it down.'

16. a wise woman Cp. the wise woman of Tekoa, II 14.1 f.

18-19. RSV follows MT. G (reconstructed) reads: 'Let them ask in Abel and in Dan whether what the faithful in Israel had established ever came to an end'; i.e., Abel and Dan were cities famed for their attachment to traditional Israelite ways and for their nurturing of the old values of life. Eissfeldt[9]

[7] Hertzberg, *ATD in loc.*
[8] S. R. Driver, *Notes, in loc.*
[9] Eissfeldt, *Einleitung*, pp. 152 f.

takes the point to be that these two towns had remained loyal to traditional Israelite ways of life despite their location in an area occupied by Aramaeans. If this is so, the proverb presupposes the event recorded in I Kings 15.20 and originated subsequent to *c.* 900 BC. This, Eissfeldt suggests, may be a pointer that the History of Succession was written subsequent to 900 BC.

a mother in Israel i.e., a metropolis, a walled city with a surrounding rural area in its jurisdiction. In time of danger the inhabitants of the villages could retire for protection behind its walls.

21. That is not true Or: 'That is not the point.'

22. Then the woman went to all the people RSV follows MT. G: 'And she went in to all the people and she spoke to all the city.' S. R. Driver[10] thinks that this is a conflation of two readings and that the latter is original. He would emend MT accordingly.

LIST OF DAVID'S OFFICIALS

20.23-26

23. all the army of Israel This presupposes a small emendation of MT. The original may have been simply 'all the army', i.e., the militia; cp. II 8.16. See Commentary on II 19.13. It thus appears that Joab has successfully restored his position (see Commentary on v. 11).

Cherethites The Hebrew consonantal text reads 'Carians' and the Masoretic vocalization 'Cherethites', in agreement with II 8.18 (see Commentary *in loc.*).

24. And Adoram was in charge of the forced labour This is an addition to the list of II 8.15 ff. and an indication that David had followed the practice of oriental kings in respect of the imposition of *corvée*—forced labour. This was a

[10] S. R. Driver, *Notes, in loc.*

demand which did great violence to Israelite feelings concerning the rights and liberty of the individual and it became a burning social issue in Solomon's reign, since he used it on a large scale in connection with his many building projects (I Kings 5.13 f.). Adoram (Adoniram in I Kings 4.6 and 5.14; Adoram in I Kings 12.18) continued in this office under Solomon and the measure of detestation which he inspired is seen from the circumstance that he was stoned to death at the division of the kingdom (I Kings 12.18). It is probable that this list which includes Adoram belongs to the latter part of David's reign, while that in II 8.16 ff. derives from the earlier part of the reign,[11] although Smith[12] has held that the longer list is the earlier and that the name of Adoram has been expunged from the list in II 8.16 ff. in order that an institution damaging to David's reputation might not be seen to have existed during his reign. Bentzen[13] holds that II 20.23-26 is a doublet of II 8.16-18 and is out of place in its present context.

25. Sheva Seraiah in II 8.17, Shisha in I Kings 4.3 and Shavsha in I Chron. 18.16. It has been argued that Shavsha is the original form of the name and that it is Egyptian.[14]

26. Ira, the Jairite Another addition to the list of II 8.16 ff. 'Jair' was the name of a group of villages of Manasseh in Gilead (Groll. p. 151, Havvoth-Jair). Ira may have become attached to David's establishment during the latter's stay in Gilead (II 17.24 ff.); cp. Chimham, II 19.37-40.

The narrative is still factual in character, although it deals with events which invite opinion. It is notable that no judgment is passed on Joab for his murder of Amasa, although the reader can hardly fail to understand what Joab's motives were from the way in which the episode is described (see Commentary on v. 11). His action is such that we can appre-

[11] So Noth, *History*, pp. 210 f., 217; Bright, *History*, p. 184.
[12] H. P. Smith. *ICC. in loc.*
[13] Bentzen. *Introduction* II, p. 94.
[14] Bright, *History*, p. 184 n. 47.

ciate why David saw him as a hard and ruthless man (see Commentary on II 16.10; 19.22), and the image of his statesmanlike behaviour projected by the previous chapters is somewhat tarnished. He is a man who will stop at nothing to regain his position of supremacy in David's military establishment and who has no intention of accepting his deposition meekly. The notice at the end of the chapter (v. 23) would indicate that he attained his objective.

This chapter tends to suggest that there was more involved in David's deposition of Joab than the latter's killing of Absalom and the former's highly emotional state. David, it would seem, was seeking a broader, popular basis for his rule in the light of the experience of the Absalom revolt and was proposing to reduce his dependence on his professional soldiers. He could not look to Joab to implement a policy which was detrimental to the latter's own position, since he was concerned that David's rule should continue to be based on the effectiveness of his professional army. Hence David relieved him of the command of the militia (see Commentary on II 19.13), and replaced him with an officer who had led this force in the Absalom revolt and in whom the militiamen might be expected to have some confidence.

The Sheba revolt was an opportunity for David to try out his new policy and so he instructed Amasa to mobilize the militia of Judah (v. 4) and to crush the rebellion. But his initiative did not produce quick enough results and, when he became anxious about the military situation, he fell back on his professional soldiers (see Commentary on v. 6). David in fact chose the wrong kind of situation to exercise this type of initiative and the political wisdom of his decision was dubious. Nothing could have served more to exacerbate the inter-tribal rivalry of north and south than the use of the militia of Judah (his own tribe) to put down a rebellion among the northern tribes (cp. II 19.41-43). In this situation there were political as well as military reasons why he should have used his professional force which was not directly involved in the inter-tribal squabble between north and south.

APPENDIX

II 21-24

CHAPTER 21

FAMINE AND ITS CURE

21.1-14

1. sought the face of the Lord i.e., asked for a divine decision through the oracle. (See Commentary on I 23.)

there is blood-guilt on Saul and on his house This is in agreement with G and presupposes a different word division of MT which, unaltered, reads: 'on Saul and on the house of blood'.

because he put the Gibeonites to death See Commentary on II 4.1-3.

2. had sworn to spare them Literally: 'had sworn with reference to them' which means 'had entered into a treaty relationship with them' (see Commentary on II 4.3). The treaty made provision for the co-existence of Israel and the Gibeonite confederacy, but Saul was not prepared to countenance the existence of foreign enclaves on Israelite soil and was no longer willing to honour the treaty.

3. how shall I make expiation? Or: 'restitution', 'reparation'. The basic idea of the root would seem to be 'to cover' and a noun formed from it can mean 'ransom' or 'bribe'. This is the sense which seems to have suggested itself immediately to the Gibeonites, since their first reaction is to tell David that reparation cannot be made by a money payment (v. 4).

4. neither is it for us to put any man to death in Israel This has been taken to mean: (*a*) There is no man in Israel whom we would desire to put to death. (*b*) We have not the right to put a man to death in Israel. (*b*) is surely correct and the meaning is that the right of blood revenge operates only among members of the same community and that the Gibeonites are not fully entitled citizens of Israel. Even if it be supposed that they had some such rights *de jure* in virtue of their treaty with Israel, it would have been suicidal for them in their position of numerical inferiority to take such arbitrary action.[1] The second and more practical consideration was probably the one which weighed most heavily with them, since they had no scruples about executing revenge on Saul's family, provided that David assumed responsibility for handing them over. Hertzberg[2] suggests that 'seven' has significance as a sacred number (v. 6).

5. and planned to destroy us An emendation of MT on the basis of G which is usually accepted.

6. that we may hang them up The meaning of this verb is obscure. Robertson Smith,[3] on the basis of a cognate Arabic root, suggests that the literal meaning is 'cause to fall', and thinks that Saul's sons were put to death by being forced to leap from a rock. (It is certainly the case that their corpses were exposed on a rock, see v. 10.) Smith's suggestion, however, has not won general acceptance.[4] Köh. suggests 'to expose with arms and legs broken' and Cazelles[5] argues that the reference is to a rite of dismemberment.

at Gibeon on the mountain of the Lord MT: 'at Gibeah of Saul, the chosen of Yahweh'. G: 'At Gibeon of Saul, the chosen of Yahweh'. The emendation on which RSV rests is commonly followed. The corruption of Gibeon (still preserved in G) into Gibeah encouraged the further corruption of the text. (So S. R. Driver.[6]) There is a double mention of

[1] H. Cazelles, *PEQ* 87, 1955, p. 170.
[2] Hertzberg, *ATD in loc.*
[3] W. R. Smith, *ROS* p. 419 n. 2.
[4] Cp. S. R. Driver, *Notes, in loc.*
[5] Cazelles, *op. cit.*, p. 168.
[6] S. R. Driver, *Notes, in loc.*

Yahweh; Saul's sons are to be put to death BEFORE YAHWEH . . . ON THE mountain of Yahweh (it was at Gibeon that Yahweh appeared to Solomon [I Kings 3.5; 9.2] and it may be conjectured that the sacredness of this mountain derived from its being a place of theophany), and thus Yahweh is associated with this act of restitution. The reason for this must be that Yahweh had been a party to the original treaty between the Israelites and Gibeonites and so was implicated in Saul's breach of faith. It was a treaty which had been concluded in Yahweh's name and so the act of reparation must also be carried out in his presence and at his sanctuary. Hence Saul's act was a sin against Yahweh and the famine is a judgment of Yahweh on Israel.

7. because of the oath of the Lord . . . See Commentary on I 20.14-17 and II 9.

8. Merab MT: 'Michal', which is obviously incorrect. The emendation is supported by two Hebrew manuscripts, G^L and S; cp. I 18.19.

The king took . . . It has been held that Shimei had this in mind when he denounced David as a man of blood[7] (II 16.7 f.) and that David had political as well as pious motives for this decimation of the house of Saul. Cazelles[8] has pointed out, however, that the seven handed over here cannot be regarded as the most dangerous contenders for David's throne. They are made up of two sons of a concubine of Saul and five sons of his daughter. More menacing from David's point of view were the descendants of Saul's sons (I 14.49; 31.2) and Cazelles suggests that they had already been liquidated.

9. in the first days of harvest MT: 'In the days of harvest, in the first days'.

at the beginning of barley harvest i.e., April or early May, so that from then to the beginning of the autumn rains (v. 10) would be a period of some six months.

[7] Cp. Bright, *History*, p. 187.
[8] H. Cazelles, *PEQ* 87, p. 172.

12. the men of Jabesh-gilead See II 2.4b.

from the public square of Bethshan RSV follows MT. G^L: 'from the wall of Bethshan'.

14. And they buried the bones of Saul . . . MT does not state explicitly that the bones of the seven were also buried, but G has a fuller text and reads: 'and those who were exposed' (or, 'hung up').

EXPLOITS AGAINST THE PHILISTINES
21.15-22

15. and David grew weary RSV follows MT. It has been argued[9] that the words AND DAVID GREW WEARY are a corruption of the name of a Philistine, and of a verb such as 'and he arose'. It has been held further that ISHBIBENOB of v. 16 is a corruption of 'and they stayed (so the Masoretic vocalization of the Hebrew consonantal text) at Gob' (emending 'Nob' to 'Gob'; cp. v. 18 where AGAIN would seem to imply the previous mention of Gob). With this phrase transposed to v. 15 the reconstructed passage reads: 'And David with his men went down and stayed at Gob and they fought against the Philistines, and X, one of the descendants of the giants, whose spear weighed three hundred shekels of bronze, and who was girded with a new sword, thought to kill David.'

16. a new sword SWORD is a conjectural insertion. G: 'club'.

17. lest you quench the lamp of Israel On the key position of the king in the community see the Commentary on II 7; cp. II 18.3. The readiest elucidation of the metaphor is the lamp which burned continually outside the veil in the tabernacle according to Ex. 27.20 and Lev. 24.2. It is likely that this was symbolic of the constant presence of God in the sanctuary. It is described as 'a statute for ever to be observed

[9] S. R. Driver, *Notes, in loc.*

throughout their generations by the people of Israel' (Ex. 27.21; Lev. 24.3), and it is the responsibility of the Aaronic priesthood to tend the sacred flame. The Exodus passage is usually attributed to P and the Leviticus passage is part of the so-called Code of Holiness. It seems a safe assumption that the lamp which burned continually was a feature of the Jerusalem temple and, since this was a royal chapel, it may be asked if the lamp was not a royal symbol in the Jerusalem cult. This view receives strong support from I Kings 11.36; 15.4 ('that David, my servant may always have a lamp before me in Jerusalem'). This lamp, always burning, may have continued to symbolize the constant presence of Yahweh in his sanctuary, but it was also a symbol of the enduring covenant between Yahweh and the Davidic dynasty (see Commentary on II 7), on which the welfare and prosperity of the Israelite community were thought to hinge. It may have been more than a symbol in the sense that the tending of the flame in the cult was believed to be an effective guarantee that the welfare of the community would be constantly maintained and so it was of vital social importance that it should not go out[10] (cp. Ps. 132.17).

19. Elhanan, the son of Jaareoregim RSV follows MT. There is little doubt that this should read: 'Elhanan, the son of Jair' (according to II 23.24, 'son of Dodo', but see I Chron. 20.5), although 'Elhanan, the son of Jesse' has been suggested on the ground that we have here the personal name of David, the latter being a throne name. If this were so, there would be no conflict between this passage and I 17 f. according to which David killed Goliath.[11] Otherwise it has to be assumed that we have two different accounts of the same incident and in that case it is likely that this is the earlier and that the heroic exploit was subsequently attracted to David, the hero *par excellence*.[12] According to I Chron. 20.5, which is an

[10] Cp. A. R. Johnson, *Sacral Kingship in Ancient Israel*, pp. 1 f.
[11] Cp. G. E. Wright, *Biblical Archaeology*, p. 124 n. 1; Bright, *History*, p. 172 n. 21.
[12] Bentzen, *Introduction* I, p. 240.

attempt at harmonization, it was Lahmi, a brother of Goliath, who was slain by Elhanan.

a weaver's beam See Commentary on I 17.7.

Cazelles[13] thinks that there are some features in this chapter which are best explained by the assumption that what is described in vv. 1-14 is a Canaanite fertility rite designed to end drought (and so famine). The seasonal ritual has been historicized and applied to the special case of blood guilt incurred by Saul's house in relation to the Gibeonites and it is this which explains the connection existing in the chapter between blood guilt and famine. Cazelles[14] cites a passage from an Ugaritic[15] text where the dismemberment of Moth by Anat is described in terms of agricultural operations, so that its relationship to fertility is unmistakable. Anat tosses Moth in the winnowing fan, scorches him in the fire, crushes him in the mill-stones and sows him in the field. This is mythology, but Cazelles argues that it presupposes a Canaanite harvest festival at which a human body was sacrificed and dismembered in order to put an end to drought.

There are one or two points which are immediately raised by this interpretation. If this were a seasonal festival, the drought for which an end was sought *cannot* be regarded as having been exceptional. In this case the intention of the rite can only have been to bring on the regular autumn rains, and it would appear from the description in the Ugaritic passage to have had the more general function of ensuring continuing fertility and of guaranteeing the next harvest. It is therefore not clear that such a ritual is particularly related to famine conditions and the point of this chapter is that a famine has existed for three years (v. 1).

Cazelles[16] finds further support for his interpretation in the fact that the coming of the rain ends the need for Rizpah's

[13] H. Cazelles, *PEQ* 87, pp. 165 f.
[14] Cazelles, *ibid.*, pp. 169 f.
[15] *Baal* iii, Col. ii, 35-37. G. R. Driver, *CML* pp. 110 f.
[16] Cazelles, *op. cit.*, p. 167.

vigil and he supposes that this is only intelligible on the assumption that, with the coming of the rain, the end of the rite has been achieved. This, however, is not what the passage *now* means and its present meaning is the commentator's primary concern. In asking, 'Why does the coming of the rain end the need for Rizpah's vigil?' Cazelles asks the wrong question. The intention of the author is not to ascribe this kind of significance to the coming of the rain. For him it is no more than a time reference. 'from the barley harvest to the coming of the rain' is simply a way of saying 'for a period of about six months' and the reason why she did not need to continue her vigil beyond this limit is indicated in the narrative. Nothing was left of the corpses but the bones and the danger of defilement by birds was past.

In any case Cazelles[17] recognizes that the extant narrative no longer has the meaning which he thinks originally attached to it and so we may ask, 'What meaning does it *now* have?' First of all let us deal with the connection between blood guilt and famine. Cain, because he slew Abel, was banished from the area of the sown (Gen. 4.14) and was forbidden to practise agriculture. The voice of Abel's blood cried from the soil (Gen. 4.10) and Yahweh said to Cain: 'When you till the soil, it shall no longer yield to you its strength' (Gen. 4.12). God made a covenant with Noah and guaranteed that the natural order of the created world would not again be destroyed by a cataclysmic flood and that nature in its ordered courses would support human life on the earth (Gen. 9.1-3). But with this promise is coupled a demand: 'Whoever sheds the blood of man by man shall his blood be shed' (Gen. 9.6). The continuance of nature in its regular processes is conditional on the operation of the law of blood revenge (cp. Gen. 4). (See Commentary on v. 6.)

The intention of this chapter is to portray David sympathetically. The country faces a desperate situation (v. 1) and David, having sought the guidance of Yahweh, conscientiously endeavours to fulfil his requirements. The Gibeonites are

[17] Cazelles, *ibid.* pp. 174 f.

adamant that they will not accept money and so David has no alternative but to hand over the seven Saulides whom they demand. He is moved by the superb devotion of Rizpah and he combines his recognition of this with an act of piety towards Saul and Jonathan. If there were political motives at work (Cazelles[18] suggests that the burial at Zela was a gesture of appeasement towards the Gibeonites), this is not evident in the extant narrative.

CHAPTER 22

This, with textual variants, is the same as Psalm 18 and its detailed treatment may be left to the volume on the Psalms corresponding to this one. The question of the meaning of the psalm in its present context is dealt with in the Commentary on ch. 23.

CHAPTER 23

THE LAST WORDS OF DAVID

23.1-7

1. who was raised on high Or, 'whom the Most High raised'[1] which, however, requires a change in the Masoretic vocalization.

3. Rock On God as Rock see Commentary on I 2.2.

when one rules justly over men Literally: 'when one rules over men as a righteous man'. 'Righteous' does not refer so much to legal rectitude as to the rightness of David's relationship to Yahweh. The subsequent verses show that it is David's loyalty to the demands of the covenant sworn between him and Yahweh which constitutes his righteousness and it is in

[18] Cazelles, *ibid.* p. 173.
[1] Gordon, *UM* pp. 304 f., No. 1402.

virtue of this righteousness that the social wholeness of the community—its material and spiritual welfare—is assured.

4. he dawns on them . . . Rather: 'Then is it as the light of morning when the sun rises—a morning without clouds. As a result of sunlight after rain new foliage springs out of the earth'; i.e., the beneficent effects of David's just rule are compared to the fructifying powers of the sun on a cloudless morning after rain.

5. Yea, does not my house so stand with God? The metaphor of v. 4 is now applied more particularly to Yahweh's everlasting covenant with the Davidic dynasty. See Commentary on II 7 and cp. II 22.51.

ordered in all things and secure The terminology is probably legal. The covenant has been formulated with legal correctness and is valid. Moreover it has been secured against every form of tampering.

6. But godless men Literally: 'but worthlessness' (or 'confusion', see Commentary on I 1.16). In this metaphor the fate of those who oppose the will of God is described. Since the first metaphor (vv. 4 f.) applied to the just ruler, the second should probably be referred to unjust rulers whose rule, unlike that of David, does not have its basis in Yahweh and so is characterized by 'worthlessness' or 'confusion'. Such men are dangerous and due precautions have to be taken in dealing with them just as with thorns which are cut down for burning 'with iron and the shaft of a spear'.

7. with fire After these words 'in the sitting' appears in MT. This has been taken to mean 'on the spot', but the words may have arisen through a scribal error.

LIST OF DAVID'S HEROES

23.8-39

8. Josheb-basshebeth The original was probably 'Ishbaal' with *bosheth* being substituted for *baal*. (See Commentary on II 2.8.) G reads 'Ishbosheth' in both these passages.

Tahchemonite Read 'Hachmonite' (cp. I Chron. 27.32).

chief of the three MT: 'chief of the officers'. The consonantal Hebrew text of I Chron. 11.11 reads 'thirty' and the Masoretic vocalization 'officers'. G^{L} reads 'three' in both passages and this is what the sense seems to require.

eight hundred 'three hundred' according to I Chron. 11.11.

9. He was with David ... RSV follows MT, but I Chron. 11.13 gives a superior reading. 'He was with David at Pas-damim when the Philistines were gathered there for battle ...' THERE presupposes the previous mention of a place name and this is supplied by the text of Chronicles.

withdrew Rather: 'had withdrawn'.

11. Lehi MT: 'to the troop' (?). The place name is presupposed by the following THERE. Lehi was probably in the Philistine country, but the site is unknown.

13. about harvest time This is a dubious translation. I Chron. 11.15: 'to the rock'.

16. he poured it out to the Lord The men had exposed themselves to such danger in fetching the water that David regarded it as the equivalent of their blood and so he says: SHALL I DRINK THE BLOOD OF THE MEN WHO WENT AT THE RISK OF THEIR LIVES? There may be an allusion here to the practice of using other liquids (e.g., wine) as surrogates for blood in libations which were poured out to the deity. This would mean that David is here making a libation to Yahweh, with the water having the value of blood.[2]

18-19. There is some confusion in these verses between 'three' and 'thirty'. According to the Masoretic vocalization of v.

[2] W. R. Smith, *ROS* p. 230.

18 (also I Chron. 11.20) Abishai was chief of the Three. However 'Thirty' is supported by two Hebrew manuscripts and by S here, and S in I Chron. 11.20. A similar situation obtains in the case of the phrase 'and won a name among the Three'. 'Thirty' is read by S in both passages. RSV follows S in v. 18a and MT in 18b. In v. 19 RSV reads 'Thirty' where MT (also I Chron. 11.21) reads 'Three'. The phrase which supports the choice of 'Thirty' amid all this confusion is that of v. 19b, BUT HE DID NOT ATTAIN TO THE THREE. RSV, BESIDE THE THREE in v. 18b would mean that Abishai shared the acclaim which was accorded to the Three, but did not attain to this rank (cp. v. 22). The translation, however, looks like a harmonistic device and is very improbable.

19. most renowned There is no reason for translating MOST RENOWNED here and RENOWNED in v. 23, since the language is identical in both cases.

20. a valiant man RSV follows G. MT: 'son of a valiant man'.

Kabzeel Groll. p. 154.

he smote two ariels of Moab G: 'the two sons of Ariel from Moab'. Robertson Smith[3] explains the obscure 'ariel' of MT as 'hearth of God', and argues that it is a pillar-shaped fire altar to which he compares the pillars of Jachin and Boaz in Solomon's temple. Benaiah's exploit was 'to overthrow the twin fire pillars of the national sanctuary of Moab'. He adds: 'On the stele of Mesha (line 12) an *Ariel* appears as something that can be moved from its place which accords with the view now suggested.'

21. a handsome man So the Masoretic vocalization of MT. I Chron. 11.23: 'a huge man'.

25. Harod Groll. p. 151.

[3] W. R. Smith, *ROS* pp. 488 f.

26. the Paltite From Beth Pelet in the Negeb (site unknown).

Tekoa Groll. p. 163.

27. Mebunnai 'Sibbecai' according to I Chron. 11.29 which agrees with II Sam. 21.18.

the Hushathite Husha is west of Bethlehem (Groll. p. 152).

28. Netophah Groll, p. 158.

30. Pirathon Groll. p. 159.

brooks of Gaash Groll. p. 149.

31. Abialbon I Chron. 11.32: 'Abiel'.

the Arbathite Probably referring to Beth Arabah, south of Jericho (Groll. p. 145).

of Bahurim MT: 'Barhumite'. I Chron. 11.33: 'Baharumite'. Probably referring to Bahurim which is north of Jerusalem (Groll. p. 144).

32-33. the sons of Jashen, Jonathan, Shammah, the Hararite I Chron. 11.33 f. reads: 'Eliahba of Shaalbon, Hashem, the Gizonite, Jonathan, the son of Shagee, the Hararite.' The Chronicles passage shows that 'Jonathan' should be attached to v. 33a in the Samuel passage. G^L points to 'Jashen, the Nunite'. Read: 'Eliahba of Shaalbon, Jashen, the Nunite, Jonathan, the son of Shammah, the Hararite.' This is the 'Shammah' mentioned in v. 11.

34. Maacah Perhaps Abel Beth Maacah in the north of Palestine (Groll. p. 140).

Gilo Groll. p. 150.

35. Carmel Probably the Carmel south of Hebron (Groll. p. 146, Carmel [1]).

Arbite Belonging to Arab which is south of Hebron (Groll. p. 142).

36. Gadite Belonging to the territory of Gad in Trans-Jordan.

37. Beeroth A city of Benjamin, south of Bethel (Groll. p. 144).

38. the Ithrite A family of Kiriath-jearim (I Chron. 2.53) which is west and north of Jerusalem (Groll. p. 155).

39. thirty-seven in all The total number of names given in the chapter is thirty-six. Elika is absent from G and from I Chron. 11 and, without Elika, the names in vv. 24-39 amount to thirty in number. This, however, can hardly be adduced as a reason for deleting 'Elika' or for concluding that the correct total for the chapter is thirty-five, since Abishai and Benaiah also belong to the 'Thirty' (vv. 19, 23) and this would raise the figure to thirty-two exclusive of Elika.[4] The explanation may be that THIRTY-SEVEN is meant to include Joab whose place at the top of the pyramid above the 'Three' is assumed but not explicitly mentioned.[5] This receives some support from the circumstance that both Abishai and Asahel are described as brothers of Joab (vv. 18, 24) and that the armour-bearer of Joab finds a place among the 'Thirty'. These facts suggest, on the one hand, that Joab was a more prominent person than either Abishai and Asahel and, on the other, that Joab could hardly have been excluded from an order of knighthood in which his armour-bearer found a place. The mention of Uriah (v. 39) must indicate that the list belongs to a period prior to his death (II 11.17) and that it has not been worked over by a reviser. Another and more important mark of the earliness of the list[6] is the mention of Asahel who was killed by Abner (II 2.23) before David's reign had begun, and a similar pointer is the circumstance that a large proportion of David's men (thirteen in all) come from Judah and the Negeb. This suggests that their association with David

[4] Cp. S. R. Driver, *Notes, in loc.*
[5] Cp. Hertzberg, *ATD in loc.*
[6] Cp. Bentzen, *Introduction* II, p. 94.

goes back to the days when he was leader of a mercenary band at Ziklag and the mention of Asahel proves that these two orders of chivalry[7] ('The Three' and 'The Thirty') were in existence prior to David's assumption of kingship.

Chapter 22 (Ps. 18) supplements the theology of II 7; 23.1-7, and it is in this connection that it appears in our book. It declares that Yahweh is David's fortress and saviour (vv. 2-3). He describes his distress and the extreme danger to which he was exposed in language which recalls the threat of the primaeval waters of Chaos. 'FOR THE WAVES OF DEATH ENCOMPASSED ME, THE TORRENTS OF PERDITION ASSAILED ME' (v. 5). In his danger he called to Yahweh who heard him from his temple and appeared to save him. The phenomena associated with this theophany are described (vv. 9-20). Then comes the thought already noted in 23.1-7, YAHWEH REWARDED ME ACCORDING TO MY RIGHTEOUSNESS (vv. 21-25, cp. Commentary on 23.3).

The subsequent verses (26-31) should also be understood in terms of the everlasting covenant between Yahweh and the Davidic dynasty. The 'loyalty' of v. 26 is the attitude of constancy which is proper within the framework of the covenant obligation. David's constancy is matched by the constancy of Yahweh. WITH THE LOYAL THOU DOST SHOW THYSELF LOYAL (v. 26a). Verses 32-50 reiterate that Yahweh is David's fortress and the supporter of his rule, and the covenant betwen Yahweh and David receives explicit mention in the final verse of the psalm in terms which recall II 7 and 23.5. GREAT TRIUMPHS HE GIVES TO HIS KING, AND SHOWS STEADFAST LOVE TO HIS ANOINTED, TO DAVID AND TO HIS DESCENDANTS FOR EVER (v. 51).

Yahweh hears David's cry for help from his temple (22.7) and from this circumstance it could be concluded that the assurance of salvation was given to the king in the context of a cultic festival. The danger of which David complains is not

[7] Bright, *History*, p. 186 n. 53, suggests that 'The Thirty' was an order formed on an Egyptian model.

disturbance of the cosmic order. He fears not a return to primaeval chaos but the activities of hostile nations. Yet the language used in v. 5a suggests some contact with the pattern of the New Year festival as it is known to have existed elsewhere in the ancient Near East, particularly in Babylon. There it was concerned with renewal and maintenance of cosmic order, so that, if this psalm does point to the place of the Davidic king in an Israelite New Year festival, the historicizing of the old theme is the distinctive Israelite contribution and this derives from the supreme value attached by Israel to history as the theatre where Yahweh revealed himself and enforced his will.

If the psalm is susceptible of this interpretation, it would reveal the Davidic king exercising the unique mediatorial role which is his in view of his unshared covenant with Yahweh. On the effective discharge of this role the continuing welfare and social wholeness of the community absolutely depends (cp. Commentary on 23.3). On it also depends the continuing security of Israel in a hostile world and the decisive moment in all this is when the king waits for Yahweh's assurance of deliverance for himself and the nation in the context of the ritual of the New Year festival (22.7). This is the climax of the Davidic king's place in the cult and the central point of the theology of kingship (see Commentary on II 7.14).

CHAPTER 24

THE CENSUS

24.1-9

1. he incited David against them Or. 'he set David against them'. According to I Chron. 21.1 it was Satan who incited David to number Israel.

2. from Dan to Beersheba See Commentary on I 3.20.

4. from the presence of the king MT: 'before the king'. The reading of RSV is obtained by a small emendation of MT in agreement with S.

5. and began from Aroer . . . RSV follows G^L. The sense of MT is poor. 'And they encamped at Aroer to the south of the city which is in the middle of the valley, Gad and to Jazer.' For Aroer see Groll. p. 143, Aroer (1) and for Jazer, p. 153.

6. Then they came to Gilead and to Kadesh in the land of the Hittites RSV follows G^L, which reads 'to the land of the Hittites, towards Kadesh'. MT, which is perhaps corrupt, reads, 'to the land of Tahtim-hodshi', the site of which is unknown. S. R. Driver[1] identifies the 'Kadesh' of G^L with the city on the Orontes which was the capital of the empire of the Hittites and which is here used to designate the northern limit of Israel. Similarly Groll. p. 154, Kadesh (2). Noth[2], although he follows G^L, takes the 'land of the Hittites' to mean a strip of city-state territories which David had subjugated, lying between Gad and Gilead, on the one side, and Dan, beside the sources of the Jordan, on the other. He presumably identifies 'Kadesh' with 'Kedesh' in Naphtali (Groll. p. 154, Kedesh [1]).

and from Dan they went around to Sidon This is a conjectural reading, based on G. MT is corrupt.

7. the fortress of Tyre Probably the mainland base of the island city of Tyre. The 'lands of the Hivites and Canaanites' are the city-states of the maritime plains extending from the north of Carmel southwards to the northern limits of the Philistine cities.[3]

[1] S. R. Driver, *Notes, in loc.*
[2] Noth, *History*, p. 192.
[3] Noth, *ibid.*, p. 192.

DAVID'S REMORSE

24.10-14

11. the prophet Gad, David's seer Gad is both a prophet and a seer. The etymology of the first word has been a subject of debate, but it is probably connected with the idea of declaration or utterance and so defines the prophet as one who speaks God's word. The second word 'seer' characterizes Gad as a visionary and so as one with whom God communicates through the medium of dreams or visions. Apparently he served David in the capacity of 'domestic seer', but his integrity and sense of prophetic responsibility had not been impaired by his close relationship to the king. Unlike the later court prophets of Ahab (I Kings 22.5 f.) he was subject to the word of Yahweh (v. 11).

12. I offer Literally: 'I lift up'. RSV margin: 'hold over', i.e., guillotine-wise.

13. three years of famine RSV follows G and I Chron. 21.12. MT: 'seven years'. The correctness of the number three is suggested by its reappearance in connection with the other two alternatives. Perhaps there is the suggestion that the intensity of the punishment grows as its duration diminishes (three years, three months, three days). The reading THREE YEARS also gains support from the consideration that there may be here a covert allusion to the three years' famine of II 21.1.

PESTILENCE IN ISRAEL

24.15-17

15. So the Lord sent a pestilence . . . RSV follows MT. The verse has been reconstructed on the basis of G to read: 'And David made the choice of pestilence, and it was the season of the wheat harvest, and the plague began among the people and seven thousand of the people died.' The chief difficulty in MT is the phrase 'until the appointed time'. This cannot mean 'until the end of three days', since the plague was halted before the end of this period (vv. 16, 25).

17. when he saw the angel . . . The scene shifts back to David and to a point in time earlier than the decision of Yahweh in v. 16, for there the angel of Yahweh had stayed his hand but here he is still dealing out death to the people.

DAVID BUILDS AN ALTAR

24.18-25

24. I will buy it of you for a price The reason which David gives for refusing Araunah's gift of the site and of sacrificial animals is that he does not wish to make burnt-offerings to Yahweh which have cost him nothing. It may be supposed that like Abraham, who similarly refused to have the cave of Machpelah in a gift[4] (Gen. 23), he was interested in acquiring a proper legal title to the land. Gordon[5] argues that Araunah (which means 'Lord') was the former ruler of Jebusite Jerusalem.

25. peace-offerings See Commentary on I 10.8.

Bentzen[6] suggests that this chapter perhaps originally stood after II 6, in which case we are to understand that, although David was forbidden to build a temple to house the ark, he was permitted to acquire the site for its future building and to build an altar there. In the extant compilation of the book, however, 24 would seem to be a continuation of 21.1-14.

There is a discontinuity between the representation of vv. 1-9 and the description of David's behaviour in vv. 10 f. Why should David have been filled with remorse, if the census originated as v. 1 states? There the primary cause of the census is said to be Yahweh's anger with Israel and it is to satisfy

[4] Cp. G. von Rad, *Genesis*, ET, 1961, pp. 242-4.
[5] Gordon, *UM*, p. 234, No. 77.
[6] Bentzen, *Introduction* II, p. 94.

this anger that he instructs David to submit Israel to the humiliation of a census. But in this case David is simply an instrument of Yahweh's anger with Israel and the feelings of guilt in vv. 10 f. seem to be out of place.

It was no doubt because the Chronicler saw this difficulty that he made Satan and not Yahweh David's tempter (I Chron. 21.1). Verses 1-9 and 10 f. should then perhaps be regarded as two differing acounts of the census, and the orientation of the first is political rather than theological, although this is somewhat obscured by the quaint theology of v. 1. This, it may be suspected, is an attempt to relieve David of responsibility for a wrong political decision—the decision to number Israel. That this was *his* decision may still be gathered from the phrase THE KING'S WORD in v. 4. Joab, who opposes it in the name of political sagacity, again appears as a loyal servant of David (v. 3) and yet a man of independent judgment who has confidence in his own grasp and appraisal of a situation. Although the grounds of Joab's disapproval are not stated, we may safely assume that they were political and not theological, and that he foresaw how the census would create friction and arouse fears among the constituent tribes of David's realm who were jealous of their liberties.

A different orientation, however, appears in vv. 10 f. David says that the census is a sin which he has committed against Yahweh, and Gad confronts him with a choice of punishments. In the nature of two of these punishments there is surely an allusion to judgments which have already fallen on David. The three years of famine glance at II 21.1 and the three months as a fugitive at his experiences during the Absalom revolt (II 15.16 f.). In the view that the third possibility comes more directly from Yahweh than the other two expression is given to the belief that plague is a particularly direct manifestation of divine judgment, (cp. Ex. 7.20 f. and, especially, II Kings 19.35) and so is administered by an angel of Yahweh (v. 16).

David asked for the plague to be stayed on the ground that he alone is guilty before Yahweh and that the innocent ought not to suffer, and the angel of Yahweh, who has been dealing lethal blows throughout the entire area of David's kingdom (v. 15), is not permitted to destroy Jerusalem. Bentzen[7] has described vv. 10 ff. as a sanctuary legend and it is clear that the narrative has a general aetiological aspect. It explains in what circumstances the threshing-floor of Araunah became the site of Solomon's temple. But the representation has a more specialized intention than this and it is hard to resist the conclusion that there is something here of the later belief in the inviolability of Jerusalem—an inviolability owing to the temple. In particular the angel of death whose activity was stayed at the threshing-floor of Araunah (which was outside David's city, cp. v. 16) recalls the angel of death who decimated Sennacherib's army and vindicated Isaiah's belief in the inviolability of Jerusalem (II Kings 19.35). Hence the temple, which was to become the guarantee of the inviolability of Jerusalem, is represented as having been built on the site where Jerusalem was once denied to the angel of death; and, on that occasion, the specific of Yahweh for the turning away of the plague was the building of an altar, that is, the foundation of the germ of the future temple. So we have here the story of a plague and how it was averted which matches the previous story of a famine and how it was terminated (21.1-14).

[7] Bentzen, *Introduction* I, p. 236.